Pain and Gain
The Untold True Story

This book proves that sometimes the truth is stranger than fiction!

By
Marc Schiller

"Despite having sat through the entire trial, and having heard the live testimony, I still find myself cringing at Marc Schiller's description of his captivity, torture and attempted murder. This book speaks volumes about the evil that some are able to perpetrate and the tragedies that others are able to overcome." Judge Alex Ferrer, October 9, 2013

DEDICATION

This book is dedicated to all those people in the world who are in physical or mental chains, who are oppressed, and who are deprived of their freedom and liberty. May the invisible hand of GOD break those chains and give you the dignity and the basic rights all human beings deserve: physical, emotional, and mental freedom.
And to the memory of my father, mother and sister, who always fought, never gave up, and instilled that spirit within me.

CONTENTS

ACKNOWLEDGEMENTS

Cover Art—Stephanie D. Schiller
Editing—Victoria Kenning, Talia Leduc
Special thanks to Alex (Moose) Schiller,
David J. Schiller, Edward Du Bois III,
And Gene Rosen.

Prologue

I no longer had the strength to conjure thoughts of rescue. My body and mind, weakened by starvation, blinded and ravaged by pain, no longer responded. I sat chained to the wall and tried one last time to garner enough strength to visualize my children in my mind's eye.

The invisible clock ticked down to what would surely be the last moments of my life. Numbly I sat there, aware of what awaited me, no more trying to fool myself that events would suddenly take a favorable twist. I knew my fate and reluctantly accepted it. The cavalry had never arrived, and I was now convinced that my ideas of rescue had been merely an illusion I'd created in order to survive my captivity.

It had been a month of torture, humiliation, and darkness that was now coming to a close. In a way, perhaps it was best that it was finally over, even though it would not end the way I had hoped.

That evening, they came to me and told me I needed to wash up and change clothes for the first time in a month. They happily announced I was being let go, since they had financially ravaged me and there was nothing left to take. They'd grown just as weary of me as I was of them. I wanted to believe them, yet I recognized their subtle hints and knew it was just another lie. Besides, I knew whom they were, and I was sure they knew this, and dead men tell no tales.

This, as everything else they had done, was comical. They

wanted me to change my urine-drenched clothes and wash up so they could kill me while I was looking and smelling good? It didn't matter to me, and I felt I might as well die with some dignity.

A month-long tour of hell with my own personal demonic guides was ending: a month filled with pain from the burns, electrical shocks, and assorted beatings. I hadn't seen any light for the whole time, and food was almost nonexistent.

Perhaps the most difficult part was the rollercoaster ride of emotions I had endured. I had never imagined that I would be chained to that wall for so long.

So I waited for them to come take me away one last time. I sat and asked for forgiveness, and I prayed for my children.

I did not know how they were going to kill me. I just prayed that it would be quick and relatively painless. But what I had learned from my experience was that my captors enjoyed seeing their victims suffer. I braced for whatever was about to come my way. They had taken everything from me, humiliated me and made me suffer, but they had not been successful in smothering my spirit, and perhaps, in the end, that was what infuriated them the most.

Little did I know that the coming evening would set off another chain of events far, far beyond my wildest imagination. That was typical of my stay in Hotel Hell; everything that happened was surreal, as if the scriptwriter were a deranged, drugged madman who saw no boundaries in a world of lunacy.

So I just sat there on the edge of darkness, waiting for the lights to be permanently turned off and to make my final exit from that stage.

~

~

~

A pile of loose papers, yellowing with age, collecting dust, has sat in a corner of the room for nearly seventeen years. Those many pages, written in January of 1995, contain ghosts and demons that are very real to me. Perhaps this is why I have made so many attempts to write these words and have only succumbed to those spirits contained within the manuscript. Each time, I put them back in the corner and hoped they would remain dormant. At last, I have found the will to confront those ghosts and demons. Perhaps external forces did finally push me into writing this, my story. Yet, deep inside, I have always known that writing these words would play a large part in cleansing my spirit and allowing me to obtain closure. Cleansing and closure are so necessary for my healing to be complete.

It is often said that time heals all wounds, and as it passes we are able to evaluate our experiences and hopefully learn the sometimes harsh and bitter lessons. This largely depends on how deep those wounds and psychological scars are that are left behind, the magnitude of the trauma suffered, and the mental strength, tenacity, and fortitude of the victim. Sometimes, healing takes more than the mere passage of time.

In all respects, I feel blessed. I have been able to move on with my life and, for the most part, leave those events of November and December 1994 behind me.

In July 2008, a television program was aired about my story on

TruTV. I was asked to participate, which I did. My interest in writing this book was revived, and I wiped off the dust from those loose pages. Naively, I believed that the television program of my story could help someone else by providing a ray of light and hope in a time when everything appeared to be darkest. My aspirations for that were soon dashed, and I realized that the program was not going to convey that message or even tell the story in a balanced manner. Disappointed, I put the manuscript back in the corner to continue its lonely process of decay.

Then, in 2011, I was told that Paramount Pictures and Michael Bay were making a movie adaptation of my story. I started to reexamine the possibility of writing the book once again. This time, I felt it was important to tell the audience what had really happened and not let them be fooled by a Hollywood adaptation, which would contain many fictionalized events and would trivialize what had occurred. I want to transmit the important lessons I learned. And so here I sit at my desk in 2012.

Incredibly, it all began in January 1995, when I first sat down and wrote about two hundred pages of detailed notes on what had occurred in the previous two months. It was not exactly a book but more like a cleansing of the soul and mind, a journal that documented the events I endured and marked the beginning of my long process of healing. Now, using those notes, I write these words in the hope that someone may read them and see that no matter how horrific things may seem, a message of hope shines through. I'm convinced there will be some individuals who, in reading these words and pages, will find inspiration and the fortitude to take on and overcome any difficulty they may face. If this book helps just one individual, then my mission is accomplished. That is my hope and the reason for this book.

Chapter 1 — Beginnings

"ADVERSITY IS A FACT OF LIFE. IT CAN'T BE CONTROLLED.
WHAT WE CAN CONTROL IS HOW WE REACT TO IT."
- UNKNOWN -

It is important for me to give the reader an understanding of who I was and who I had become through my personal experiences prior to my kidnapping in 1994. This will help explain my acts during these events and, more importantly, why I was able to survive them and continue on with my life afterwards.

I was born on a rainy winter day in August 1957 in Buenos Aires, Argentina. My family and my country were going through turmoil. My grandparents had emigrated from Russia in the early 1920s and had chosen Argentina because of its economic prowess and political stability. Of course, all that changed after Juan Peron took power in a coup in the 1940s and the country began its long slide as the world's third-largest economic power.

As went the country, so did the economic condition of my family. I was the second child. My older sister, Michelle, was born almost five years to the day before me. When I was born, my family's situation had become precarious, and we were forced to move into my grandmother's house, which was also shared by my father's younger brother. I always joked with my dad. I said it looked as though I had brought bad luck, since prior to my birth they had lived a comfortable middle-class life.

So that was where I spent the first six years of my life. We had

1

three families sharing the same house, trying collectively to make enough money to pay for food and other necessities. In 1964, a distant uncle who lived in the United Sates visited us. Dismayed at what he saw, he persuaded my father's younger brother and his mother to immigrate to the US. He tried to talk sense into my father and make him move also, but my father decided that he was a patriot and would sink with the ship.

So, at the end of 1964, we were basically homeless. My father's economic situation had gotten worse, and the only thing he could do now to get enough money to eat was selling socks door to door. We were forced to move from the city to a rural area called Gonzalez Catan. Here was the Wild, Wild West, and gauchos still roamed the prairie. Our little house had no running water, and the scarce electricity was not enough to light two lamps at the same time.

It was a little pink house with two bedrooms and an old-fashioned kitchen. It was rustic, simple—bare bones, as certain prefabricated houses can be, but it was home. At least we had a small parcel of land where we could grow some food and have a few chickens to provide us with eggs. Our closest neighbor was about two miles away; it was pure desolation. My school was a one-room building with a dirt floor about four miles from the house. I made the trek every day and hunted for frogs or tried to kill snakes along the way. Once or twice a month, the garbage truck would actually show up on the one and only paved road. I caught a ride to school by hanging on the back of the truck.

During the summer, we went swimming at the water hole where horses drank. I spent most of my free time wandering the fields, inventing new adventures. That year, my brother, Alex, was born, and the situation seemed dimmer than ever. My father's brother came to visit and again tried to persuade my father to leave and immigrate to the US. Father was adamant. He would not budge.

Finally, in 1965, the situation became so dire that my father gave in and left for the US. The four of us, my mother, my sister, Michelle, who was twelve, my brother, Alex, who was a few months old, and I, at seven, were left behind to fend for ourselves in a hostile environment. After my father left, our situation deteriorated further. We had no one to tend the few crops we had. Our few chickens were dying and laid no more eggs.

We resorted to eating a mush my mother prepared, and to this day I have no clue what was in it. It just looked like white paste that you could use to hang wallpaper. We also had plenty of wild blackberries that my mom used to make compote. Sometimes, we ate that five days a week. I have never been able to eat anything with blackberries since those days. Years later, my sister sent me a ten pound jar of blackberry jam for my birthday—very funny.

After a while, my father was able to send some money so we could buy food. That was wonderful, but there was no supermarket or convenience store in our neighborhood, so my mother had to go into the city to buy groceries. She left at five o'clock in the morning and did not return until one o'clock the following morning. She had to carry the grocery bags for miles, since there was no public transportation where we lived. We three children were left to fend for ourselves, and after dark we simply sat in a room together and waited.

Finally, in May of 1966, my father had saved enough money to bring us to America. Michelle stayed home to care for Alex while Mother and I went to the city to see if someone could give us some hand-me-down clothing for the trip. Our wardrobe was nonexistent; you really didn't need much clothing where we lived. We lucked out after going from place to place and received enough clothes to get on the plane to our new home. It may be surprising that those days as grim, difficult or sad as they may sound. Bring back no bitter memories, no sadness, and no negative feelings.

In fact, my memories are happy ones. It was a time when I felt totally free. There was no pressure, and I was able to grow up free from the complications that can often deluge a child in big cities. Because I was free to explore the environment, I developed the self-assurance I would need to be able to survive no matter what circumstances I might encounter. This episode in our lives gave me the internal fortitude and self-reliance that would help me survive in the difficult situations that were to come.

Chapter 2 — The Journey

"YOUR STRUGGLES ARE ONLY BIGGER THAN YOU WHEN YOUR
THOUGHTS CONVINCE YOU TO BELIEVE THAT YOU ARE
INCAPABLE OF OVERCOMING THEM."
- EDMUND MBIAKA -

We landed at JFK airport on May 10, 1966. Sensory overload! I felt as though my head was spinning, for I had just left a place where everything was green and grew wild, and now I found myself in a concrete jungle that was totally foreign, even alien, to me. Father had saved some money and bought a little bit of furniture and a TV.

A television, wow! I didn't even know such things existed. My father had done well, but his rebellious self caused us problems again. Instead of getting an apartment in the same neighborhood where my grandmother and uncle lived, one that was somewhat safe, he moved us to one of the most dangerous neighborhoods in New York. We got our welcoming the following week. One day, while Michelle and I attended school, my father was at work and my mother was running errands. Someone took the door of our apartment off its hinges and carted off our few earthly possessions. No more television—my novelty item lasted for only one week. It was again time to start from square one.

My adjustment was difficult and painful. I was going to a school where I was one of very few white children. This was the sixties, when racial tensions in this country were at a peak. Bewildered, puzzled, confused, I could not understand what was happening and why so many of my fellow classmates harbored such ill feeling towards me. Adding to the dilemma was the fact that I could not yet speak a word of English and could not communicate with anyone. I wanted to be back in my little house in the middle of nowhere, eating the white pasty mush and going to school barefoot.

School was a survivalist camp for me. I was often harassed and beat up while going to and from school. The teachers were themselves lost and had their own battles to survive in the jungle; they offered no help and no way out. I fought back, but I never understood why I was fighting, just trying to survive. During the two years I spent there, it never got easier, but I eventually managed to avoid the craziness that surrounded me by becoming as invisible as possible.

Shortly after we arrived in this country, I decided to become an entrepreneur. Never mind that I was eight years old and could not speak English. That was not going to stop me. There were necessities I needed, such as shoes and clothes, and, from the beginning, I learned to rely on myself for those things. I guess I was not a normal child who craved toys. I made my own from whatever material I could scrounge. I wanted a bicycle, but that was because it created new opportunities to generate income. My first capitalistic venture involved simply standing in front of the supermarket, asking ladies if I could carry their groceries home for them. Perhaps my shabby appearance made them sympathize with me, but I was very successful and would get a dime, a quarter, or sometimes even a dollar! I often did this every day for three or four hours, so I began to see some real money in no time. My parents were never opposed to what I was doing, and to this day I'm not sure if they even knew.

My next venture was to get my mom's shopping cart and stroll up and down the street, hunting and collecting returnable bottles. This was not as lucrative, since the amount they gave back was small, but I got anywhere from two to six dollars every other day. I found and returned many bottles. As an early recycler, I did a service to the city also, helping to remove trash.

As a result of my effort, in a very short time I was able to buy a bicycle that cost me the princely sum of thirty-six dollars. I bought it by myself, without any adult help. Imagine me doing this when I was just eight years old, no parents involved. This gave me the opportunity to start delivering TV guides, another source of income. That was how I began my career as an entrepreneur. At the time, I was not instructed in the principles of capitalism; to me, this was the instinct for survival that would always serve me well.

We lived in that neighborhood for two years until it was decided that enough was enough. My father was getting mugged on a weekly basis. His earnings were small, but he knew that was all we had, and he never allowed his take-home pay to be taken away from him. He often came home bleeding, beaten to a pulp and with bloody hands, to give my mother his pay. He finally took the advice of his brother, and we moved to Brighton Beach, Brooklyn, where we were close to him and my grandmother.

I lived in that neighborhood until I finally left home seven years later. To me, it was an opportunity to go to school and not fear what awaited me. By now, I spoke English pretty well and my assimilation process was much easier. I had lost my sources of income, but that was temporary. I began delivering newspapers and actually got odd jobs. I worked for Robert Kennedy and other political campaigns, handing out flyers. It didn't seem they cared about my age. I started getting any odd job that I could. Convincing the owner was sometimes difficult and other times not, since I would work for less than minimum wage, which was a tantalizing incentive for many to hire me.

In 1969, I joined the Boy Scouts. It was an opportunity to be in a safe environment and become friends with other kids my age. It was difficult being accepted because I represented a different perspective and reality than did most of my peers. I stuck with it anyway and was glad I did; it was a refuge from the outside world. That summer, the troop I belonged to was planning a trip to Washington, D.C. The cost was reasonable, but my parents were not in the position to pay, nor did they want to give me their support. There was going to be a fund drive to raise money for the trip. It involved selling boxes of candy, and the one who sold the most would win the prize of going on the trip for free. Well, that was all I needed to hear. It was a solution, and it was up to me whether I could go or not. I began an insatiable selling campaign, selling candy at every free moment I had.

We lived in a vast area of tall apartment buildings. Every day after school, I targeted a certain area and went from building to building and door to door. I would knock on the door, and as soon as someone opened it, I would start my memorized sales pitch: "Hi, I'm

Marc, and I'm selling Boy Scout candy to help me go on a trip to Washington, D.C. Would you like to buy some?" Most of the time, I did not receive an answer. They would simply either shut the door or, worse, slam it shut on me. That never discouraged me, and I just simply kept going to the next door or next building. I spent over a month selling tenaciously, and I even got mugged once, having all my boxes of candy stolen.

The day I got mugged, the police just so happened to be driving by. I stopped them and told them what had happened, and they let me hop into their cruiser and took me around the neighborhood to look for the perp. We never did find him, so that day represented a severe setback. Now I was not only looking at the prospect of selling enough to win but also to pay for the stolen candy. That was not going to be my downfall. I was determined and just kept on going. In the end, I did win, and I went on the trip with all expenses paid. I not only sold over five hundred boxes of candy for the competition but also enough candy to pay for the boxes that had been stolen. That was who I was, even at that age. I was tenacious and hardworking when I wanted or needed something and never expected my parents or anyone to give things to me. I let nothing stop me or deter me from reaching my goals. That was who I was then and still am today.

The junior high school and high school years were uneventful. I started playing sports on a regular basis and ran track until my sophomore year. When I was not playing sports, I was working. I worked in a pharmacy, a beauty supply store, a deli, and a supermarket as a cashier. I always had a job, and it was not only a necessity but also a way for me to earn my self-respect. I hardly studied in those years, but it did not affect my grades. I always managed to maintain a B-plus or A-minus average with minimal or no effort. Most of the classes I took were honor classes, which demanded more from the student. Fortunately for me, school came easily, and I even managed to get ninety-eight and ninety-six percent in my state algebra and biology exams.

Chapter 3 — Confusion

"SUCCESS IS NOT FINAL, FAILURE IS NOT FATAL: IT IS THE
COURAGE TO CONTINUE THAT COUNTS."
- WINSTON CHURCHILL -

"WHAT LIES BEHIND YOU AND WHAT LIES IN FRONT OF YOU
PALES IN COMPARISON TO WHAT LIES INSIDE OF YOU."
- RALPH WALDO EMERSON -

The last year of high school was tumultuous for me, and I felt very lost. Most of my peers were making early plans to go to different universities. I did well in my SATs, but the problem was that I did not know what I wanted to do. There was nowhere to turn for help. My parents were too busy struggling to survive each day. They neither had the knowledge nor the energy to help me at such a critical time. At the last minute, I enrolled in Baruch College in Manhattan, New York. Why I enrolled and what I was going to do still remain a mystery to me.

As strange as it may sound, my parents never took me on a vacation when I was a child. In 1975, my last year of high school, a couple of school acquaintances asked me if I wanted to go on Spring Break to Miami, Florida, with them. That would be my first vacation. I decided to go with the hope that perhaps I could get my thoughts straight as to my future. We made the journey by bus, and the total booty that I took for my one-week stay was ninety-eight dollars. I found out when we got there that we had a hotel room for three days, and the rest of the time we would have to find somewhere else to sleep. Somehow in the chaos, we were always able to find some floor to lie down on and get a few hours sleep. During that trip, I met Andrea from Milwaukee. She was from a rich family, and her father was a prominent lawyer. Little did I know then, but, as fate would have it, she would play a very prominent role in my near future.

Reluctantly, I started my college education in 1975. It was a period of confusion and uncertainty for me. I did not like the school, and I still didn't know what I wanted to do with my life. I was alone to make all my decisions, with no one to turn to for a word of advice. My grades were slipping. I was not interested and paid no attention to my education, yet I managed to somehow pass all my classes with very low grades. The following year, I decided I was not going to return to school. I had no idea what I was going to do, since working at menial jobs would not be sufficient.

In the summer of 1976, I received a call from Andrea, the girl I had met during my trip to Miami. She persuaded me, which was not hard to do, to go to Milwaukee, where she could maybe help me sort out my mind. In October, I took all my possessions; two ripped jeans, four torn shirts, and a light jacket, and moved to Milwaukee.

My welcome was anything but exuberant. On my second day at her house, which to me was a mansion, her brother approached me and told me that I needed to leave because he did not want a homeless bum like me in the house. In retrospect, I could not blame him. My appearance was that of a street beggar, complete with long hair. My sister wrote me a letter asking me to come home. She reasoned that I could go to a trade school and become a plumber. Me, a plumber? No. I neither liked nor was adept at anything manual. Later on, I was thankful for that letter because it made me realize how I needed to find the strength and fortitude to do something with my life.

Andrea helped me get a job at a local diner, where I flipped eggs for eight hours. I was making a dollar and sixty-five cents an hour, and my survival was tenuous. The following five months were to be the most difficult test in my life so far. I was able to get a room in a boarding house. There was barely any heat, and the ritual every night was to wrap two towels around my feet to fight off the cold. Most of the time, I slept with my clothes on, for it was unbearable otherwise. I cooked all my meals in a toaster oven I had found at a garage sale.

I had to take two buses to work, and I was ill prepared for the northern weather. I sloshed through the snow with my worn and torn sneakers, and by the time I got to work, my feet were soaked and painfully cold. I had a light jacket, a real joke in the sub-zero weather. It did nothing to warm or protect me. Sometimes, when I waited for the bus, the cold was so painful I often had to go into a store to get warm. Nearly every time, I was thrown out. That taught me a lot about human compassion—basically, it didn't exist.

After I was in Milwaukee a month, I applied for admission to the University of Wisconsin-Milwaukee. Two months later, I was accepted on probation. That was all I needed, a chance and an opportunity. I went back to school in January 1977. That was my salvation in a time of despair and near insanity. I moved into the dorms, and even though the rooms were minuscule, they looked like a five-star resort to me. I quickly got a job doing janitorial duties in the school so I would not have to make a long trek every day to the diner. Eventually, I ended up working as a chef in the restaurant that was situated in the commons area of the school. From the beginning, I knew what I was going to study and set out to finish as quickly as possible. I decided on accounting since numbers had always come easily to me. I attended two summer school sessions and also took seven classes one semester. Although everyone thought I was crazy, it ended up being the semester in which I received my highest grades.

Chapter 4 — Career

"THE HARDER THE CONFLICT, THE MORE GLORIOUS THE
TRIUMPH. WHAT WE OBTAIN TOO CHEAP, WE ESTEEM TOO
LIGHTLY; IT IS DEARNESS ONLY THAT GIVES EVERYTHING ITS
VALUE. I LOVE THE MAN THAT CAN SMILE IN TROUBLE, THAT
CAN GATHER STRENGTH FROM DISTRESS AND GROW."
- *THOMAS PAINE* -

In 1979, with my studies almost complete, I was interviewed
and hired by Ernst and Whinney, a prestigious accounting firm.
When I found out that my salary was going to be almost eighteen
thousand dollars a year, I was in shock; that was so much money to
me.

In September of that year, I began my employment. As at other
times in my life, my first work clothes and shoes were items that
someone had handed down to me. I was on top of the world, and felt
I had finally made it. That feeling was fleeting with the onset of new
problems around the corner. At the firm, I was always treated as an
outsider and given the worst assignments. Along with an African-
American girl who was also new, I was isolated in a far corner of the
office. We knew we were the token minorities and that they had
hired us to satisfy their affirmative action program.

When it came time to take the CPA exam, all the new hires
were given time to study. I was sent to Tomahawk, Wisconsin, on a
project that demanded fourteen hours of work each day and gave me
zero time to study. I was brought back to the office the night before I
was scheduled to take the exam. Three weeks later, when the results

were in, all twelve new hires stood in line by the phone to hear their results. I was last, of course, and they all asked why I was waiting in line, since I could not have passed the exam. They told me not to waste my time and go back to my corner, where I belonged. They were rooting for my failure and did not try to hide it. As I picked up the phone, they all stood around me, staring. They were confident of the result; they just didn't want me to lie to them and say I had passed. But I passed the exam the first time. You cannot imagine the disappointment on their faces as they busily searched for answers, wondering how I could have done so well. They didn't understand the triumph of the human spirit and the desires of the heart.

Things deteriorated rapidly from there. Finally, as I drove home from an auditing assignment, the senior in charge embarked on a two-hour tirade of insults for no reason. That was the breaking point, and I once again knew it was time to move on.

That year I bought my first car, a Nissan 200SX. Shortly thereafter, while driving to an assignment one snowy Wisconsin day, my head in the clouds, I had a head-on collision at sixty miles per hour. My car ricocheted from the retaining wall into other cars like a Ping-Pong ball. I flew out of the front windshield and landed on the pavement. The car was totally destroyed. I walked away from that accident with a few minor bruises. People who had seen the accident on television assumed that the driver of the Nissan was dead. Wrong. That was my first experience escaping sure death, and that marked a turning point.

I decided to quit my job and look for opportunities elsewhere. I interviewed with different companies across the country and finally decided on a company called ENSERCH, located in Dallas, Texas. I moved to Dallas in 1980, and this time I was welcomed by my colleagues. The storm, for now it seemed, had passed. One of the projects I participated in was an acquisition audit in South America. That audit was to significantly impact my life in a few years. Life in Dallas was good. I worked for ENSERCH and then moved on to Sabine Oil & Gas and finally Easley Investment. There I managed the money and investments for a multi-millionaire. I was happy and had stability. I had a well-paying job, friends, and great coworkers, and those stormy days seemed like a distant memory. In 1984, the company at which I had participated in the acquisition audit called me and asked me if I wanted to go to Colombia as a controller. It was an offer that was difficult to refuse, because the compensation was very generous.

I moved to Colombia in 1984 and met my wife that year, who also worked for the company. We got married in 1985, and she retired from working. In 1988, our son was born, and things seemed to be on autopilot. Those years I worked in Colombia were professionally satisfying, and I had peace of mind. Just when I thought everything was perfect and nothing could go wrong, my world was turned upside down again.

In 1989, the lull in the storm was over, and all hell broke loose at the company were I worked. Leftist rebels in one of our field offices had kidnapped my boss and employer. The focus of the company changed from making money to getting him back alive. The atmosphere in the office changed, and it was not pleasant to go to work anymore. We were a ship without a captain, and we just

17

drifted with the tide. The ordeal lasted seven months, and company officers were continually in meetings, working to meet the ransom demands. The man was finally released and flown to his home in Houston, Texas. A month after his release, he called me. I was told that all Americans would have to leave Colombia. In other words, I had no job. It was a shock that I should have been prepared for, but I was not. I decided to come back to the United States. My wife wanted to be close to her family, and so, at her urging, we moved to Miami instead of Dallas.

Chapter 5 — Life in Miami

"THE HUMAN SPIRIT IS STRONGER THAN ANYTHING
THAT HAPPENS TO IT."
- *C. C. SCOTT* -

In January of 1989, I arrived in Miami. This time, I was pretty sure what I wanted to do. Instead of seeking employment, I was going to start my own accounting firm. I rented an office and purchased the necessary furniture and equipment. I hired three employees. One of them was Linda Delgado. The company was a success, and we were able to sign up nearly a hundred clients in the first six months. Things were going as well as one could expect for a startup company. I had a sales representative who was doing great work, but we were getting more interest from clients than he could handle.

Linda was aware of this and came into my office sobbing one day. She was a good employee, and she was excellent at her job setting appointments with prospective clients. She told me that her husband, Jorge, was selling cars and they were very tight on money. She wanted me to give him a job as a second sales representative. They were living with Linda's parents because their combined income was not sufficient to move out and get their own place. Well, seeing that I'm a bleeding heart, I caved in to her request, and that was how Jorge Delgado came to work for me. Jorge was a very good worker and was always willing to do whatever was needed. He was soft spoken, and I never saw him mad or frustrated. Years later, he

19

would be the one who wanted me murdered while I was in the warehouse.

The company grew and prospered. Magnanimously, I shared the profits with my employees. I helped Jorge buy a new car, which was also good for me since he needed to visit the clients. I also helped them buy their first house. In 1991, the wear and tear of the long hours was getting to me, and I decided to sell the company. The agreement was that the new owner would also continue to employ my current employees, including Jorge and Linda. It was to his advantage to do so since they knew the business and the clients so well. I was going to look at other business prospects, and since I had received a monthly payment from the buyer, I could take my time.

Things started to go sour from almost the beginning. Jorge and I kept communicating, and he told me that clients were not being taken care of and the work was not being done. The first payment was the only one I received; after that, it became a game of cat and mouse. After three months, I decided to retain a lawyer and to get the accounting practice back before there was nothing left. Surprisingly fast, a court date was set to settle the dispute, and both Jorge and Linda attended on my behalf. With their help, I won back the accounting practice.

There would be no office this time, and I was going to work out of the house. I subcontracted half the work to one of my ex-employees, who was well versed in the work that had to be done. Jorge continued to work for me, picking up the work and delivering it to the clients. This meant that he was at the house almost every day and also became friends with my wife. He knew every nuance of our home and our lives. When we went on vacation, he took care of the house for us. He had the alarm codes and was on the list of people the alarm company could call in case of an emergency. I trusted him completely and had no reason not to. Perhaps I was naive, but I never saw any malicious or violent tendencies in Jorge. At that time, I could never imagine how the trust I placed in him could bite me in the back and almost cost me my life.

Chapter 6 — The Storm

"WE DON'T SEE THINGS AS THEY ARE. WE SEE THEM AS WE
ARE."
- ANAIS NIN -

In 1992, my house was in the direct path of Hurricane Andrew. My brother was visiting us at the time. On the day of the hurricane, I sent my wife to a friend's house further inland. She was six months pregnant with our daughter. In what turned out to be one of the most ridiculous things I've done in my life, my brother and I stayed behind to guard our possessions.

As the storm approached, I realized I had made a terrible mistake. We were initially in the kitchen, and as the storm got closer, our windows blew out, and then the doors. My brother and I knew we were in trouble, but we could not find anywhere to hide. We finally holed up in a closet on the second floor. It took us almost an hour to get there. As the storm raged, we could hear the house being torn apart. We noticed that water was leaking in from the roof, and we knew that if the roof went, there was no refuge and we were most likely dead. The roof held, barely, and after six hours in the closet, we came out to inspect the damage.

All of the possessions that I had stayed behind to guard were gone, replaced by total destruction. All the furniture was gone from the house and had been replaced with debris blown in by the wind. There were no windows or doors, and other people's furniture occupied my pool. At first, I didn't recognize where I was. When we had gone upstairs the previous night, there had been furniture and walls—now it was all gone. We had waist-high water in the house, and when we went outside, we could not comprehend what we were looking at.

It seemed as though a nuclear bomb had hit my neighborhood. Most of the homes had lost their roofs, and my neighbor's house had collapsed. There were things where they shouldn't have been, utility poles in the middle of a house, bricks embedded in walls, and in the park across the street, not a single tree remained. It was total devastation. It dawned on me then how lucky we were to have survived. The magnitude of our stupidity was alarming.

My wife left for Colombia, and I stayed back to rebuild our house. That year, my daughter was born, and by the beginning of 1993, our house was rebuilt. It helped that some of my good clients were contractors and put me first on the list when it came to repairs.

My brother was living in Miami, and he was looking for something to do. I decided to open an Schlotzsky's deli and have him run it, and we would split the profits. It looked like a pretty nice deal all around for the both of us.

Chapter 7 — The Handwriting on the Wall

"EVIL INFLUENCES ARE A VIRUS THAT THE WEAK MINDED
HAVE LITTLE IMMUNITY AGAINST."
- UNKNOWN -

That year, things started to change with Jorge. He was still working for me, and I was surprised at his reaction when I told him about my plans to open the deli. For some reason, he thought that he had a natural right to participate in it as well.

That year, he began going to Sun Gym. At first, when he told me, I couldn't help but laugh. Jorge was a skinny, wiry guy, and I could not imagine him as a bodybuilder. Shortly thereafter, he introduced me to Danny Lugo, his personal trainer. Danny disturbed me from the very first day. He seemed manipulative, and there was something about him that flashed like a neon sign: *Don't trust me. Don't trust me.* He was a muscle-bound bodybuilder who stood over six-feet four and supposedly played professional football for the New Jersey Generals, but of course most of what he said was a lie. The thoughts that came to mind whenever he spoke were *con man* and *stay away.*

After our first encounter, it was impossible to see Jorge without Danny. He became his shadow and stuck to him like glue. He brought him over to the house on a couple of occasions, and I told him that I would rather he not bring him. Jorge was always offended when I mentioned negative things about his new friend. Jorge was changing or being changed and I was not quick to pick up on it. One afternoon, I had to go visit a client, and Jorge was going to go with me. When he picked me up, Danny Lugo was with him. I was surprised and showed my disapproval. During the drive, Lugo began to speak of frauds he had committed and started making comments insinuating that we should do something similar. That day, I realized that not only did I have to get away from that character but also try to help Jorge pry himself loose from the bodybuilder's grip.

Late in 1993, I was already building the deli and making plans to open in the first quarter of 1994. Jorge was spending more time with Lugo, and he was still resentful that I had left him out of the deli. So I proposed to him that we start another company that would be involved in buying and selling mortgages. I told him that I had worked for someone who had done it very successfully, and, in fact, I was managing that business for him. He agreed and seemed enthused, and we agreed on the amount we each would put in.

The next time I saw him, he threw a virtual cold bucket of water on me: He insisted that Lugo also form part of the company. I refused and told him there was no way I getting involved in any business with his friend. He pouted and was very displeased, but he agreed to go through with our deal. In retrospect, I should have never entered into that business, considering the circumstances. But I was grateful to him for the help and support he had given me when he was my employee in my accounting practice.

We set up the company and called it Jo-Mar Investment, Inc., and we both put seed money in. I put more money in than he did, but

I was in a better position to do so. I stayed away from the business and let Jorge do most of what needed to be done. That was another mistake, because I feared that he was working with Danny Lugo. In the beginning of 1994, Jorge started acting strangely. He was not his jovial self and was pouty and moody. I didn't recognize his altered personality and thought I was talking to a different person from the one I had known for the past four years. During all that time, it had become a ritual for him to call me several times a day. Now, days passed during which he did not call me or return my calls. These ominous signs were present, but I did not heed their warning.

In February of that year, we decided we needed additional capital to do the business properly. So Jorge set up a meeting with a banker he knew who was willing to listen to our proposal. I met them at a Miami Lakes restaurant where we proceeded to talk about what we were doing, how much capital was needed, and all the rest of the specific details. The banker told us that he would present it at the bank and would let us know.

As the meeting ended, the banker turned to Jorge and said, "Jorge, what are you and Danny Lugo doing that you're depositing so much money in the bank?"

I will never forget Jorge's reaction; he turned pale white, he stared and stuttered, he could not answer the question, and he immediately said he had to go. The banker insisted. Jorge danced around the question. The banker realized he was not going to get a straight answer and desisted. After saying our goodbyes to the banker, I followed Jorge outside. I demanded to know what was going on. In what strange business was he involved with Danny

Lugo?

Jorge got mad, and it was the first time I'd seen him that way. He told me it was none of my business and to stay out of it. I told him he was my friend and that his wellbeing concerned me. I implored him to break his friendship with Lugo that it would only get him into trouble. He told me that it was none of my business and that I had no right to tell him who he could and could not be friends with.

My last words to him were "Remember what I'm telling you today. If you continue to be friends with that character, you will end up being sorry and in some deep problems." I walked away in shock. In a short period of time, Jorge had transformed into a person I did not know.

My mind was spinning as I drove home. I asked myself what was going on. What were they up to? I reluctantly decided that I had to end my business relationship with Jorge that day. I was dealing with a total stranger and did not want to get dragged into any mess he was concocting with Lugo. As soon as I got home, I called him and told him I was pulling out of our business. There was almost no reaction, which I thought was strange. We did not talk about financial arrangements and agreed that those would be discussed later. I did not hear from him for another month. In early March, I called him to discuss the financial arrangements. I decided to take a ten-thousand-dollar loss and give a little extra to him so that he would not harbor ill feelings. It backfired on me, and he was immediately upset. Thinking about it now, I could have left him all the money and it would not have made any difference. This was a different person I was talking to.

He decided to meet me to give me a check. Our meeting went as though we had not known each other for years, and he was rude and resentful. I tried to explain that he had come out better and I was taking a loss. He would have none of it and walked away. That was the last time I would talk to or see him. At least that was what I thought. There were surprises to come, and, unbeknownst to me, we would meet again in much different circumstances.

I concentrated my efforts on opening the deli, and it seemed there were numerous obstacles to overcome. The first and most important was that my brother no longer wanted to participate, and I was now facing the need to run it myself while continuing with my accounting business. The opening kept getting pushed back further and further, and now September seemed to be the most likely date when we would finally open.

In September 1994, we finally had our grand opening of the deli. Several acquaintances were invited to try out our menu. Jorge was not one of those invited. I don't suppose he would have attended. September and October were busy months for me as I tried to keep both the deli and my accounting practice going. I hired a manager to run the deli, but the results were disastrous, and he ended up making me work harder than if I had not employed him.

But the deli had really started well, and by the end of October we were actually breaking even. Our close proximity to several TV stations, the warehouse district, and the Metro-Dade Police kept our business going and growing. It's amusing to note that one of our biggest and most consistent customer bases were law enforcement officers. Not a day went by without a large group of Metro-Dade's finest eating lunch in our new establishment. Of course, the day I needed them most, none were present.

I didn't hear from Jorge between the last time I saw him and the time the deli finally opened. I had no idea what he was up to, and there was no communication at all. There was no possible way I could have imagined what he and his new handler were planning. In retrospect, I was oblivious to what was happening and should have been more vigilant. But I could never imagine the dastardly plan they were concocting, and I would never have believed that Jorge could actually be manipulated into going so far. Perhaps I was not a good judge of character. Perhaps I was naive to think that human beings could actually stoop to such low levels for money. Nonetheless, I should have been paying more attention, and the events caught me off guard.

November was the tail end of hurricane season, and as the storm clouds rolled in, I never suspected that it would be the month of my own personal hurricane, a month that would change my life forever. But sometimes you cannot know what is coming. Had I known, I would have run, hidden beneath a rock, and never come out.

Although what I am about to narrate may seem like a story out of some pulp fiction crime novel or movie, the events actually occurred. I still somehow wonder if they were real or some nightmare that I dreamed. One look at my scars affirms that, unfortunately, it was all too real. Now buckle up and get ready for a wild ride through the world of evil, greed, and mayhem. A word of advice: Please don't read this before you go to sleep. Some of the scenes described are disturbing. Now let's go.

Chapter 8 — The Second Storm

"KEEP A FIRE BURNING IN YOUR EYE, PAY ATTENTION TO THE OPEN SKY, YOU'LL NEVER KNOW WHAT WILL BE COMING DOWN."

- FOR A DANCER, JACKSON BROWNE -

November 15, 1994, was the day that changed my life forever. It was a hot, muggy day in Miami as the clouds that preceded tropical storm Gloria rolled in. The humidity was heavy and seemed so thick you could almost cut it with a knife, the type of day where you wanted to roll over and go back to sleep. I did not want to go to the deli that day, and if the manager I'd hired could have handled it, I would have stayed home. But he was inept, and I feared that if I stayed home, everything would go haywire. Besides, there was a very specific reason I needed to go in that day.

I had placed an ad in the Miami newspaper to see if anybody was interested in buying the business. Sure enough, the previous day, someone had called and said he was indeed interested, and he would be coming to see the deli and discuss terms. I had only had the deli for two months, but the hectic rhythm and the fact that it took time away from my other areas of interest had made it clear to me that selling it would be a good move. So I had to go even if, for some unknown reason, I didn't want to. I told myself the reason I didn't want to go and the strong feelings of negativity simply meant I was being lazy, tired, and affected by the bad weather. Nevertheless, I told myself that if the prospective buyer was really interested, I would not need to make that trip many more times. In reality, I was being set up, and I went for it hook, line, and sinker.

Many people close to me said I had been acting funny the previous two weeks that I was irritable and withdrawn and at times appeared preoccupied with some matter that could not be pinpointed. A few events had occurred which I shrugged off, but paying greater attention would have been wiser. Perhaps it was my melancholy state that was behind my lack of attention to those events. I have never been, nor am I now, very observant. I miss many things others see, and they have to point them out to me.

We had a sophisticated alarm system in our house, which was both good and bad: good because you could isolate precisely where the alarm was triggered and bad because Florida can sometimes suffer from daily thunderstorms, making the alarm go off during the more severe ones. The two weeks prior to my kidnapping, the alarm had gone off a few times. What was different about these occurrences was that there had been no thunderstorms to cause them. Another curious thing was that the alarm was being set off from the window in the garage. In previous storms, those windows had never set off the alarm.

On a couple of occasions, I went down and looked to see if the window had been pried open. Of course, in the sleepy stupor I was in and with my lack of observational skills, I could have missed something. I was just checking to see if the windows were open and not if something else was amiss, and I crawled back to bed when I saw nothing. Later, I found out that I had unwelcome guests roaming my lawn, guests who had probably tried to open the windows.

The second and probably more telling occurrence happened two days prior to the commencement of the actual festivities: We lived in an enclosed community situated in what was considered a pretty safe neighborhood. Robberies and other crimes were not common, and we scarcely heard about such things. When I went out to get the newspaper, I noticed glass on the driveway. I walked over to my Toyota 4Runner, which I had just purchased a month before, and the window on the driver's side was shattered. Nothing had been taken from inside the car, not even a cell phone on the passenger seat.

This should have been a wakeup call, but not to me it wasn't. I only considered it to be rather strange and inexplicable. I hadn't even heard when they broke the glass during the night, either. I talked about it with my wife and took it no further. I simply shrugged it off and made plans to get new glass installed. Apparently, I needed someone to post a sign in front of my face that said, *Wake up, something is wrong. Snap out of it, something smells fishy. Yo, Marc, wake up!* Anything less than that might not have worked. I have tried to justify my thinking by asking who could have foreseen what was about to occur. Nonetheless, the signs were there, and I simply didn't recognize the danger that lay ahead.

Grudgingly, I got in my car and started my trek to the deli, which was about twenty minutes away in light traffic. During the ride, my thoughts were on the prospective buyer, who I would be seeing at three o'clock that afternoon. I decided I was willing to consider a low offer to get rid of it. I got to the deli at about nine o'clock, and the employees started straggling in. The usual routine began as we prepared items for the lunch crowd. This included making the bread, cutting the cold cuts, making soup, cleaning the restrooms, and other miscellaneous chores. Lunchtime arrived, and we had a decent but not overwhelming crowd. Maybe it was the menacing weather outside making it a slower day. We had our usual crowd from Metro-Dade police, and that day we even had the bomb squad as patrons.

By two o'clock, the customers had subsided to a trickle. It was time for me to prepare the daily deposit, send the manager to the bank, and then go home. I was a creature of habit, and my routine never varied, which I later learned was not wise. I always left the deli by two-fifteen and went home to have my coffee while I watched TV or read. That day, I had to stay, and you could not imagine how much I dreaded doing so. I sat down at one of the tables and waited, and I was joined by one of my employees taking a break. We chatted until three o'clock, the time I expected the buyer to show up.

By three-thirty, no buyer, I was seriously bored and ready to go home. I told my employee that I would wait another fifteen minutes; maybe the weather or traffic had slowed him down. I tried to call him to confirm that he was still coming; there was no answer. By three forty five, I gave up and told my remaining two employees that I was going home before the evening's rush hour. I picked up my briefcase and headed for the back door. Normally, I parked out front, but that day, when I arrived, there had been no spaces, and I had to park in back, which had less traffic and was more desolate.

I joked with an employee as I opened the door and stepped outside. The air outside felt heavy and saturated with moisture; it was one of those days when a person could break a sweat by only raising an arm. The back parking lot was mostly deserted. It faced the rear of the shopping strip, which lodged the deli. All the stores in the strip were occupied, and at one end was an auto repair shop with bays facing the back lot. That day, the bay doors were open, and there was movement in them. It was almost a hundred yards from where my car was parked, and they had good visibility of the entire lot.

I walked into the lot, nonchalantly carrying my briefcase, thinking I just wanted to get home before the rain started. As I said, I'm not observant, and I did not see the white Astro van or its occupants as I walked toward my car. I looked back briefly and saw my employee close the door of the deli.

I was oblivious. It never crossed my mind that I could possibly have some badass enemies that wanted to hurt me. Besides, carrying out such an act in the middle of the day, in a parking lot at a busy intersection, was so brazen and stupid that no one would do that. Obviously, they did not concur with me. I had seen such a similar act in New York City, but that was a different jungle, and anything can and does happen there.

As I approached my car, I saw three men walking towards me. Two were Hispanic, and one was African American. I thought nothing of it. Why should I have? There was nothing about their appearance that made them stand out. They were dressed in blue jeans and t-shirts. They could have been going to any of the shops on the strip, and people sometimes liked to park in the back because of traffic patterns. I cannot be sure, but I didn't see if they were carrying anything. If they were, it was well concealed.

In retrospect, everything seems to have occurred so fast that time is distorted in my mind. As I inserted the key into the lock and opened the door, one of them grabbed me from behind, trying to push me towards their van. The struggle for survival began.

The first thing I said instinctively was "If you want my car, just take it."

My thoughts were initially that these were car thieves, and I was not going to fight them for the car—they could have it. It just was not worth it; I had insurance on the car, and it could be replaced. There was no response, and now the two others joined the first guy. Collectively, they were trying to force me towards the white van.

In desperation, I said, "Tell me what you want, and maybe I can give it to you."

No response, no negotiation, nothing, nada.

I fought back, and the struggle lasted a while. I'm not the biggest person in the world, but my years of playing sports gave me strong legs, which I used to resist them. They tore my shirt to shreds in the struggle, and even today I cannot believe no one saw the commotion. Even worse, if they did see, they didn't care or didn't want to get involved.

They were getting exasperated and decided that their intended victim needed to be subdued. One of them brought out a Taser and started shocking me with it. My body was sweating profusely, and it made an especially good medium to apply electric shock. Even with the constant painful electric shock, I kept fighting until the electricity weakened my body. I did manage to yell for help several times; either no one heard me, or it just went unheeded. At this point, I noticed that one of them was packing a gun. I could not fight any longer, and they dragged me to the van and threw me inside. Believe it or not, this ordeal lasted at least ten minutes, no joke, and no one; I mean no one, supposedly saw it. No one called the police.

The joy ride to hell was boarding, and I was the VIP passenger. I was thrown face down between the driver's seat and the first row of passenger chairs. A silver-plated gun appeared in front of my face, and one of them said, "See the gun? If you make a sound or wrong move, I will kill you."

I believed it; there was no doubt. At that point, they were jubilant. Just for fun, they shocked me again with the Taser.

The next order I received was to put my hands behind my back, and they proceeded to handcuff me. They also put cuffs on my feet. I was totally at their mercy, and they knew it. They taped my eyes with a roll of gray packing tape, and the world went dark. They celebrated their conquest as cavemen would by taunting and abusing their prey. They kicked me repeatedly in the ribs, punched me in the face and body, all while laughing loudly. This was only the beginning of a long and very scary episode.

They covered me with a moving blanket, and I started to hyperventilate. I could not catch my breath. I think it was a combination of fear and the effort I had exerted in struggling against them. I was bewildered. Like bullets from a machine gun, thoughts shot through my brain. Questions, many questions, but there were no answers. Who were these creatures, and what did they want? Where were they taking me and why? I could not comprehend this. Why was it happening to me? I was terrified and thought of my family. I wondered if they were all right. I even thought this might have been a nightmare and I was really safe in my bed at home. I wished I was, and I wish I had been.

They proceeded to loot the carcass they had just captured. They took my watch, my wallet, a chain I was wearing, and a bracelet. Then one of them said, in a cry of joy, "We got ourselves a Matzo Ball." They were talking among themselves the entire time, but I could not decipher much of what they were saying. From what I was able to sense, there were five occupants in the van: the driver, the two seated in the middle seat and shotgun seat, and the two in the bench seats in the back.

We made a right turn onto Seventy-Ninth Avenue, and after that, I lost track of the various directions we were heading. From that point, we could have gone anywhere, including the moon, and I would not have known where I was. My mind raced so fast I thought it would explode. I thought that these goons were going to kill me and ditch me somewhere in the Everglades. I was convinced that was how it would end. I was helpless. Whatever fate awaited me, I had no choice but to accept.

One comment I clearly heard was "Everything went so well, it was a piece of cake."

I didn't think so, but that didn't matter now. I needed to clear my head and calm down so I could deal with whatever awaited me.

We drove for fifteen or twenty minutes. It was hard to tell, but it couldn't have been much longer.

During the ride, one of them made a comment: "You have no right to live a good life when we don't."

I thought it was a strange comment since I did not live an extravagant or lavish life. Nonetheless, I realized that my captors knew me better than I had thought and this was not a random snatch. I had never felt as helpless as I did then. Always in control of my life and the choices I made, I now had to submit to their will, and nothing I could do would change that. There was no comfort and not the slimmest ray of hope.

When we reached our destination and the van had come to a complete stop, the driver called someone and said, "We're at the warehouse, and we have a present for you." Then he said, "How far away are you? Okay, we'll drive inside and wait for you."

They drove the van into what they called the warehouse. One of them got out and opened the sliding door, and the rest got out of the van, leaving me in the same facedown position I had been in since we left the deli.

One of them said, "What are we going to do with his car?"

Another one replied, "We'll wait till the boss gets here."

"Yeah, we go do it quick so no one gets curious," the first one responded.

"He'll be here in a few minutes" was the reply.

I could tell they were trying to disguise their voices. Were they afraid I would recognize them? Or were they concerned that if anything went wrong and they got caught, I would be able to identify them by their voices? Someone came over released the cuffs from my feet, and yelled, "Get up!"

I was shoved out of the van and dropped face down on top of what seemed to be a cardboard box just a few feet from where the van was parked. They checked to make sure the tape was affixed to my head and added more for good measure. It was hot and muggy, and I was sweating profusely from the temperature and the fear, as well as from the exertion. It felt as though I had submerged myself in a pool with my clothes on. But that was the least of my concerns then. They made me lie on my stomach and proceeded to cuff my ankles again, and then they raised my feet and linked them to the handcuffs on my wrists. I was a human circle, a big zero, and a doughnut. This position became very uncomfortable almost immediately.

They took my boots off, and I lay there, playing my role of human doughnut, trying to concentrate on other things as the pain increased in my arms, legs and back. The items on my thought menu were not pleasant. Either I thought of the pain and numbness that kept increasing throughout my body or happy thoughts of the wonderful things that probably awaited me. Trying to think of anything pleasant to distract my mind was of no use. The handcuffs were really tight, and they started eating into the skin of my wrists and ankles. Someone walked up and faced me from the front.

He asked, "Do you want some water?" My throat was parched, and I felt that I had just walked a long trek in the Sahara.

I managed to reply, "Yes."

He said, "Pick up your head."

I obeyed. He threw the water on my face and laughed as he

walked away.

I could tell this was not going to be any picnic. These sadists enjoyed taunting and humiliating.

I lay there for what seemed like an hour. My arms and feet had gone numb, and I could hardly breathe. The heat and mugginess just added to the misery I felt, and I was soaked in my own sweat. Faintly, I heard them speaking in the background, and apparently the boss had arrived and given the order to go pick up my car. They were using code names so that I could not identify them later. I was Eagle, and the other names I heard were Sparrow and Robin. I guess whoever made up the names liked birds, or they were as crazy as cuckoos. This gave me a faint glimmer of hope, realizing that if they were trying to disguise their voices and names, maybe, just maybe, this ordeal would be short lived.

Then I heard a conversation that sent chills up my spine and increased the terror.

One of them said, "Do you have someone watching the house?"

Another one replied, "We have a car out there."

"We'll make sure he stays out there so we don't have any problems," the other said.

The nightmare had just entered a new phase. Not only was I in a situation wherein I was totally helpless and at their mercy, but now my wife and children were also in danger, and there was nothing I could do about it. I know it may sound bizarre, but I hoped she would not call the police. First of all, if she did, the thugs watching my house would call the thugs holding me, and, without a doubt, they would dispose of me. Secondly, calling the police could have caused them to take revenge against my family.

I was panicky, but the more I thought about it, I came to realize that there was only a slim chance that she would actually make the call. She spoke limited English, and her personality would make her freeze and probably not react. She wasn't a person who would seize the initiative. When our son had nearly drowned in our pool in 1991, I gave him CPR while yelling for someone to call 911. She had frozen in horror, and it was I who called them. I suspected that she would not call, and I needed to find a way to get them to a safety from which she might rethink her strategy and call the authorities. My wife told me later that she was being followed when she picked up our son from school that same day. They were so inept in doing so that they nearly collided with her. We were all in danger, and each move needed to be measured if we wanted to survive.

It seemed like forever, but eventually, someone came over and released my ankles from my arms. They rolled me over, and an object was pressed firmly against my face. It was either an aluminum bat or some kind of club. He said, "Feel this, asshole? You know what it is?"

I didn't reply.

"Well, do you?" he said.

"Yes," I replied. I had two choices, either yes or no, and no didn't seem like a good choice at the time.

"You make one wrong move, and I'll break your head," he spat.

"Yes," I replied. I had no doubt that he would do so and would enjoy it immensely.

They picked me up since trying to get up by myself would have proved to be impossible. I sensed they enjoyed the power trip they were getting from dominating and manhandling me. The power to control and humiliate another human being and the smell of fear and terror that poured from their prey were like a drug, an adrenaline kick that they seemed to thrive on.

A hand held my arm firmly, pressing me forward. I shuffled ahead; it was difficult to walk because of the tightly pressing ankle cuffs. The games had begun. They made me walk in circles so I would get disoriented. There was no need for that; with the pounds of tape on my face, I could not tell if I was on Earth or Mars. They took me into what I perceived to be another room and put me in what seemed to be a large top of a box or maybe one that had been cut out. It felt as though a moving blanket or something similar was in the bottom of the box. This was going to be my home away from home for a while, even though, at that point, I still thought my ordeal would be short.

I was placed face up with my hands still handcuffed behind me. The box appeared to be six feet long by two feet wide. My ankles were also still cuffed, which afforded me very little range of motion. In other words, I was not going anywhere. The handcuffs were put on very tightly, and the friction they caused sent bolts of pain shooting through my arms. The position was uncomfortable, and I could not wiggle to any degree to make it less so.

A few minutes later, someone came in and said, "We'll be back later. There is someone who wants to see you."

Geez, what if I don't want to see him. Do I have a choice? Can I have a good book or watch a movie until his highness gives me an audience? I guess the answer would have been no and the repercussions even worse, so I said nothing.

And then, I heard music. Loud music. Once it started playing, it seemed to never stop. They turned on music to drown out their conversation and, I'm sure, to drive me crazy. Not only was it loud, but also it was not at all to my taste. It played almost constantly for the entire time I was there, twenty-four hours a day. Maybe you can understand why I couldn't listen to music for years afterwards.

Chapter 9 — Rules of the Game

"WHEN BACKED INTO A CORNER, A VICTIM HAS TWO OPTIONS: HE CAN LIE DOWN AND DIE, OR HE CAN FIGHT REGARDLESS OF THE ODDS."

- UNKNOWN -

As I lay there, I kept wondering whether someone had noticed yet that I was missing. I was as punctual and reliable as a Swiss clock, and so was my routine. I was not the type of person to go wandering off anywhere without previously informing my wife. I was a homebody and went straight home from the deli. I didn't even like to stop to run errands. My affection for being at home was so extreme that I had moved my accounting office there.

Now hours had passed, and I had not called or shown up. It was obvious to me that my wife must have realized something was wrong, but what? Had I gotten into an accident? The thought of me being kidnapped was so farfetched that I doubted it would ever cross her mind. She probably thought I was in some hospital, unable to call. I also knew she wouldn't know what to do under the circumstances. She would have no idea where to turn for help. There was no family: My brother had recently moved to Tampa, and my sister lived in New York. There were no friends to call.

Who was she going to call, Jorge Delgado? Later on, I found out she actually had contemplated calling him. That would have been interesting. So I knew she was in a quandary and would most likely do nothing, hoping to hear from me. I later learned someone had called her about five times to see if I was home. The calls were strange. They were not from anyone my wife could identify. Perhaps they were checking up to see if she was home and to check on her mental state.

So I lay there, knowing that no quick solution was going to be forthcoming. At that point, I didn't expect my rescuers to come charging through the doors. I was hopeful that I could give my captors whatever they wanted and the ordeal would soon end. The other possibility also existed that they were going to kill me and were making final plans. My mind raced as I searched for answers that didn't exist. Why were they doing this to me? Who were they? What did they want? It went on and on, and I revisited each question a thousand times. Although it was to no avail, under the circumstances, I understood that this was normal and expected.

I always try to live my life correctly, doing no harm to anyone. A person can become almost a recluse and have very little contact with strangers and no friends, as I did, and also try to help anyone in need if the circumstances permit it. That does not mean that others are not looking at you and wanting whatever you have. There is no perfect way to find shelter from of a world of insanity and madness.

So, I just lay there, time becoming insignificant. A minute seemed like an hour, an hour like a day. Then there was commotion and several voices—something was happening. I was sweating so much that the tape on my face had come loose. I could wiggle my face and peek through the tape. I saw one figure in the distance and a light behind him. It was blurry, and I could not make anything out too well. I looked directly above me and saw that I was below a window with mini blinds. The strain to see was immense since I had to contort my face in funny ways. It was just too much, and I finally gave up. Those were the last things I saw for the next month. In that moment, I didn't know if they were the last things I was ever going to see.

I had to go to the bathroom, and there was no way to ask someone to take me. If I could, would they actually let me do so? My bladder was going to burst, which it actually did later. There was no shame. It was a survival instinct that kicked in. I urinated as I lay there on the box, soaking my pants in the process and adding to the misery I already felt. But humiliation and shame were the last things I was concerned about at that point. It was the first of many unthinkable acts to which I would have to resort. I would have to muster any resource available to me just to survive.

Bent on survival, I reverted to what I feel was some sort of ancient animal state that had lain dormant in my DNA. I didn't know I had this capability, but the ancient reptile brain I had not acknowledged demanded my survival. I discovered that at the same time, my spirit gained ascendance as my guiding force, enabling me to pass through circumstances and obstacles that seemed impossible to withstand.

Someone came in perhaps an hour or maybe five hours later. I didn't know, nor did it matter. He said, "Someone is here to see you."

Gee, do I have time to get myself together and fix up?

He said, "Get up."

I can't, moron. I have chains on my ankles, and my arms are handcuffed behind my back, or didn't you notice? He pulled me up and almost fell over the edge of the box doing so.

"Be careful, or you might break your face." He snorted as he let out a boisterously mad laugh. I was sure that sort of accident would cause them great sadness. We shuffled along as we played the let's-go-around-in-circles game.

I was taken to another room and pushed into a chair. I could sense the presence of various people close by in that room. It's amazing how, when you lose one or more of your senses, the remaining ones pick up the slack and compensate for the loss by becoming more finely tuned.

I knew whatever was coming would not be pleasant. I was almost in a drunken stupor from the physical and mental exertion. At some point, I considered throwing in the towel. This feeling would return to me again, but I could not do it. I wasn't going to allow them to break me that easily, even if it meant dying in the process. I could not let this evil have its way without a fight. So the ceremonies began.

Chapter 10 — Torture 101: Basic Torturing

"THAT WHICH DOES NOT KILL US MAKES US STRONGER."
- FRIEDRICH NIETZSCHE -

So there I sat, in front of the great council of madmen. It comprised greedy and sadistic psychos who got drunk on the power they created through acting out their violent fantasies. It would be proven later that financial gain was not their only objective—they wanted to hurt and destroy their victims through their bloodlust.

As I sat there speculating on what was to come, I never imagined what actually would transpire. Were they going to question me or threaten me? Would I answer the questions, and how would I play my cards? Would I bluff? Was it going to be a matter of giving them what they wanted until they let me go, or were things going to get considerably more complicated? I willed myself to snap out of my stupor; I knew that I had to be alert for what was to come.

They began by saying, "We are the family."

At that point, I didn't know whether to laugh or cry. How ridiculous, just a bit melodramatic.

One of them continued, "We brought you here because you stole from the family, and we want it back."

Now I was thinking this must have been a case of mistaken identity. I had no knowledge of any family, and I had certainly never stolen anything from anyone. This was just bizarre. I was in the twilight zone.

Suddenly, things escalated to the physical, and they punched me twice in the face. Maybe they were mind readers or aliens and could tell what I was thinking. Anyway, it hurt.

"We want a list of your assets," he growled.

I thought he had to be joking. Nonetheless, I replied, "You want a list of my assets?" I guess they could hear the sarcasm in my response.

The next thing I felt was a series of vicious blows to the back of my head, neck, and back with what I perceived to be the butt of a gun. For some reason, each blow started to hurt less as I tried to become oblivious to them.

They whispered among themselves, and I could not discern anything they were saying, not that I cared much. Hearing them would not change my circumstances, though it could give me a clue as to their identities.

The next thing they asked set off an explosion of fireworks and alarms ringing in my head.

"Is the alarm code to your house one-seven-four-nine?" he asked.

Now I knew at least one person who was involved: Jorge Delgado. He was the only one who knew the old code to the alarm at the house. I had not published it in any newspaper, nor had I advertized it. He was the only one who had been privileged to know it. Of course, after things went sour with him, we had changed it.

I made a mistake and said, "That was the old code."

"Don't lie," my interrogator snapped back.

"I'm not lying," I said, realizing that I should have done so.

"If you don't cooperate, we're going to bring your wife and children here and do the same to them. They are easier to get than you," he continued. "We have people in front of your house, watching."

I was confused again. I realized how badly disadvantaged I was, since they had all the leverage while I had none. Could I cooperate and avoid a bigger tragedy? If I did cooperate, how could I guarantee that something would not happen anyway? I was in a quandary, and, in the labyrinth of my mind, could not find a way out. I hoped their interest was purely monetary and nothing else, but how could I be sure? I was still reeling from the fact that Delgado was playing a role in this fiasco. There were two possibilities: Either he was directly involved, or he had sold me out by giving information to these criminals. Either way, it didn't matter. He had betrayed me after I nurtured and trusted him. It was unforgivable, and that hurt more than some of the physical blows.

I realized that I was playing with a bad hand. I had the two of clubs while they had the ace of diamonds.

Reluctantly, I said, "I'll cooperate." I did not see any other way. I could gamble with my own life, but I could not gamble with the lives and wellbeing of my family.

He said, with bravado in his voice, "If you don't, we'll bring your wife here, and each of us will take turns raping her."

I didn't believe this to be an idle threat and knew that not only would they make good on it, they would probably enjoy inflicting the pain. This confirmed that I had no choice but to cooperate and pray that things ended shortly and well. But I started getting the feeling that things were not going to be that easy. They didn't stop there, for he continued, "And for good measure, we'll bring your kids and chain them to the wall, like you."

For a brief moment, the image of my six-year-old son and two-year-old daughter blindfolded and chained to a wall flashed before my mind's eye before I could shake those disturbing thoughts loose. They were trying to mentally torture me and were succeeding. How could I possibly risk such a fate for my children? I had no doubt that they were serious. These were some sick minds. It was not a gamble I was willing to take. I was going to give them what they wanted and hope that it would end there, but the fact that there was no guarantee kept nagging at the fringes of my mind.

First question: "What is the gate code for your community?"

I was trying to think of so many things at the same time and hear their questions.

"One-one-nine-six?" he asked. Again, this was the old code. The community changed the code periodically, and this confirmed that Delgado was the traitor. He had known that code, as well.

"That's the old code," I mumbled.

"Stop lying," he snapped.

Maybe I should start lying, since you have hard time believing the truth. They hit me in the face a couple of times just to make sure I understood. This was getting exasperating. I had told them the truth and still paid the consequences. The truth was no good, and lies were no good. I wished they had given me a script of exactly what they wanted me to say. It may have saved me a few knocks to the head.

"Do you manage money overseas for your wife's relatives?" he inquired.

"Yes."

I received a couple of surprise electrical shocks with the Taser. I guess they were testing it to see if it still worked after using it that afternoon. It did, and I felt it.

It already sounded like they knew everything, so why were they asking me? If Delgado was involved, as it surely seemed, then all this questioning was a waste of time. He knew what I had and where it all was located. They couldn't have been that stupid. Didn't they figure that by telling me they knew the alarm codes, I would realize Delgado was involved?

Apparently, they didn't like that answer either, for they put me face down on the floor on my hands and knees.

"Well, you should have cooperated." He laughed. This was bewildering. I was cooperating. It dawned on me that it didn't matter if I did or not. These boys were sick sadists and needed to release their primal savagery on me just to make themselves feel good.

They put the barrel of the gun next to my ear and made sure I heard when they inserted a lone bullet into one of the chambers. They pressed it against my temple. Perhaps they wanted me to piss in my pants again. Sorry, not this time.

"We are going to play a game. Let's see if you know the name of the game," he said.

I felt the game must have been over for me, and this was going to be the end of it. They were going to kill me, and the rest had been a charade, a way of having some fun at my expense. I thought it was strange they were not after money or other assets, just toying with me and preparing for the kill. The gun was pressed into my temple. Clenching my teeth, I braced for the impact of the bullet that was about to penetrate my brain. The only comfort available was that it was going to be a quick and relatively painless death. He pressed the trigger, and I heard a click. First round, and I had not won the big prize; as far as I could tell, my brains were still inside my skull and not splattered on the floor. They were laughing uncontrollably, and I was shaking. I wondered how many other things they were going to put me through for their enjoyment before they killed me.

He spun the cylinder and pressed the gun against my temple once more. Click, no bullet to the brain. It must have been my lucky day, because they were zero for two. Again they laughed uncontrollably. Perhaps they were rolling on the floor with amusement. I didn't find it funny at all. It amazed me how much they enjoyed making another human being miserable. Then I received a sharp blow to the back of the head as a reminder that I was not out of the woods yet.

They picked me up and threw me into the chair again. I guessed that the game was over. So far, I was still alive, but I didn't know if that was good or bad.

"Let's make a deal, okay?" he said.

"Fine," I replied. I wondered if they were getting bored already or if they were sore losers. I couldn't wait to hear the gem they were about to lay on me.

"We will let your wife and children leave the country if you give us all your assets," he said.

I didn't have to think about it to respond.

"Once I know that they're safe and out of the country, you can have whatever you want," I replied.

It was the best deal possible for me. I could not handle my captivity and their imminent danger at the same time. I could not put a value on their lives, and material possessions meant nothing now. Material things didn't figure into the equation. With my family safe and sound, I could concentrate on surviving this captivity and eventual release, if that was actually going to happen. If not, then I would be able to accept my death knowing I would be the only victim. But the problem remained: I did not know if it was all a trick to dupe me or not. There was no question that I could not trust anything they said. I had to have irrefutable evidence that they had kept their end of the bargain.

"Okay, you're going to call your wife tonight and tell her you're going on a business trip and you won't be back for a couple of days," he ordered.

That was so ludicrous, to think my wife was actually going to buy such a story when I had never done anything similar. What? The business trip just came up out of the blue? It was a total joke, and surely they could have thought of something better. It was so out of character for me that it would have been like George Washington telling his wife that he was going to fight for the British for a couple of days.

Nonetheless, I replied, "Fine." I didn't really have many other choices for a response.

"If you say anything to get her suspicious, or if she calls the police, we're going to have to kill you," he barked.

I didn't have to tell her anything to get her suspicious. The story they concocted would be enough to do that. As far as calling the police, I was hoping that she would not call them either until she was out of harm's way. But if they thought she was going to believe this story, they had a few brain cells missing. There was no doubt they wouldn't hesitate to kill me if she did call the police. I was not sure whether they would kill me either way.

"Fine," I responded again. What else could I say?

I thought we had reached an agreement and their games were over, but I was wrong. It didn't matter to them. They enjoyed inflicting pain. They shocked me several times with the Taser they had introduced me to in the parking lot. I felt like a laboratory mouse they were experimenting on to see how much electric shock it could take. After I recuperated from the last shock and they stopped laughing, my torturer told me, "If you cooperate and everything goes well, you'll be out of here and back with your family in a couple of days."

I wanted desperately to believe those words, because it is said that the last thing you lose is hope. I needed to cling to whatever hope there was, even if it was minimal. However, my rational mind told me they would probably kill me anyway after they got what they wanted. First, I needed to make sure my family had left. Second, I had to refuse to have my spirit broken and keep fighting until the end. The one remaining wish I had was to say goodbye to my family.

"Okay," he said. "You have a house that is paid for, your wife's family money that you invest, your wife's jewelry, your

Rolex, your ring, an apartment in Miami Beach under construction, insurance policies, your jet skis, is that correct?"

I was astonished and could not respond. The only thing missing was how many rolls of toilet paper we had in the garage. I could not respond, but it should not have shocked me, since I suspected Delgado's involvement. This sealed my suspicion, and I definitely knew that he was playing some role there. No one could have given them such a complete and accurate list of my assets except Delgado. I guess I took too long to respond, since I was trying to digest what was happening, and as a result received two blows to my head. They had no patience.

"Yes," I replied, the terror now giving way to sadness. My most trusted and loyal employee, whom I had always tried to help, had sold me out. I had always been there for him, and that traitorous turnabout was now inflicting great pain on me, both emotionally and physically.

"Okay, in a little while, you are going to call your wife and tell her what we told you," he instructed. He then zapped me with the Taser without giving me a chance to respond.

"Fine," I replied quickly, trying to avoid another blow to the head or another shot of electricity. It appeared that the torture and humiliation session was over.

One of them showed some concern and asked me if I needed to go to the bathroom. I said yes, not knowing when my next opportunity would come. They took me to the bathroom and placed me in front of what must have been the toilet. Performing such a simple task while blindfolded becomes a major challenge. Next, I had to figure out how to lower my pants. I had both hands handcuffed behind my back, and lowering was going to take some effort. Fortunately, the pants were loose fitting and I was able to slide them down. At that point, someone yelled, "Stop masturbating, your time is up," and started to laugh, knowing full well that I had not finished or even started the chore. It was just another way of humiliating me, and they had no intention of actually letting me relieve myself. It was just another game to them. I slid my pants back up as well as I could. It seemed like I was going to have to rely on the POM method of relieving myself, better known as the pee-on-myself method.

I was taken back to the cardboard box where I had been before and put in the same position. I started recounting all that had been said to me, along with the shock and sadness I had felt when I realized that Jorge Delgado was playing a role in this. I didn't know which was worse, the physical pain or the pain in my heart. My mind was working overtime, but I was exhausted both physically and mentally. I reasoned that things were at least settled and the worst appeared to be over. I told myself that all I had to do was wait and the ordeal would be over. I was wrong on both counts.

Chapter 11 — Torture 201: Advanced Torturing

"THE GREATEST EVIL IS PHYSICAL PAIN."
- ST. AUGUSTINE -

I lay in the box, recounting all the events that had just transpired. I thought about my choices, which were not many—there were, in fact, none. I could not afford to get distracted by Jorge's traitorous act. I would have time for that later, maybe. I didn't know what time it was. It already seemed that days, not hours, had passed since I walked out of the deli's door.

Someone came and said, "If you try taking your blindfold off, or if we think you're trying to peek and see any of us, we will kill you." I wondered if they had seen when I tried to peek before. I didn't think so, but I couldn't be sure. My second thought was they were looking for any pretext to kill me. The urine on my clothes had dried, which was the only comfort I could find. It is often said that misery loves company. I had misery but no company.

I reached the point where my mind was overcome with all that had happened … was happening, and my mental circuit breakers tripped. I passed out for a period of time. How long? I'm not certain, but in retrospect it was a welcome relief, and my body must have known that it had to shut down for a while or my brain was going to overheat. I was rudely jolted awake by them turning up the volume on the radio to a nearly unbearable level. Fortunately, this time the station was changed to soft rock, so it wasn't as bad as the previous music they had played.

They came back a short time later. As I said before, time had become irrelevant. One man said, "You're going to call your wife and tell her what we told you. Do you understand?" As a peace offering, or better yet, to manipulate me further, they gave me a cigarette. I smoked half a pack per day and, under the circumstances, could have chained smoked a couple of packs or maybe more. They were trying to soften me up again and knew that I wanted my nicotine fix. I was left alone to smoke my cigarette. I soon realized that I had nowhere to put it out. I used the floor next to me; if I started a fire, it wasn't my fault.

Soon they came in, picked me up from the cardboard box, and sat me down in a chair in the same room. There was some sort of desk in front of me, and I could hear when they brought in a phone and plugged it in.

"If you say anything to make her suspicious or anything that we don't like, we're going to have to bring her and the children here and chain them up next you," he said.

Right, like she is not going to be suspicious. I disappear, and that's normal. To this point, it had always been the same person talking to me, and I could not recognize the voice. He tried to distort it and at times he forgot to, but I did not recognize it.

"I'll do as you say. Just leave them out of this," I replied.

"How long do you think she will last, chained to that wall?" He snorted. I knew they were referring to my wife's medical condition. She had suffered from Lupus for the past fifteen years, and Jorge knew that she had her good and bad times. I did not respond, and perhaps this was a mistake. They probably thought they had hit a nerve and might use it later on to get further concessions from me.

"Make it short, and don't get wise. We'll be listening on another phone," he said.

I heard them as they brought the phone and dialed the number. This was irrefutable evidence of who was involved—they hadn't even needed to ask me for the number.

My wife and I called each other China and Chino, names that are commonly and affectionately used in Colombia, her native country.

She answered the phone, and her voice was shaky. After I said hello, she said, "Chino, where are you? What's happening?" She was in despair, and I thought it would be wiser to make the conversation as short as possible.

"I'm okay, don't worry. I have to go on a business trip for a couple of days. I'll call in two days. How are the children?" I asked. I always asked about the kids, and I was putting on a great show for my captors.

She started to get hysterical and go over the deep end—not good. She said, "Tell me what's happening and who you are with."

I wish I could tell you, and you wouldn't believe it if I did. I replied, "I'm alone and need to finish some urgent business. I'll call you in a couple of days. I love you," I said, and I hung up without giving her the chance to say anything else. It was better that way. If my captors thought she was not suspicious, they were total fools or totally blinded by their greed and stupidity.

Amazingly, they approved the conversation and said, "That was fine. We hope she doesn't do anything stupid, or both of you will pay the consequences."

I replied, "She won't. Just let her and the children leave as soon as possible." To me, that was priority number one, but it was not up to me to decide if and when they could leave.

Next, I was taken back to my cardboard box and given a cigarette. It was as if I were one of Pavlov's dogs, given my reward for performing the trick correctly and being obedient. In order for me to smoke it, they untied the chains behind my back and retied them in front. That alone was a great relief. It was getting painful to have them in that position for so long. The music was blasting away. Trying to think of anything was difficult. I didn't know how my wife was going to react, nor did I have sufficient information.

What was the situation at the house? I just hoped she would sit tight and wait it out for a couple of days. At that point, hopefully, they would let her leave and she, being supported by her family, could regroup and think of a way to contact the authorities or someone who could obtain my release. Maybe I was being too pessimistic, and in a few days there would be no need for that. They would let me go after they got what they wanted: money. I did not have many choices at this juncture, and the possibility of escaping seemed remote to me. Being shackled and blindfolded did not afford me the advantage I needed to be able to carry out an escape. I didn't know how many of them there were. I didn't know how well armed they were or the location of this supposed warehouse. At this point, the possibility seemed too risky, and attempting to do so could put my family in danger. I quickly pushed away those thoughts to wait and see what would happen. It would all be over soon, I thought. But I was wrong again.

I lay there for what must have been a few hours, dozing in and out of consciousness. I was so weary by then that I couldn't think even if I wanted to. I needed to go to the bathroom and had to use the POM method, so my pants were once again wet. They came back in again, and one of them asked me if I wanted a cigarette. I wondered what I had done to deserve that prize, but it turned out that the visit was not being made in peace.

He told me that he would light the cigarette for me and ordered me to hold my hand out to grab it. With difficulty, I did, and he proceeded to burn the top of my hand. I could hear the skin sizzling as I cried out in pain. I was too slow in retracting my hand, and he burned me again between my middle finger and my index finger, emitting deep laughter again. This was not fun at all. I flinched in pain.

They picked me up forcibly and took me a few steps to a hard chair. I was totally perplexed. Hadn't we reached a deal? Then again, when you make a deal with the Devil, you really don't expect him to abide by the terms, do you?

One of them said, "You lied to us about your assets."

"I did not," I responded, to no avail.

So this was a fishing expedition to see if they could intimidate me into confessing about other assets I may have had. For some reason, they were not satisfied with their list. But they pretty much had covered everything that I owned, so this was pointless. Then a realization hit me like a ton of bricks. I recognized the voice I was hearing. It had a New York accent with a very discernible lisp. There was no doubt about it, it was Danny Lugo, and this was the Danny Lugo show. Now I understood Delgado's involvement. That was a short-lived moment of lucidity.

The next thing I heard was the sound of a lighter, and whoever was in the room with Lugo whispered in my ear with a sickening madman's groan, "FIRE … FIRE … FIRE," and proceeded to burn the top of my arm near my shoulder with the flame. The smell of burning flesh filled the room, and I could hear the sizzling of my skin as the flame penetrated through it. The pain was mind numbing, and I groaned, unable to muster the energy to yell. He did this three times, each time whispering the madman's groan, "FIRE … FIRE … FIRE," which actually made it worse because I knew what was coming.

After each time he burned me, he would start laughing uncontrollably, and I could hear him do a little dance. I realized that this was better than sex for him. He was in pure orgasmic joy. This fellow was sick, and I could tell this was what he had been born to do. I would have wanted to meet this psycho alone in a dark alleyway. While most kids grew up playing sports or video games, this dude had probably prowled the neighborhood looking for defenseless animals to torture and kill.

The last burn was in my lower arm, near my elbow. I tried to brace for each one, but it was useless. I was ready to vomit from the combination of the reek of burnt flesh in the room and the immense pain that was coming from the open wounds in my arms. In between the second and third burns, I was also hit in the back of the head with what I thought was a baseball bat. This hurt, but my arm hurt so much more that it distracted me from the new bump I had just received.

Lugo said, "Do you have a safety deposit box?"

"No," I replied, which was the truth. Unfortunately, it didn't seem to make a difference.

"Where do you keep your will?" he said.

"I don't have one," I told him, though I wondered whether I would need one soon.

He laughed and said, "Bad mistake," as he hit me with what I thought was the butt of the gun on the back of my head. Well, it looked like I had an answer to my unvoiced query.

They burned me once more, this time with meaning and gusto, just in case the previous three had not driven home the point. Of course, he repeated the sick chant, "FIRE ... FIRE ... FIRE," prior to doing it and laughed like a hyena after.

"We're going to find everything, and if you lied to us, we are going to kill you," Lugo said.

"Fine," I replied. *It sounds like you are going to kill me anyway, so what difference does it make?*

He continued, "Tomorrow you're going to call your wife and tell her that she is going to leave for Colombia on Friday. Tell her to leave everything, including the jewelry, and take nothing except some clothing, do you understand?"

How benevolent of them, I thought; they were going to allow her to take a change of clothing for her and the children. These guys were pigs. They wanted everything, and I mean everything.

"Yes, I understand," I replied. At the same time, I was thinking these guys wouldn't be winning any intellectual challenges. They didn't want my wife to get suspicious, but they told me to give her an order that would automatically make her suspicious, as if she wasn't already.

"How much money do you have in the house safe?" Lugo asked.

I always kept a good sum of cash in the safe in case an emergency arose. After Hurricane Andrew, I found myself short of cash, so it became a custom. Thinking about it, Delgado had mentioned that he did the same and that I should do it also.

"Five thousand," I told him.

"You are going to tell your wife to cash another check for eight thousand. Tell her to put the money in the safe."

"Okay," I replied. This brain trust did not want to get anybody suspicious, but they were doing everything just short of holding up a neon sign saying, *something is wrong*. Very smart.

I was in such pain from the open burn wounds that I was almost incoherent. It really didn't matter what they were saying or how absurd it was. I could not concentrate. However, the next thing he said really caught my interest.

"One more thing, we are going to receive some boxes at your house. You are to tell your wife not to open them and leave them in the garage, not to open them, understand?" Lugo emphasized.

They were using my house for their new mailing address. I wondered what would be in those boxes: guns, other tools to kill or torture me or somebody else, drugs? Anything was possible with this gang of madmen, anything.

"Yes," I replied. What was I supposed to say? *Well, that depends what's in the boxes?*

They picked me up and took me to the cardboard box and made me lie down in it. I lay there with the smell of my burnt flesh still in my nostrils. The ache in my open wounds was maddening, and I could not even reach up and touch them because of my handcuffs. I would not even say I was miserable at that point; it went beyond what words could describe. The only thing I could achieve from my vantage point was to make sure my family was out of harm's way. After that, it didn't matter. They could have what they wanted. It was all I could do.

After this latest torture session, I was convinced that they were probably going to kill me after they got what they wanted. But I couldn't let myself slip into a state of self-pity and give up hope, though my future seemed dreadfully dim. I had to keep fighting and keep my spirits up even as difficult or impossible as it might have been. I was determined to go down fighting. I said to myself, *Okay, bitches, let's get it on.*

They came back a little later and took me to the bathroom. This time, they actually let me go, not because they were compassionate but because I think the smell of urine seeping from my pants was getting to them. Good, I could play games, too. As usual, it took a while to get to the bathroom as they walked me in circles to fool my senses, not that they needed fooling.

They brought me back to the box and took the handcuffs off

my feet, then removed the ones on my hands, and while they were pressing a gun to my temple, they tied one of my hands to what seemed to be a heavy leather chair. It seemed they had formed a chain with two pairs of handcuffs, one being attached to me, the other to the chair. I had only a small leeway of movement, but the added freedom and the fact that the handcuffs were not pressing against my skin was welcome. I was a little more comfortable, if you can call it that in those circumstances. They gave me a cigarette, and I sat up in the box to smoke it. This time, there was no trick of burning my hands. While I sat there, Lugo came in and said, "We are concerned about your wife."

"Why is that?" I asked, trying to act stupid so I could get more on their wavelength.

"We have your phones tapped, and she made a couple of phone calls late last night that we didn't like," he said.

Was that even possible? Was he telling me the truth? I couldn't imagine that these clowns could possibly have the ability to tap a phone. But I decided to play along anyway. Playing stupid sometimes has its advantages.

"I wouldn't be too concerned about her doing anything. Just let her leave," I replied. The only option was downplaying it and minimizing their fear. No matter what they projected externally to me, they had to be nervous and have their doubts.

"Who do you think she called?" he asked.

"The only people she would talk to are her mother or sister in Colombia. She has no one to talk to here," I told him, which unfortunately was the truth.

"Well, I hope she doesn't start causing trouble," Lugo said.

"She won't. Just let her leave," I said, almost pleading. My worst fear was that these people would change their minds and not let my family leave, instead keeping them prisoners in the house or, worse yet, here in the warehouse where I was.

"Okay, you're going to tell your wife and children to leave Friday. Remember to tell her to leave everything and put the extra cash in the safe, and about the boxes she is to leave in the garage," Lugo repeated.

"Fine," I said with a sense of relief. For a moment, I had thought he was going to change his mind.

I lay back against the wall and just tried to think about whether there was anything I could possibly do. Nothing, blank. My brain could not come up with any solution that was feasible. The next thing I did was probably stupid, but at the same time it gave me information that I needed. I thought I was alone in that room and could not hear anyone or anything. I knew that a short distance in front of me was some sort of furniture.

The last time they had given me a cigarette, I realized they had placed them on top of whatever this thing was. I could tell this by the sounds they made. I needed a cigarette and decided to be brave and stretch myself and try to get one. I did find the cigarettes and the lighter. I took a cigarette and tried to light it. Before I was able to do so, I received a tremendous kick in the head that made me see stars. I was not alone, and someone was keeping watch over me constantly. That was a painful but valuable lesson.

Whoever was in the room said to me, "Can you see?" which

was a logical question since he did not understand that my other senses had picked up the slack created by my lost eyesight. I told him I couldn't. "Well, if you can, and you see any of us, we will have to kill you," he said.

I tried to tell him that I had not seen anyone, nor could I see. Whether he believed me or not I couldn't tell. It did not matter to me. I was just too weary to care.

I sat there with a stupid grin on my face. Surely, when my wife left and was in a secure area of the airport, she would call the police or FBI, and they would come to my rescue. I felt smug in knowing that my stay would be short and the cavalry would soon arrive to set me free. My captors would never receive any money or anything else. So I convinced myself that I had not given them anything and had tricked them into their own undoing. This would have made perfect sense in a world where events happened according to plan. I did not know it, but I had entered some black hole where reality had become totally warped.

I sat back against the wall, and whoever was with me gave me the cigarette anyway. I smoked it slowly, as if it was going to be my last one, which was possible under the circumstances. I could not even think at that point. My brain had been over exercised, and the mental weariness along with the pain in my arms just made my thought process shut down completely. Maybe it was for the best. I needed to gather myself and find the fortitude to face whatever lay ahead until the cavalry arrived. I finished the cigarette and lay down for a while. I drifted off to the only place I could find comfort and peace: sleep.

Chapter 12 — Sitting on the Edge of Darkness

"IT IS DURING OUR DARKEST MOMENTS THAT WE MUST FOCUS
TO SEE THE LIGHT."
- TAYLOR BENSON -

Someone woke me, and I sat up, disoriented, and then it dawned on me where I was. I was a little bit disappointed, as you can imagine that I was not home and the past events had not just been part of a very vivid and awful nightmare. The burns on my arm ached, and I wondered if they were already infected. But I brushed that aside, knowing that I had to deal with a far bigger problem: survival.

I surmised that it had to be Wednesday. I had been kidnapped on a Tuesday and was sure that only one day had passed, even though it had seemed like eternity. I decided that somehow, through the radio, I needed to keep track of the days and time, at least until Friday, which seemed so far away, when I knew my family would board the plane and leave. After that, the day and time would become inconsequential.

Lugo and his alter ego came into the room. They whispered something to themselves. It was nothing I could hear or understand. It was obvious that Lugo was the one that they called the "boss" and was in charge. Not a big surprise. They released the handcuffs from the chair I had become married to. I was picked up from the box and taken to the same chair I had sat in the day before to call my wife and perhaps get burned. It couldn't have been more than a day since that call, even though it seemed so.

"You're going to call your wife and tell her what we told you," he said.

"Fine," I said. I was happy to oblige and tell her to get away as far as possible.

"We'll be listening in on the other phone, so no funny stuff. We sent your wife flowers, if she happens to mention it," he said.

"Okay," I said. I thought to myself that the flowers would probably make her more suspicious under the circumstances. I always gave short answers—no point in discussing anything with them.

"Make it short, and if she asks you why she's going to Colombia, tell her you are moving there and that you will join her when you sell everything," Lugo said confidently. Did these thugs actually think my wife would believe the story they were concocting? This was beyond comical. Did they actually believe she was so gullible that she would believe something that outrageous? Obviously, they did, or they would not have been barking those orders.

I heard them as they plugged the jack into the wall and handed the receiver to me. Then they dialed the number, and I heard as someone picked up the extension somewhere else in the warehouse and my wife picked up the phone. I needed to tell her what to do without answering any questions.

"Hi, China, how are you and the children doing?" I said.

"Chino, where are you? Who are you with?" she replied. *You would not believe it if I told you.*

"I'm fine, I'm alone," I replied. *The goons standing next to me, pointing the gun at my head, are invisible*, I thought. "Listen to me. Pack up some clothing for you and the children and go to your mother's house on Friday."

"I'm not leaving if we don't leave together," she replied. This was not the answer I was hoping for.

They pressed the gun to my head. I guess my wife was giving more resistance than they expected, and they were getting nervous. Did they really believe she was going to be so easily convinced?

"China, listen and do as I say. Call Liliana and get tickets for Friday. I will join you in a couple of days, as soon as I get things wrapped up here. Leave everything, go to the bank, and take out eight thousand dollars and leave it in the safe," I instructed her. "I will call Liliana and confirm you got the tickets."

I noticed that she had gathered her composure somewhat and was calmer than she had been during the last phone call. I did not need for this to be harder than it was.

"What are these flowers for and from whom?" she inquired. The flower thing was really stupid on their part, but what did I expect?

"I sent them to you because you're leaving," I replied, trying not to laugh. Sending flowers was not my style unless it was our anniversary or someone's birthday. There must have been something with the card they sent with the flowers, because if they were from me, she would have had no doubt.

"How about the deli? Who is going to take care of it?" she asked. Good question. Didn't the deli employees find it strange that I hadn't shown up or even called?

"I'll take care of it," I told her. "China, you're going to receive some boxes for me. Don't open them, and just leave them in the garage."

"Boxes?" she asked. I could hear the incredulity in her voice.

"Yes, boxes. Just leave them in the garage for me," I said. I got no argument but knew she thought that I had either gone off the deep end or was being forced to say those things. Fortunately, she caught on and didn't argue or ask me anything further.

"When will you be joining us?" she inquired.

Lugo was getting nervous and whispered in my ear to cut the phone call.

"Soon. Tell the children I love them, and give them kisses for me. I have to go. I love you," I said as I held out the phone for them to hang up. I just hoped that she would do what I had asked her and leave on Friday. If not, things would get very messy quickly.

They made no comment about the phone call. It appeared they were satisfied and felt that I had put on a good show. It was for my family's safety and not to help them achieve their goals. They pushed me towards the cardboard box, and I tripped over the edge, which made them laugh. I got in and lay down, and they handcuffed me to my friend the chair.

I sat there, lost in my thoughts. I wondered if that was the last time I would speak to my wife. Now it was a waiting game. Friday was two days away and there were too many things that could go wrong between now and then, things that would affect my family leaving. There were too many variables, none that I could control from the position in which I found myself. I just had to hope everything would go smoothly and they left as instructed. Then, with that resolved, I could concentrate on meeting their demands and getting my release, if that was even possible. Better yet, perhaps the cavalry would arrive to save me.

The next two days were going to be mentally tortuous, and the pain I felt in my arms became secondary. At times, it didn't even seem to exist. My face was starting to itch from the tape, and it was driving me crazy. I lay there in quiet desperation. I continued to hope my wife would not call the police until she was out of harm's way. So I sat there waiting, listening to the loud radio, as it played nonstop. Lugo came in and put another roll of tape on my face. I probably looked like a gray version of a mummy.

He said, "You're going to call your travel agent and make sure your wife bought the tickets." It was an order that I was more than happy to oblige.

There was no food. I had not eaten for twenty-four hours, but I don't think that I could have, anyway. They brought me a glass of warm water—at least I think that was what it was—and a cigarette. I guess I had said what they wanted, and this was my reward. The water glass became my Porta Potty, and it was better than urinating on myself. When it was full, I would dump it on the carpet and reuse it. I felt no shame. I was a chained animal that had its needs.

They turned the air very cold. Without any shirt to speak of and in my deteriorating physical state, I shivered. I had to lie in a fetal position to get some warmth. I could only lie on one side since the chain did not have much give. The music blasted away, and for the first time I noticed that they played the same songs over and over to the point that I was getting nauseated hearing them, though this was only the beginning. After a while, it felt like a drill boring into my skull. I liked to listen to music, but after this experience I promised myself not to listen to anything for a long while.

I thought about my captors, and they seemed to be flying by the seat of their pants. The limited contact I had with them had given me the feeling that none of them were very intellectually endowed, as though they had taken too many drugs. Both of these things troubled me, because I felt they would make rash decisions and resolve any situation based on brute force and not logic.

I do not consider myself a religious person, nor do I follow any particular religious philosophy, but I have great faith. I know that many people under these circumstances would start praying. That's fine, and I respect that. I have my own way of believing in God and my communion with Him. Throughout the ordeal, I never felt that God abandoned me. I know He was there with me all the time, giving me the courage to survive and to continue fighting towards that end.

I always felt that people sought God only in their moments of need and felt disappointed if they did not receive what they asked for. They look at the trees, not the forest, and fail to see that sometimes it's better not to receive what we wish for in the grander scale of things. I knew that He was always there for me and that His light would lift me from the darkness.

Lugo came in that afternoon to inform me that it was time to call my travel agent to make sure my wife had booked the flight and in fact was leaving. So it was the same ritual: They took me from the box and over to the chair. I was asked for the phone number, and they dialed while someone else listened on an extension. The conversation was brief, and it was confirmed that my wife had booked the first flight on Friday. I wondered if the person on the other side was aware of my predicament or whether I sounded strange. Probably not. It was only wishful thinking on my part that the SWAT team would come busting through the door. They took me back to the box and tied me to the chair. It was a relief to find out that my wife and children were leaving. Now it became a waiting game until Friday.

I would lie down in the box, sit in the box, lie down in the box, and sit in the box and so on, changing positions when I could no longer stand the position I was in. The chains did not give me much freedom of movement, so the positions I could assume were limited. I had no sympathy for those who complain about having to wait fifteen minutes, thirty minutes or even an hour for something or stand in some line for service. They don't know what it really is to wait.

With the music blaring away, I tried to go to sleep so the time would pass. It didn't work. I had no escape anywhere from the music or the reality I faced. That night, I met my night guard, who seemed to be a little less deranged and less violent than the others by the few comments he made. He was probably just a paid babysitter and nothing more, but, being blindfolded, I didn't know.

He said to me, "I have a gun pointed at you, so don't try any funny stuff." I felt this bravado was more out of fear and that he just wanted to get through his shift without problems. He wanted to make sure I was no threat.

"Don't worry. I'm not in the mood," I replied, trying to find some humor under the difficult circumstances.

"Just give them what they want and you'll be out of here and back with your family in a couple of days," he told me.

"I wish I could believe that. They can have what they want. Just let my family leave," I replied, knowing that he would probably relay the message.

He gave me a couple of cigarettes and sat next to me most of the evening without saying much. There was not much to say, and I'm sure he was instructed not to talk to me. He gave me some water to drink, and I had a couple of new cups I could relieve myself with. I had a complete bathroom with three possible toilet bowls. Oh, joy, things were certainly improving.

"They're leaving tomorrow. Just don't cause any problems between now and then," he said.

"Don't worry. I won't."

"Look," he said confidently, "these guys are good. They have everything covered. They even have witnesses that will say they saw you during these days."

"Oh, really?" I answered, trying to sound surprised and impressed, though I wasn't. That was not the impression I had, but the tidbits of information I was receiving were interesting. These thugs were different, and that was what made them so dangerous.

"Believe me," he continued. "If you ever tell anybody about this, nobody is going to believe you." At the time, I thought that was ridiculous, but it proved to be true. I gave no answer, spinning what he said in my mind.

"You want a soda and a cigarette?"

Wow, a soda. "Sure, thanks," I replied. I needed to stay on good terms with this guy, and maybe I would be able to get some information.

"You'll have to smoke one of my brand. We're out of yours," he said with relief.

Beggars can't be choosers. "Fine."

He gave me a menthol cigarette that was either a Kool or a Newport. I sat back and smoked it while I thought of everything I had just been told.

That night, I could not sleep. I tried, but it would not come. I could find no way to give my tortured mind a rest. Whirlpools of thoughts kept churning through my head. Delgado, Lugo, and why this was happening swirled in my mind, with no answers to be found.

Thursday morning rolled around, and the boss and his merry band of madmen returned. I could never tell how many there were, but I knew at times there were several present. I was only useful to them until they got what they wanted, but they couldn't take the risk of something happening to me before then.

So Thursday was uneventful, and they practically left me alone for most of the day. There was no actual torture; it seemed illogical that they were going to starve me to death, but then again what made sense? But there was no food, and I only got a couple of glasses of what seemed to be water to drink. I continued to urinate in cups since they didn't seem concerned about my needs and didn't offer to take me to the bathroom. My face, now covered with about two rolls of duct tape, itched so much that at times I was tempted to rip it off.

I sat there and most of all contemplated how Delgado could have gotten involved in something as heinous as this. He was meek, soft spoken, and the feeling I had gotten when I met him was that he wouldn't have hurt a fly. I guess I underestimated Lugo's power of persuasion, but there is a limit to what people let others talk them into. This was something that I thought he would never contemplate. Even though there was irrefutable evidence of Delgado's involvement, I still refused to fully believe it. We had not departed the best of friends, but we had developed a strong bond that stretched for four years, and we helped each other mutually during that time. I had learned that anything is possible and anyone can do anything if the right mixture of influences is present.

At that point, I didn't contemplate confronting them. First, there was still my family to think of, and I didn't want to put them in danger. Second, it went against the grain of my personality. I'm a passive and non-confrontational person. I believed that confronting them would have complicated the situation. I still wanted to believe that if they got what they wanted, they would release me in short order. If I opposed them, I would give them no other choice but to kill me. The unfortunate mistake I made was that I was thinking within my own terms and the framework of my rational mind. I needed to try to think as they did. This A seemed like an impossible task.

The chairman of the board and the directors of Madmen Inc. left, and my night guard arrived. This was the way I was able to distinguish between night and day. He made little conversation, gave me a few cigarettes and a soda. No sleep that night, either. Despair could not even begin to describe what I was feeling.

Friday morning and my fourth day of captivity rolled around. Lugo and his sidekick came into the room. By now I was sure the smell in that room was anything but sweet. I had not bathed or brushed my teeth in four days, there were cups of urine next to me, many of which had spilled onto the carpet, and I was still wearing the same clothes that had also been soaked in urine. He threw something at me that hit me in the face and said, "Here, eat this. Since you're a Jew, you probably like it."

I touched the package, and it was round. It felt like some kind of bread. I opened it, leery of anything they were giving me, but I had to eat something. I took a bite and knew that it was a raisin bagel with cream cheese. I didn't like raisin bagels, but food was food, and it was not like I had a choice. They gave me a glass of warm water. I tried to eat the bagel, but it would not go down. It wasn't because it was not the kind I liked. It simply was that I was anxious about my family leaving that day. I managed to eat some of it. It didn't matter. I was past the point of feeling hunger, anyway. I needed some sort of fuel to maintain some energy. I ate as much as I could before revulsion overtook me.

I sensed someone was standing next to me. It was Lugo. "Eat up. We don't want you getting sick, at least not yet." He laughed. Again, I felt his comedy routine was lacking something.

I put the bagel aside, and they gave me a cigarette. Lugo said, "Your wife is leaving today. We are going to follow her to the airport and make sure she does." I didn't respond.

Right after that, they brought me a new present. These guys were full of surprises. They took the chair away and replaced it with some kind of metal railing that appeared to weigh a ton. It was big, too, the length of the box. I guess they figured that I might be tempted to run out of that warehouse with the chair in tow. This new contraption they tied me to removed all possibilities of doing that.

One of them said, "This will give you a little more freedom and make it more comfortable." *Right, I'm sure that me being comfortable is of prime concern to you,* I thought. I knew the real reason was that they wanted to make sure I couldn't go anywhere.

They brought me a beer for lunch. I don't drink beer, and if I have had more than one in my life, I can't remember. I put it aside with my collection of urine-filled glasses.

That afternoon, they surprised me and came to take me to the bathroom to urinate. But I soon found out that was not the real reason. At first I thought that the urine on the carpet and glasses was getting to them, but I was wrong. They released the handcuffs from the railing and helped me up. Boy, was I dizzy. I walked as if I had drunk a hundred beers. Then we went into the circle game, which made me dizzier. They took me straight and released me. I walked into a wall. They took me back a few steps and did it again with the same result, as I walked into the wall. Each time there was a chorus of laughter. The boys needed some free entertainment, and I was it. After doing this five times, they finally took me to the bathroom, where I did my duties. The whole point of the exercise I assumed was that they wanted to see if I was able to see anything at all. The conclusion of their experiment was that I couldn't. On the way back, we did the circle dance, and I finally dived into my box, having to lie down because of the dizziness and exertion of my little adventure.

My wife told me later that before she left on Friday, she received various strange phone calls. The caller would ask her why she had not already left and what she was waiting for and would then hang up. She told me that she had received three or four calls that afternoon, and by the time she left, she was in a total state of panic. She got an overwhelming fear that she and the children were in grave danger if she did not leave immediately. She was also sure the house was being watched. She was so scared that for three days she had not gone outside to get the newspaper or mail. She figured they could have my garage door opener and might waltz uninvited into the house at any time. Not a pretty thought. Their repeated calling seemed brazen and stupid to me. I guess they couldn't wait to get their paws on everything that was in the house.

Sometime that afternoon, around five o'clock, I surmised, Lugo came into the room. He was as jubilant as if he had just won the lottery. He said, "Your wife and children left. We followed them to the airport."

I said nothing. That was the only time during my captivity that I felt relief and a fleeting moment of happiness. They had left, which meant that they could not be used as a bargaining chip and that they were out of danger. That was a big burden that had been taken off my shoulders, but I couldn't take their word for it. I would not feel totally assured until I spoke with my wife and confirmed for myself that she and the children had, in fact, left. So now it was relief mixed with anticipation and anxiety until I was able to talk to her.

Lugo said, "We are going to your house, so what is your alarm code?"

They couldn't wait even a little bit to go rummage through my things. It was like talking to children who were promised a trip to the candy store and couldn't wait any longer.

"Three-zero-zero-two," I told him. I had no choice in withholding information from them, as there was nothing to gain.

"What's the gate code?" Lugo asked.

"One-four-nine-nine," I told him.

"Where do you keep the papers for the house and mutual funds you have?" he asked.

"In the studio in the file cabinet," I replied. It was obvious their intention was to clean me out.

"Where's your safe?"

"Upstairs in the master bedroom, on the floor on the right-hand side of the closet," I said. I thought this questioning was ludicrous because they must have known all the answers, as Delgado was involved. Maybe it was their foolish attempt to make me believe that he wasn't, or maybe they forgot what they had told me the first day that had given it away.

"What's the combination?" was the next question.

"Forty-one, three times to the left, seventy-two, two times to the right, and fifty-three, one time to the left," I told him, thinking that I should have told them just to ask Delgado, which would have been easier. Maybe they were testing me, and Delgado was probably standing in the room even when I gave those responses. Delgado was probably present much of the time, but he obviously could not say anything, lest I recognize his voice. Lugo thought I would not recognize his own voice, yet it was impossible not to recognize it. It was distinctive.

"Forty-one, three times to the left, seventy-two, two times to the right, and fifty-three, one time to the left," he repeated.

"Right," I answered.

"Are you friendly with your neighbors?" he asked.

"I only speak to them on occasion, when I see them outside, not on a routine basis," I said, which was the truth. I mostly kept to myself. Then I said something else. In retrospect, I wonder why I said it.

"Can I have my wedding band and family pictures?" I told him. I did not wear my wedding band to the deli, because food would get under it and it was not hygienic. I guess I said this because I felt that they were going to take absolutely everything. I was right, but I was amazed at the extent of their pettiness.

"You can have them, and we'll send your furniture to Colombia. We don't want it," he said.

Yeah, right.

"Give him a cigarette," he yelled to one of his buddies. I guess I did my tricks right and got rewarded with a treat, good boy.

They left to go ransack my house and personal belongings. The financial ravaging had begun. I sat there and was completely depressed, and for the first time, tears flowed from my eyes. I felt violated, raped, and naked. The sanctuary of my home, the only space in the world that was mine and no one else's, was gone. I felt miserable at my helplessness and could do nothing about it. I felt betrayed. I had lost my privacy, dignity, and identity.

It is one thing to come home and have your house burglarized. It's a random act, and you don't know those involved in most cases. You grieve for your losses and move on. In this case, I knew the people doing it and had given them the key. I sat there, imagining them going from room to room, through my children's toys and clothes, and that only brought me more misery. I imagined them going through my wife's and my personal belongings and cracking jokes about things. They would be eating my food and sitting at my kitchen table. God only knew what else they were thinking of doing there. But what could I do? I knew that I could never go back to that house if I actually survived. I was angry, and I wanted to lash out at my captors, but I knew that was not going to occur.

As I sat there, I told myself that I needed to control my emotions and concentrate on getting out of that warehouse alive. I could not afford to expend energy on something that was already done and that I could do nothing about. I managed to get a hold of myself, but the sadness would not go away. My family was safe now; at least I wanted to believe that, which meant that now I was all alone.

The night guard strode in and said, "Hey, Marc, how are you doing?"

"Okay," I lied. *Just great, can't you see I'm having the time of my life and there's nowhere else I'd rather be than chained to this railing?*

"You want a soda and cigarette?" He was trying to be friendly, though I don't know why. They probably wanted some information.

"Fine," I replied.

"Hey, I heard about the cigarette incident, and they were really worried about that. Can you see?" he asked as he handed me my dinner, the cigarette and soda. So that was what this was all about, this and the walking into the wall thing.

"No, I can't. I knew by the sound where they had put them. I was having a nicotine fit, so I remembered," I reassured him.

"If you have a problem with your blindfold, let me know. These guys are scared to death that you can see them, and that's not good for you," he said, sounding worried.

To me, "these guys" and "death" sounded like a likely combination.

My only problem with the blindfold is having it on, and the itching is going to drive me nuts.

"I made a mistake. It won't happen again. I'm blind as a bat, so don't worry," I said, hoping to convince him. Besides, I was in no mood to talk to him.

"Okay, just sit back and relax. I'll be back to check on you soon," he said jovially. That was easy for him to say. I could not imagine relaxing while they ransacked my house and I wasn't sure if my family was safely out of the country.

A few hours later, Lugo bolted into the room, and I knew something was wrong.

"Sit up!" he yelled angrily. *Oh, the shit is about to hit the fan again.* This was the first time I heard him this angry.

"We have a problem," he snarled. I felt a brief rush of fear run through me. This dude was scary, to say the least. I didn't know what to expect next.

"Why is that?" I asked innocently.

"Where are the jet skis?" he snarled.

"I sent them to Colombia to sell," I lied. I had no clue where they were unless my wife had done something with them.

"The bitch took all the jewelry and your gold Rolex," he said, sounding disappointed.

Smart girl, I thought, *good move.* "I don't understand. I told her to leave everything," I said sheepishly. They knew that was true and whatever she had done was out of my control, but I was enjoying that moment.

"I guess she doesn't listen to you or give a shit about you, that bitch," he said, trying to goad me. No way was that going to happen. They must have been pretty stupid if they thought that she had bought my story and thought everything was okay. Obviously she knew it wasn't and had acted accordingly.

"I guess not," I said, trying to sound sad, but at the same time trying to hold back a snicker.

"She left less money in the safe than you asked her to, also," he said.

Of course, she knew that if everything was all right, I could just go back to the bank!

He calmed down somewhat but was still angry.

"She must have misunderstood me," I told him, knowing full well that it was not true. I couldn't believe they actually thought their story was so foolproof that nothing could go awry.

"How come your neighbors knew your wife was leaving to Colombia?" he wanted to know. I thought this was a lie. She never ever spoke to the neighbors, and for her to do so would have been highly unusual, even more so under these circumstances. Why he was telling me this, I had no idea.

"Really?" I said, trying to sound dumbfounded. "Maybe one of them saw her putting luggage in the car and asked her where she was going." I doubted that very much.

"You keep very neat records, fortunately for us," he said, boasting, while I was thinking how unfortunate it was.

"Monday you are going to start calling all the banks and get the money transferred to D. J. & Associates," he told me. D. J. & Associates was my accounting and consulting company.

"Fine," I replied. *I'll help you financially rape me, but do I have to enjoy it?*

He gave me a cigarette without burning me to reward my good behavior. I sat back and thought about what had just transpired. Now I was reasonably sure my wife and children had left, which was good. I tried to go to sleep for a while. I didn't want to think anymore, but sleep would not come. The night guard came in, and we did not chitchat much. I sat and lay there but could not find any way to be comfortable for more than a few minutes. Friday rolled into Saturday, my first weekend in captivity.

The boss and some of his goons came in and again threw some food at me. It was a raisin bagel again, and this time he told me explicitly that I had to eat it. I passed each bite with sips from a warm glass of water and managed to eat most of it without gagging. At this point, I did not feel hungry, nor did I have the energy to eat. It had all been spent in the state of fear, anxiety, and despair that I had endured the previous four days.

Later that morning, they came in and unshackled me from the railing. They picked me up and we did the circle dance. I thought that they were taking me to the bathroom. I was both right and wrong. They did take me to the bathroom, but not for the purpose I had thought. They had a chair and instructed me to sit in it, which I did. It appeared that they were going to hold me here, for how long I did not know. There was no air conditioning, and the air was hot, stuffy, and humid. I started to sweat immediately. There was no water to drink.

By early afternoon, I was almost unconscious and incoherent. Someone came in and saw my state and became concerned, so much so that they immediately took me to another room and I was allowed to lie on the bare carpet. I just lay there, unable to move, in an almost comatose state. Their concern was obvious, for if I croaked, they could not get their greedy paws on my money and assets. I thought that day was the end of the line. I was feeling terribly ill and could not foresee lasting much longer. By early evening, I was feeling better, and they returned me to my box. I bet they breathed a sigh of relief then, knowing that I was not going to die just yet and maybe they could still get what they were after.

That night, when the night guard came, he had a surprise for me: a can of Chef Boyardee ravioli. It was served cold. I didn't care. I did not get utensils, so I had to eat using my dirty hands. My napkin was my urinated pant. While eating, I felt as though I had been reduced to the level of a wild animal or a caveman. That day, I was hungry, and I ate despite what I was feeling. It tasted like a gourmet meal to me. In fact, I asked the night guard if there was any more. I was disappointed that he said no, but I had no choice in the matter. I guess my physical state earlier that day had, at least temporarily, concerned them.

That extra concern would prove to be short lived. The night guard came in after my scrumptious meal and asked me if I wanted him to read to me. I politely declined his offer and managed to pass out after a while to escape from my reality into the safer and sweeter world of dreams. I woke up in what must have been the middle of the night. I know I did not sleep very long. I thought to myself that at least the torture was over. As usual, I was wrong. My wounds still ached, and by now I surmised they must have been infected. So I just sat there all night. I sat at the edge of darkness.

Chapter 13 — The Conversation

"A MAN'S CHARACTER MAY BE LEARNED FROM THE
ADJECTIVES WHICH HE HABITUALLY USES IN
CONVERSATION."
- MARK TWAIN -

Sunday rolled around, and to my surprise I got a cup of coffee and an apple. I guess they thought I got sick the day before because of the bagel and decided to change the menu. I could not believe that I was drinking a cup of coffee. As I said, I'm a creature of habit, and coffee was one of the items I never missed. I always had my coffee in the morning and another cup punctually between two and three in the afternoon. After I finished my breakfast, they came in, and back to the bathroom we went. They sat me in the same chair and chained me to some unknown object. They gave me a bottle of warm, probably dirty, water for the day. I guess that yesterday's scare didn't concern them enough to avoid trying it again today. They may have figured the only reason it occurred was the lack of water. The fact that it was infernally hot in that room did not cross their minds as a possibility. Their concentration was on getting their grubby hands on my assets.

"We had to change arrangements and put you in here so we could make room for another guest," Lugo told me. Another guest, I thought? Were these criminals running a kidnapping and extortion factory? Was this Hotel Hell, where your guests check in but never check out, at least not alive? What were these out-of-control maniacs up to? Anything and everything my mind could conjure up was possible. I didn't respond to what he told me, mostly because his statement left me speechless.

He continued, "Don't worry. Once we get everything organized, we'll bring you back to your room."

I never did find out if someone else was being held there against his or her will. I never heard anything to lead me to that conclusion, either, so this was most likely said to throw me off or make me think that they were some professional, high-level organization.

He checked the tape on my face, which now ran from the top of my forehead to my upper lip. He added some more for good measure and left. I sat in the bathroom in the sweltering heat for most of the day. The temperature had to be over a hundred degrees. I sat and stared into the darkness. My mind numb from the heat, exhaustion, and dehydration, it was not a pleasant day for me in Miami.

I sat there, just thinking how I had learned the true meaning of the words "humiliation" and "loneliness." Although dictionaries try to give accurate descriptions of their meaning, they do not come close. Now I knew those words well, all too well. I was not only humiliated constantly, but I felt I had been dehumanized. People are not supposed to treat animals the way they were treating me, much less other human beings.

I thought I knew where the front door was and was actually contemplating trying to escape. I did not hear anyone, but as I had learned before, that did not mean anything. I tried my handcuffs to see if there was some way to pry them loose. Then reality set in. I did not know if there was anyone watching me, I would probably have to take my hand off or break my wrist to get the handcuffs off, and I didn't know where the warehouse was located. I sat back realizing escape was not possible. I wondered if anybody was looking for me, and why no one had arrived at the warehouse to save me. I guess despair was setting in and this was just the beginning of my stay. My only hope, I reasoned, was that they had gotten what they wanted and would let me go soon.

A little later on and still in despair, I listened closely to see if I could hear anything: nope, nada, only the distant playing of the radio. Bravely, I loosened the tape in order to be able to rub my face, which itched uncontrollably. While I was at it, I took a good peek at the bathroom through the wedge I had created between my face and the tape. The bathroom was small and had a painted cement floor. They had put the radio right outside. This observation took a matter of seconds, and I did not stretch my luck by peeking for much longer.

Just as I finished, I heard someone walk up and say, "What are you doing?"

Of course, I replied "Nothing, my eyes are just bothering me." I heard my heart pounding as I said it. Another close call, and I thought that, under the circumstances, trying to escape was too much of a risk. I did not know if someone was there or how many of them there were. The person who had come into the room didn't respond, just walked away. I sat there and wondered whether this had created greater uncertainty among my captors and if that would be detrimental to me. I couldn't worry about that now. There was nothing I could do to change things. By the time they came in to get me, I was barely a limp lump on that chair. They took me back to the box and gave me a cigarette.

Lugo came in that night and said to me, "You're going to call your wife and tell her that everything is going well and you're liquidating all your assets and will soon be joining her in Colombia. Make it short, and no funny stuff. We'll be listening on the other phone."

They actually expected me to tell my wife that simply, out of the blue, I had decided to sell everything, and she was supposed to think everything was all right. The least she could think was that I had come down with a severe case of mental illness. They picked me up and carried me over to the chair from which I had made the last phone calls. They dialed, and my wife picked up the phone.

"Hello, China," I said as best as I could. These phone calls were becoming more difficult for me.

"Chino. How are you? What are you doing?" she asked.

Oh, I'm just sitting here with a couple of criminals, discussing world events. "I'm, okay. How are the children, David and Stephanie?" I said. Without giving her a chance to respond, I continued, "Listen, China, I'm in the process of selling the house and the deli, and as soon as I finish everything, I'll join you in Colombia." *If you believe I'm not being coerced into saying this, then I have a bridge to sell you, also.*

"Chino, I don't understand. Who's with you? Why are you doing this?"

96

Insanity would have been the only logical response. She told me later that she had heard breathing and other noises that were coming from the extension they were listening from. It appeared that they were inept at this, also: scary and stupid.

"I'm alone," I said. *Just the guy holding the gun to my head is with me.* I continued, "You always wanted to live in Colombia, near your family. We are finally going to do it." *I may arrive in a coffin, but that's a technicality.*

"Chino, tell me the truth. What's going on?" she said.

Better you don't know, but I'm sure you can figure it out for yourself. "Everything is okay. I'll call you soon. Give the kids hugs and kisses, and tell them that I love them. I love you." I thought these call were so stupid. I gave them the phone.

Lugo said, "I'm worried that your wife is going to start causing trouble over there."

I hope she raises hell. "I wouldn't worry about it."

"I hope so, for your sake," he replied. I thought that it didn't matter anyway.

Lugo spoke as though he was a tough, brilliant boss and a guy who always had every situation under control. I don't know if it was just to stroke his ego or impress his comrades in crime. I found him and his demeanor pathetic, but he definitely had the advantage. Lugo had a present for me that night. They put wax balls in my ears to lessen the amount that I was able to hear. Just great. I had lost my eyesight and now my hearing, as well; this was getting worse. The balls were very uncomfortable, and wax started to drip out of my ears almost immediately. They put me back in the box, and Lugo and his sidekick left me to enjoy my new misery.

I sat and wondered what my wife was thinking. I was talking to her as if I were a lunatic. I was opposed to living in Colombia, and she knew it. Besides, any decision taken on that subject would have been through mutual agreement. She had to know that something was wrong and that I was probably being held against my will. Was she going to call the authorities or hire a private detective to investigate? I reasoned that if she did not know what to do, she would call my sister, who would have an infantry unit knocking down the doors. She would not rest until they found me.

Each morning, I woke up hoping it would be the day the cavalry would show up to free me. When they didn't, I went into a deep state of depression and despair. I was aware that the clock was ticking, and as more time went on, my chance for survival diminished.

I found out later that my wife was going to send someone that afternoon. When he got to the airport, he was turned back because his passport had expired. After that, there were no subsequent attempts. It seemed that the difference of opinion between her and her family caused an impasse that resulted in inaction. Good thing I didn't know about what was going on, or I might have asked them to shoot me. I know that sounds crazy, but there are moments of despair that are very difficult to handle. Fortunately, I did not know this and had not yet lost hope that I would be rescued, though the chances diminished with each passing day.

That evening, I had two night watchmen. They came in and were in a jovial mood. You could tell by the way they were acting that they were feeling smug and filled with self-confidence. Each day that passed, their superiority seemed to increase. The new one who had not been there the previous nights said, "You are taking this very well. Other people that have been in your position haven't handled it nearly as well."

I said, "Oh, really?" What, I wondered, was he trying to tell me, that I was not the first but one among many in a chain? Was this their business, kidnapping, torturing, and extorting unsuspecting victims?

"Yeah," he continued, "some of them break down and cry because they don't want to give up their money and belongings."

"Well, I don't care about that. All I want is to get reunited with my family." I could not determine if what they were telling me was to see what my response would be or even if it was true. I thought it best to play it safe and tell them what they wanted to hear.

"Cooperate and you will be back with them in no time," he said. I had a hard time believing that this was going to be as quick and easy as they were telling me.

"I sure hope so," I told them, but my thoughts told me that they were repeating this too often, probably so I would give them what they wanted and not oppose them. It would have done me no good anyway and probably earned me a few more beatings.

I got a little bold, since this conversation was frustrating me, and asked him, "Who the hell are you people, and why are you doing this to me?" I had nothing to lose at this point by asking the question, and I thought the way I said it was measured.

The response was so ludicrous and preposterous that I wanted badly to laugh. I had to use all my willpower to resist. These guys were out to lunch, and I was in trouble, deep trouble.

"We are the FBI, and we are investigating you," he replied confidently and calmly.

"The FBI?" I asked. *I imagine the FBI now kidnaps, tortures, and extorts money from people they are investigating.* I knew that the agency had changed after Hoover, but certainly not to this extent. This was crazy, and the next response got better.

"Yeah, the FBI," he said, matter of fact. "I used to work for the CIA during the Reagan administration. They booted me out because I didn't like the president and spoke out against him. Then I got my current job in the FBI."

I couldn't help myself and had to ask the next question, just to hear the answer. "If you're FBI, what happened to due process under the law, or is this the way the government handles all investigations?" Well, it seemed I hit a nerve, or he thought that I was mocking him.

"I wouldn't ask too many questions if I were you. You could get into a lot of trouble. I could easily kill you and dump you in the Everglades. I've done that before, and it wouldn't faze me a bit," he said. He seemed flustered.

Well, it seemed that if someone confronted his bullshit story, he simply threatened to kill them. That he had killed before and it would not trouble him to do so again did not surprise me, and that was the one thing I did believe to be true.

"I understand," I told him. My understanding was that this individual was a total nut job with a violent and unpredictable temper.

He wanted to drive home the point and continued: "And besides, if we were to do that, who would care, the police? Don't make me laugh. Do you think they give a shit about you? Or they would make some big hoopla after they found you? You would be another statistic with no questions asked."

After his little discourse, I wondered if that was the fate that awaited me. What could I possibly do to change it, if anything?

He calmed down and said, "You know you gave quite a fight when we got you." Was that supposed to make me feel better?

"I thought it was a piece of cake," I said, referring to what I had overheard in the van.

"No, you put up quite a fight. It was piece of cake after we got you and no one interfered," he said. I was still not feeling any better.

"Usually, someone from the deli walks me to the car. It just so happens that no one did that day. What would've happened if someone had walked out with me?" I asked him. This was true; very often, one of the employees walked me to the car to talk to me.

"We would have had to get him and take him with us," he said. Right, easier said than done.

"What would you have done with him?" I asked.

"We probably would have to dump him somewhere on the way," he said confidently. *Right, let him go and have a witness running around.* "I see," I said, knowing full well that the answers were absurd and that they had made no contingency plans.

This goon left the room and a short while later the watchman who had been there the previous evenings came in.

"Would you like me to read to you?" he asked me.

"No, thanks," I said. *I'm not ready for my bedtime story yet.*

"Thursday is Thanksgiving. Maybe I can talk them into taking the blindfold off for a few hours so you can watch TV or read a newspaper," he said sincerely.

I replied, "That would be nice." *Fat chance they are going to allow that, and you may lose your job or worse if you ask them.*

Good thing I was sitting on the floor, because the next thing he told me would've made me fall off any chair.

"Hey, don't take this personally. I think you're a nice guy, and maybe a few years down the road we could even be friends."

Friends with the people who kidnapped and tortured me? Was this guy real? I played with him because I needed to have some fun and told him, "You never know. The world is a funny place." Becoming friends with him would be the last thing I would ever do, and even then I wouldn't do it, I thought to myself.

The other night watchman, Mr. FBI, came in the room and gave me a cigarette and a soda. He asked, "Do you want some sleeping pills?"

I told him I would. After all, they couldn't hurt, and if I actually got to spend time in la la land, it would be a much better place than this location. The mental torture to have to sit there, chained to that railing, was enough to drive anyone crazy. A reprieve was welcome. If they were going to kill me, then I would be out and would not have to go through the anguish preceding it, but I doubted that was going to occur prior to cleaning me out of everything.

They gave me a couple of pills that I washed down with the

remaining soda. I smoked the cigarette and afterwards lay down to go to sleep. Before I drifted off, I thought about the strange conversations with Mr. FBI and my future friend. These people were far beyond mentally disturbed, which was not good for me. Mr. FBI was playing out some fantasy that he was law enforcement and on a secret mission. The problem was he probably believed it. When I had tried to convince him otherwise, the reaction he gave showed he had a few screws missing. He made it clear that he had no qualms about killing me and throwing me to the alligators in the Everglades. Of course, this was all going to be done under the auspices and blessing of the federal agency that employed him.

Mr. Friendly wanted to be my friend in a few years if they didn't kill me first. He did not see anything wrong with the fact that they had tied me up in that warehouse against my will and tortured me. In his thinking, this would all blow over and we could sit down and watch a football game and drink some beers someday. I had never heard of anything so far beyond bizarre. Lugo had hired some intellectual midgets who had less intelligence than he did, surely a difficult task. This made sense because they could easily be manipulated and cajoled into doing his bidding.

But there were others involved, the guy who enjoyed inflicting pain while sickly whispering about fire. Where was Delgado during all of this? I suspected he was not too far away and perhaps sometimes right in front of me. I drifted off to sleep and away from the madness that surrounded me.

Chapter 14 — Liquidation

"YOU ONLY HAVE POWER OVER PEOPLE SO LONG AS YOU
DON'T TAKE EVERYTHING AWAY FROM THEM. BUT WHEN
YOU'VE ROBBED A MAN OF EVERYTHING, HE'S NO LONGER IN
YOUR POWER — HE'S FREE AGAIN."
- ALEKSANDER SOLZHENITSYN -

Monday morning marked a new week of captivity. Lugo came storming in, kicked the box, and screamed, "Get up, you piece of shit!"

Geez, good morning to you, too. Have a bad night?

"We transferred all calls from your house to here. So when we get a call, you'll answer as if you were in your house. If you say anything stupid, you're dead. Do you understand?" he barked.

Great, now I got to answer phone calls, too. I didn't like that one bit, as it would be too easy to make a mistake when I was under duress. He enjoyed telling me over and over again that he was going to kill me if I didn't obey. It worked. I didn't believe his threats were idle. They had limited their choices by backing themselves into a tight corner.

"Yes," I replied meekly, knowing that was what he liked. And he liked an immediate response.

"Today you're going to start calling the banks and start transferring money to your company account," he demanded.

"Fine," I replied. I wanted to believe that the quicker this transfer went, the faster they would release me. But something kept nagging in the back of my mind that no matter what I did, I was not leaving their warehouse alive. What choice did I have? Not cooperating meant certain death, while giving them everything represented only a small glimmer of hope that I might live. I knew very well it did not guarantee me anything, but I didn't want to think about the fact that they would probably kill me anyway; I needed to hang on to my illusion, at least for the time being.

"Who is on the deed to your house?" Lugo asked.

"My wife and I," I replied. This troubled me because they were not only after the money but the house, which was totally crazy and meant that I had to disappear.

"It's not owned by a company?" He seemed skeptical. It looked like he had gotten bad information.

I simply responded, "No."

"Then we have a problem," he said. "We want your house, and in order to transfer it, we need for her to sign. So she will have to come back, and she can bring your watch and ring," he said nonchalantly. This guy was an idiot, or his ego was beyond comprehension. He actually thought my wife was going to get on a plane and come back and sign the house over to him, and at the same time expected her to bring my watch and ring and give it to him.

I had to draw the line somewhere, and this was it. I couldn't believe the incredible greed and stupidity they were displaying, and they wanted everything, absolutely everything. They obviously were so overconfident that they never measured the risks of their actions.

That was good for me. I was going to set them up so that even if I were dead, they could get caught. They had opened the door, and I was going to take the opportunity. Still, this was beyond comprehension.

"Well, we'll see about that," he said. "You're going to call the manager at the deli and tell him to fire all the employees and close permanently on Friday."

This was shocking; they wanted to leave not only me out on the street but all of those people who worked for and depended on me. Wasn't the manager going to find it strange that I just disappeared one day and then called him a week later to tell him to close the deli? Maybe not. Maybe this world was crazier than I thought, and people did things like this all the time. These thugs were brazen and showed no fear of getting caught or making a mistake.

"How is he going to pay the employees?" I asked. This was probably a stupid question, but I'm Mr. Responsible and thought that if they worked, they deserved to get paid. I was the only one who signed the checks. Okay, you might say to yourself, this guy is looking at certain death, and all he can think about is paying his employees. But that's who I am. I believe in handling my responsibilities. To me, it was a big deal.

"Tell him to pay them out of whatever comes in sales," he said. Well, I hoped that there would be sufficient cash sales. Maybe the deli was closed already, since my manager could not even do the smallest thing without assistance.

"Fine," I replied. I was not going to win anything except a few knocks to my head by arguing.

"Who is your agent for your life insurance policy?" Lugo wanted to know. I had two one-million-dollar whole-life policies. One had been paid off altogether, and the other I was paying.

I told him the name.

"We want to borrow five hundred thousand against your policy," he said confidently.

"Fine," I said. I knew that it was not feasible and the cash value was one fifth of what he wanted. I felt too defeated to argue. Where would that get me? The only way they could get that much money from the policy was by changing beneficiaries before my death. There would be repercussions later, I was sure, after they found out that they could not do certain things, but at that point I didn't care.

He ordered the goon with him to give me two cigarettes. I guess he was fanaticizing about of all that money in his head and got carried away. He and the sidekick left, and they turned the music to maddening loudness. It looked like they had things to discuss and didn't want me to hear them.

I sat there smoking one of the cigarettes and wondering where the cavalry was that was sure to save me. I was in despair that morning and had to consciously get myself in control. They wanted everything, including my underwear, and I had a choice to make: fight and resist them, or cooperate in the hopes that after cleaning me out, they would let me go. It was no easy decision, but I decided to give them everything because I wanted to believe that my rescuers would arrive before they finished taking it all from me. I still held hopes for that, even as slim as it appeared with each passing day. I could not lose hope. I refused to.

About an hour later, Lugo and one or more of his cohorts came back in, and I sensed them standing right in front of my box. Lugo was the one who always talked to me. I guess Delgado couldn't, and the other guy just liked inflicting pain. There had been no food that morning, and I was relieving myself in the various cups I had been given water in.

"Get up," Lugo snarled. He had a hard time comprehending that it was almost impossible for me to do so by myself.

They released the handcuffs from the railing, roughly picked me up, and took me to the usual desk and put the phone in my hand.

"Nothing funny," Lugo told me. Again, they put the gun to my head, their normal operating procedure while I spoke on the phone.

The first banker thought my call was rather unusual, and he kept asking me questions that I could not answer. This made him more uncomfortable, and he did not give up even though I kept insisting. Of course this was strange to the person I was talking to. I had met him personally not a month before and had told him my objectives were the opposite of what I was telling him now.

Lugo and his buddies appeared to get antsy and nervous and pulled the hammer of the gun, and I heard a distinct click. At that point, I was either getting the transfer done or a bullet to the head. I didn't know which was better. The bank official finally gave up and took the information as Lugo whispered it to me so I could pass it on to the banker. This must have really sounded funny because of the start and stops that occurred. I knew that the banker was not satisfied when I hung up with him. If I could have sent him a mental SOS message through the telephone lines, I would have gladly done so.

All Lugo said was, "Good, now you're going to call the second one." The second bank did not give me any hassle.

Next, they had me call Freddy, the manager of the deli, to tell him to permanently close on Friday. They dialed, and Freddy answered.

"Freddy, it's Marc. How is everything?" I said, trying to sound as normal as possible.

"Man, where you been? We need your help. I'm having a lot of problems here. Business is bad." Freddy sounded ruffled. Good old Freddy, I thought. I can always count on him to take care of the problems. *Didn't I hire you to take care of those things so I wouldn't have to?* It didn't matter; disappearing for almost a week without a call was indeed very strange.

"Look, Freddy, I'm out of town. You'll have to take care of the problems, as I won't be back for a while," I told him. I wanted to add that I might never be back at all.

"What do I do about payroll today? Can't you come in, or your wife? What am I going to do? The employees want their money," he said despairingly.

No, Freddy, I can't come in, because I'm all tied up, really tied up. "Freddy, pay the employees from the sales. Tell everyone that Friday is their last day, and put a sign on the window that as of Friday, we are closed," I told him.

"You want me tell everyone they're fired and close on Friday?" he responded in a disbelieving tone. I knew how this must have sounded to him. I hadn't shown up for a week, not even one call, and now I was telling him to close the deli and fire everyone. He probably thought I must have gone off the deep end, if not worse.

"Yes, Freddy. Do as I say and close on Friday, and fire all the employees. If you need anything, you can reach me through my beeper," I told him, knowing that if he needed me, he was up shit creek without a paddle.

"What about me?" he said. Freddy was in shock, understandably so. The person he had known as a pillar of stability and reliability was all of a sudden talking like a lunatic.

"We'll talk about that later," I told him, thinking we probably would not. It would turn out that Freddy already had his own plans and also took the opportunity to rob me. It was not a great amount, but it added insult to injury. I guess my assets became available to whoever was quick enough to get their hands on them.

I was taken back to the box and re-chained to the railing. I was depressed and despairing. The thugs were wiping me out financially, and I was letting them do it. How had I gotten myself into this situation? Why me? I asked myself these questions a million times over and found no apparent answers. That day I began to seriously despair. I kept wondering about the house. If they had any thoughts of releasing me, then taking the house made no sense. How were they going to explain that? It was becoming more and more evident that they had no plans to release me. It was the beginning of an even greater emotional rollercoaster ride, from pinnacles of hope to dark pits of utter despair. The psychological torture was at times worse than the physical. It was hell on earth, with all exits sealed shut.

What I was certain of was that my wife was not coming back to sign the house papers. If it meant that they killed me for it, then so be it. One casualty was better than two, and there was a point at which I would stop cooperating. I was not going to be pushed into having her return, no matter the consequences. But I had a plan, and it would provide clear evidence of their criminal activities. I hoped they would go for the bait and try to get the house. They weren't too intelligent, or else they would not have gone after it in the first place.

Physically, I was feeling miserable, which added to my downbeat mood. I had not showered, shaved, or brushed my teeth for a week now and must have been interesting to look at. I knew I had a foul smell coming from my body, but it seemed to bother them more than me. My pants, saturated with dried urine, added to the eclectic odors I was emitting. I was no spring flower. I knew that, but they did not seem concerned about my hygiene, and they withstood the smell for the short periods they were next to me. The tape around my eyes itched and hurt as it ate into my skin. I did not feel human anymore but as if I had descended the evolutionary ladder and was closer to so some primordial state. The only thing left of me was my spirit, and I could not let them crush that, even though I faced death.

They came a little later and released me from the railing, and they took me over to the phone again. They told me I had a phone call and to act naturally, which was easier said than done. It was an accounting client that needed some advice. It was almost laughable when I told him that I was tied up and could not chat with him. If he had only known how really tied up I was. I told him I was going out of town for a week and would call him when I got back, which meant never, and hung up.

Returning to my box, I sat there in a stupor. I could not think anymore. A little while later, Lugo came in and told me he wanted me to sign some documents. Signing documents blindfolded is a real challenge. He would put my hand on the spot where he wanted me to sign, and I did. I purposefully tried to mess it up, but I didn't have to try too hard under the circumstances. I was not told, nor did I have any idea what I was signing. It could have been my death sentence. In fact, that would turn out to be true later on. He gave me a cigarette as a reward.

That evening, the night watchman, Mr. Friendly, who was always with me, came in. Mr. FBI was not around. The first thing he did was check the tape to see it was safely secured. He determined it was loose and added a bit more for good measure. I had so much tape on that I could hardly hold my head up from the weight.

He said, "First, I brought you some chicken and beans, and second, it looks like you're going home on Friday." I was happy about the food. Soon, I was going to look like a concentration camp survivor, and I needed some energy. The second piece of news I wanted to believe, but I couldn't. I felt it was a ploy to get my spirits up so they could complete their mission of greed. I was down most of that day; perhaps they noticed my sullen mood and told this hired goon to tell me the happy lie.

"Thanks for the food," I told him. I said nothing to him about the other news he had given me.

"Would you like me to bring you eggs for breakfast tomorrow?" he said cheerily. This new show of kindness did it not last long.

"That would be good," I said.

"Sausage or ham?" he asked.

"Sausage," I said, showing no emotion.

"Coffee?"

"Coffee would be really good," I said. Then I had second thoughts; coffee stimulated my bowels, and I had not defecated for a week now. If I had to go, the cups I was using would not suffice, and it could be a real problem.

"Okay," he said. "Tomorrow, I'll bring you coffee, eggs, and sausage."

He left me alone so I could eat the food he had brought me. No utensil, so I used my filthy hands. I felt like a caveman eating his prey after a hunt, except I was their prey and they had hunted me. I was so hungry. I contemplated eating the bones, but, after second thoughts, decided against it. If I had choked, they wouldn't be able to get their money or other assets. That was one of the better meals I had during my stay at Hotel Hell.

He came back after I finished and said, "Good?"

"Yes, thanks," I replied.

"Cigarette?"

"Sure," I said. I didn't have to do any tricks for this one—amazing.

He gave me a cigarette, which was becoming more difficult to put in my mouth because of the amount of tape, and said, "The boss said that once the money clears, the deed to the house has been transferred, and a few other things are wrapped up, you can go home to your wife and children."

The boss was Lugo, and he was a psychopathic liar, so he was probably lying to his own henchmen.

"When is that?" I asked just to see what he would say.

"They made the reservation for Friday. I saw the tickets. They think everything should be wrapped up by then," he said. Well, there were a few problems to this story. How were they going to take me to the airport looking like I did? Did they believe I could board a plane with my ripped shirt and urine-coated pants without having taken a shower or brushed my teeth for two weeks? Secondly, how would they leave me at the airport without me seeing them? They could not take the tape off until they dropped me off there, which, of course, would have been ludicrous with so many policemen present.

Thirdly, how could they guarantee that I got on the flight and didn't look for a policeman in the airport to report my story? The story was nice, but it made no sense. There was no practical way for them to do it. I wanted to believe the story so badly but realized doing so would be foolhardy.

"Good, I'm glad," I said, trying to sound convincing, even though I had just come to the realization that releasing me would have been an almost impossible task. Later on, I found out that they really had made reservations. In fact, they had used my credit card. I guess they changed their minds when they realized how impossible the plan was.

Then he did something that surprised me. He released my handcuffs from the railing, got me up, and made me walk. On the way, he stabbed the gun in my back and said that if I did anything stupid, he would shoot me. He took me to the bathroom.

He said, "I'll handcuff you to here so you can go to the

bathroom in privacy. Just tell me when you're finished."

"Okay," I replied. I was thankful he was actually letting me go. It was the first time I could defecate in a week, and it was a painful experience.

After finishing my chores, I realized that I had no toilet paper. I found a tiny piece of plastic that I used instead. As filthy as I felt already, it didn't matter or make much of a difference. This was typical of the humiliation and degradation that I had to endure during my captivity.

I yelled out that I was finished, and he came back and took me back to the box. We didn't play the circle game this time. I guess he was not in the mood.

As I lay there, the second night watchman came in, Mr. FBI. He gave me a soda and a cigarette. Wow, all these goons were bearing gifts. It almost felt like Christmas.

He said, "We are all impressed about the way you care about your family." Any normal human being would have gotten them out of harm's way, I thought, but these people were not normal.

"What else is there in life?" I said, not knowing how else to respond.

"Yeah, I got a daughter. She's an honor student in high school. I'm separated from my wife," he said.

Well, that's a surprise. Imagine that she would leave you! Your daughter must take after her mother. "Oh, you must be very proud of her," I responded. This guy had so many stories that I wondered if any of them were true.

"Yes, I got married while I was in the Service," he continued.

"What branch?" I asked him.

"Marine Corps. I know how you feel about smoking. When I was in the Corps, I had to sneak out behind the barracks and have one," he said, reminiscing.

"They don't let you smoke in the military?" I asked.

"No, they don't"

"How long were you in the Corp", I asked him.

"Four years. I wanted to make a career of it but had problems with seizures."

"Seizures?" I asked, wondering if it had not been more like multiple personalities or some other deep psychotic disorder.

"From heavy drinking. Alcohol was probably why I didn't make it in the Corps," he confided.

"Too bad. Probably would have been a good career." I thought that since he could not make the military his career, being a career criminal was his second best choice. At least he had a career.

"That's life." He sighed.

He went on and talked to me about religion and what a good Christian he was.

"Thou shalt beat, torture, and kidnap your neighbor" was not one of the Ten Commandments I had read. He must have had his own unique set of rules that he followed, I reasoned. He also made references to how unjustly African Americans were treated in this country. So it was not too hard to come to the conclusion that he belonged to that race. During the conversation, I kept thinking that this guy was either making all of it up, or he was not very intelligent. He gave me so much information about himself that it could have been used to prepare a profile of him if I got out. I guess he thought I would never get that chance, or why would he have volunteered so much info? Perhaps he had a few screws missing and didn't even realize what he was doing.

He gave me a cigarette and left. I sat there thinking. The next day would be one full week since I had been kidnapped. I did not see any ray of hope of being rescued—their story of releasing me on Friday was nice but unrealistic. I didn't want to think about how they were going to kill me. I didn't want to think at all. I lay there for hours, it seemed. Sleep would not come. I lost all sense of time, and my internal clock malfunctioned because of the blindness and disorientation. I just lay there for what seemed to be forever. There would be no escape from Hotel Hell that evening.

Chapter 15 — Lost Hope

"WE MUST ACCEPT FINITE DISAPPOINTMENT BUT NEVER LOSE
INFINITE HOPE."
- DR. MARTIN LUTHER KING, JR. -

Days passed in much the same way as the previous days had. Tuesday morning, two weeks into captivity, with no end in sight and no sleep for the weary. Monday night, I had not slept again, which denied me the only place where I could find escape. I was beginning to lose hope that I would be released soon, but I could not afford that. They say hope is the last thing you lose. Doggedly, I was trying to hold on to it. When they came in, they had the breakfast they had promised: eggs, sausage, toast, and coffee. To say the least, I was in shock. I ate with my hands, as usual, but eggs had never tasted so good, and I ate the very last crumb. They gave me a cigarette and sat back and smoked while I drank the last of my coffee. My ashtray was the same cups I had used to urinate in. I never knew these plastic cups were so versatile and had so many uses. I wondered why they had maintained the comparatively good treatment and how long it was going to last. If found out soon enough that it was going to be short lived, very short lived. Their behavior was inconsistent and based on the mood of the boss, Lugo.

They arrived in what felt like midmorning and told me that I had a phone call. They released me from the railing and took me over to the desk with the phone. They gave me the phone, and I answered it. As usual, they pressed the gun to my head. I wondered if it was loaded. There was only one way to find out, and I didn't think that was a good idea. It was my sister, and besides the call to my wife, this was the hardest call to handle. Michelle had a very determined and poised personality. She knew where she stood and didn't take crap from anybody. I admired her for that and had always wished I could be more like her. We had a very close relationship, and we counted on each other no matter what the circumstances were. If there was one person that I trusted to be able to get the forces moving to gain my release, it was absolutely Michelle.

Unfortunately, there was no way for me to give her a hint of what was going on, none, unless I wanted to risk a bullet to the head. I told her that I had to run errands and couldn't talk to her. This was highly unusual, as I had always put her first, no matter what. She tried to ask me some questions and talk to me, but I brushed her off. This was not Marc she was talking to. I found out later that the reason she had called me was that on the day I got kidnapped, she had found out she had breast cancer. She tried calling me repeatedly, and I would never answer the phone. She called for my support, and I could not give it to her. She knew something was wrong—she was very astute—but who could have ever imagined the conditions or the situation I found myself in? With the people I talked to on the phone, I tried to make no sense and hint at some problem. Nobody caught on, and my hopes for a quick resolution dwindled. I was taken back to the box and re-chained.

Lugo said, "Who was that?"

"My sister," I replied gloomily.

"What did she want?" he asked.

Isn't it normal for your sister to call just to talk to you? "She calls me once in a while to see what's going on," I said.

"Is she going to be trouble?"

If there was anyone who could make these thugs pay and at the same time make their lives miserable, it was she. But she didn't know what was going on. I had no way to tell her, or else she would be on a plane heading the rescue operation, no doubt about that.

"No, she couldn't give a shit about me. I would not be concerned," I replied. It was the biggest lie I could think of. If she wanted to stir up trouble, they would find nowhere safe to hide. She would have them squirming for mercy.

"How about your brother?" he asked.

"I don't even know where he is," I lied to him. Alex would do anything for me, but unlike Michelle, he would not take charge of the situation. But I could always count on him. I hoped that by telling Lugo that I didn't know his whereabouts, they would leave him alone.

"Does he talk to your sister?" he asked.

I guess he came from a dysfunctional family. Of course he talked to my sister. Maybe Lugo sensed correctly that my sister was a tornado to be feared.

"We haven't talked since June. I don't think he cares much, either. But I don't know if he talks to my sister or not," I lied. I just wanted to keep my sister and brother from being endangered.

"If he starts causing problems, we'll have to put out an APB and pick him up," he said smugly.

An APB? I wanted to piss in my pants, even though I had already done that more than once. These clowns wanted me to believe they were law enforcement. They'd been watching too much TV. This was beyond comical. If it were not for my circumstances, I would have laughed in their faces. There was a good side to this. They actually still thought I didn't know who they were.

"I really don't think so," I told him while trying to keep myself from laughing.

"Well, he is another asshole, and we'll get him after we're finished with you," he said. Great. Not only did I have to worry about my circumstances, but my brother was now also in danger, and there was no way to warn him. The difference was that my brother would not give these thugs anything. He would rather they killed him. Delgado barely knew my brother, so this made no sense. Maybe it was a show of bravado to keep me focused and in line. I didn't understand anything. *Good luck trying to find him. I'm not going to tell you where he is, and you have no idea.*

Back to the box I went. I sensed that maybe they were getting concerned, as so much time had passed. My sister was calling, my wife was out there and so was my brother, and who knew who else was wondering about my disappearance? They were so full of themselves and they exuded so much overconfidence that they seemed to shrug off these possible risks. Maybe they would let me go on Friday because as time went on, their risk increased.

Towards midday, they came to take me to the bathroom. I was looking at spending another day in sweltering heat, sitting in an uncomfortable chair that did not give me much room to change positions. That's exactly how it turned out, and I sat there until evening. I was already feeling numb and dehydrated when the night watchman, Mr. Friendly, came in.

"How are you doing?" he asked.

Just peachy. In fact, I have never been better. Jerk.

My throat was so dry, and my tongue felt as if it were made out of leather, but somehow I managed to lie and croak, "All right."

"You know the other guys don't like me taking you out of here," he said.

"How long do you expect me to sit here with no water and this heat?" I asked, making sure he realized I was mad, however much good that did.

"I know, but—" he replied.

But what?

So he took me to the other room and put me in my cardboard box. It actually felt like heaven compared to the bathroom. I was starting to lose it if I thought I liked my cardboard box, but the bathroom was torture, and here I could at least lie down and change my position once in a while. He brought me a fast food burger, fries and Coke for dinner. I wondered how long they were going to let me have food, so I thought I had better enjoy it while I had it. I finished, and he gave me a cigarette.

He said, "Thursday is Thanksgiving. You want anything special?"

For starters, I thought, *how about letting me go home, or at least somewhere away from here?*

"Yeah, to go home," I told him.

"Soon you'll be going home. Soon."

"I hope so," I replied, knowing full well it was all bullshit.

"They're waiting for the funds to clear, and then you're gone," he said. The funds should have cleared that day, so that was a lie, and the way he said "you're gone" didn't sound too appealing to me.

"That should be by tomorrow, Friday at the latest?" I said to him, looking for a response.

"We'll see. That's what they told me. They want two million dollars, and when they have that, complete you're out of here," he said. I thought that meant I was not leaving.

"I don't have two million," I replied.

"They think you do," he said. This was going to be a tough issue. They weren't that bright, just greedy.

"If they add everything up, it doesn't come close to that. What about the deli?" I asked.

"They said you could keep that," he said. Great, they had closed the deli and fired all the employees, and I would inherit the mess that was left. How nice of them.

"You could reopen it," he said. Well, I knew I was not talking to Albert Einstein. Yeah, right, they were going to let me go and open the restaurant as if nothing had happened.

"Yeah, I could do that. We'll see," I replied, but the first issue at hand was surviving and getting out of that warehouse. Who cared about the deli at that point?

"Hey, listen, once you are let go, you should charge as much as you can on your credit cards. You can never come back, so what is

123

anybody going to do to you?" he said with pride. He thought like a criminal and did not have a reference point for right and wrong. That was how his mind worked. Defrauding the credit card was all right by his standards, and he saw nothing wrong with it.

"Good idea," I said, like that was the first thing I was going to do if they let me go.

He left for a while, and I just sat there, thinking about what this genius had told me. It was obvious that everything he told me either originated in his warped mind or he had been sent to tell me specific things to see what my reaction would be. It also appeared that Lugo and his principal cohorts had lied to Mr. Friendly to keep him off balance. He had been hired to babysit me, and there was no need to keep him in the loop or updated about their decisions. I could not rely on or believe anything he told me because he was an unimportant cog in the wheel and his employers treated him that way. They were using him. My conversation with him boiled down to entertainment and amusement.

I was not going to be able to obtain any really useful information from him. Mr. Friendly was a criminal, but he did not possess the same violent streak as the others. That was obvious. He was the only one who had bothered bringing me food, a soda, and a cigarette. I felt that he didn't harbor hate for me and sometimes even felt sorry for my condition. His profile was one that resembled Delgado. He was easy to manipulate, and that was where Lugo excelled. So I did not know if they were going to let me go on Friday or ever. I had to deal with that, and the only way to fight them was to make life difficult, like messing up my signature in all of the documents that I could. I had another trick up my sleeve. I hoped I would be able to use it.

No sleep that night and I just went from sitting down to lying down and repeated that a few hundred times. I often had to go to the bathroom at night, and there was no to take me, not that they would anyway. So I kept using the pee-in-the-cup method that I had perfected so well. It was not as easy as it sounded. I was blindfolded, so it posed a challenge at times. Many times I had several urine-filled cups near me. It must have been a beautiful sight for them. I don't think they cared.

Since I could not sleep, I thought about many things. One of those recurring thoughts was of people who had spent years in captivity or as prisoners of war. I guess the toughest part was the beginning. Then, slowly, acceptance that you cannot change your situation unfolds, and you do the best to adapt to your surroundings in order to survive. I admired the fortitude those people had and the spirit that had guided them through their dark days.

Wednesday morning arrived, and I had not slept a wink all night. This was the second week of my captivity, and I was worn out both physically and mentally.

Sometime that morning, Lugo and one of his cronies came in.

"Get up!" Lugo was really twisted, and I could tell he enjoyed his power trip. There was nothing nice about his demeanor. He had never tried to hide it. Besides, he had to show the boys' who was in charge.

"Whose number is 592-0105?" he asked, almost yelling.

"That's the deli," I said with no interest, pretending his

demeanor didn't affect me, although it did often startle me.

"Well, they beeped you, so you have to call them back," he ordered. I wanted to tell him to call them and tell them I was busy or, better yet, tied up at the moment.

"Okay," I said. No sense in arguing with loco boy.

So we went through the usual procedure, and they took me to the desk where I was becoming accustomed to the procedures required of me. They dialed, and my star manager, Freddy, answered.

"Yeah, Freddy, what's going on?" I asked him.

"You won't believe what happened. I sent Ricardo to the bank, and he set the money down somewhere near the espresso machine, and one of the employees stole it," he said, almost crying. Good old Freddy, you could always count on him. Well, the fact that one of the employees had stolen the money didn't surprise me. They had stolen whole hams and other cold cuts before, and it could have even been Freddy who took the money. Geez, that deli was such a great idea.

"Freddy, I'm out of town. You will have to take care of the problem," I told him.

"Now I won't have the money to pay the employees," he said. Why he was depositing the money anyway when I had told him to pay the employees from it, I wondered. It made no sense. To me, it sounded as though Freddy had pocketed himself some cash and was making up this entire thing. That would not have surprised me. Criminals surrounded me everywhere, and they were all trying to fleece me. This was unreal.

"Take the missing money from the safe," I said. *If you haven't put that in your pocket already.* I kept four hundred dollars and perhaps a little more in the safe for emergencies.

"Okay, I'll do it. When are you or Diana going to come in?" he asked.

Never was the correct answer, but I couldn't say that. I never did go back to the deli.

"I don't know, Freddy. We are both out of town. You will have to take care of anything that comes up between now and Friday. All right, Freddy, I have to go," I said. *Because the guy holding the gun to my head is getting antsy.*

I gave the phone to Lugo, and he hung up.

"Very reliable manager and employees you have." He laughed as he said it. Unfortunately, I had to agree with him on that one.

"What kind of food do you like?" Lugo asked.

"I like everything. Italian, pizza, everything," I responded.

"You like steaks?" he asked.

"Yeah, I pretty much like everything," I replied.

"We'll see what we can get for you tonight," he said.

Well, that meant I was not getting any breakfast or lunch, but I might get dinner. It was moments like these that I thought Lugo was a true schizophrenic and perplexed me. One minute he was barking at me, and then he seemed genuinely concerned about what food I liked. That didn't mean I was getting anything, but he was one strange creature. Most of the time, he barked at me, and showing any concern for my welfare was a rare and infrequent event.

Lugo was perplexed as to how he was going to steal my house. How could he sign over the house to his criminal organization without my wife's presence? As nice as I am, I told him I would help him with that predicament. What I suggested to him was that I could sign my wife's name for her on the simple quitclaim deed. That day, he brought over a deed transferring my house to a company he owned. I signed both our names where he placed my hand. I'm sure that neither signature looked like our real signatures. He said he had someone who would notarize the signatures but would need some ID for my wife. I told him that was not a problem—there was a copy of her driver's license in my files. You may wonder why I did this. Simple: It was a way to trap them. If they actually recorded that deed, they would have to answer a few questions, namely, how could they have possibly gotten my wife's alleged signature on the document when it was stamped clearly on her passport that she was out of the country? They went for it, and that was all I cared about. Their greed blinded them to the obvious stupidity of this plan. Yes, maybe they thought I would be dead and my wife would not come back and challenge them. But it was a foolishly unnecessary risk they chose to take anyway. They were, in effect, signing a confession that they had done something wrong and never realized it. I was getting things in order in case I survived.

Instead of taking me to my box, they took me to the bathroom. By now they had given up on the circle game for one reason or another. I was looking forward to another day in this Turkish bath, sitting in an uncomfortable position for seven or eight hours, so I guess he was not too concerned about my condition. They gave me a bottle of warm water and a cigarette and left me to my own misery. At least the radio wasn't as loud here, and that was some sort of temporary reprieve.

That day something changed, and, like everything else, I didn't understand it. When the thug came to take me to the bathroom, I noticed that, for the first time, the person who grabbed me was wearing gloves. It was a little late to think about not leaving fingerprints, I mused. But the fact that he was wearing them concerned me. These criminals' behavior had always been so unpredictable that they were capable of doing anything. Perhaps they had seen a movie the night before, and the criminals in the movie wore gloves, so they thought it was a good idea. That was probably where they had gotten all their ideas, from watching movies. They weren't capable of differentiation between fantasy and reality. I truly believed that.

So I sat. There was nothing to do but just sit. I didn't want to think anymore. I felt it had become useless; nothing could be resolved. When I was in the bathroom, I actually missed my box. There, even though my movement was limited, I could lie down or sit up. Here, there was no choice.

There, in that chair, I felt that I was alone in that warehouse. Still, the only time I had tried to find out if that was true, I found out that I was not really alone but being quietly watched. Later, it was confirmed that I had indeed been alone several times while I was in the bathroom. But being blindfolded and having wax balls in my ears did not afford me a good sense of my surroundings. Even if I could determine that I was alone, it would have been difficult, if not impossible, to get loose from the chains that bound me.

About six or seven hours later, the night watchman, Mr. Friendly, came in and gave me a cigarette and asked me if I was all right. I didn't know what to answer to that question anymore; I couldn't possibly have been all right.

He sat me in a different chair, which I knew was in the same room as my cardboard box, and gave me a soda and a cigarette. He said he was going to clean up around my box. I was hoping he would leave me my cups; they were my private toilet after all. The steak dinner or whatever they were going to feed me did not arrive. In fact, there was nothing at all. What Mr. Friendly told me next was amusing.

"You have to stop urinating in these cups. It's not healthy having them next to you like that."

Okay, but what was I supposed to do? Use the POM method and keep getting my pants totally wet or, better yet, bust my bladder? Talk about not healthy. Being tied up was not considered healthy, either, not to mention the sporadic food or water they gave me. He didn't like the fact that he had to clean it up. Sorry, not my problem.

"Well, I'll talk to the other guy," he replied. I knew he was referring to Lugo, who didn't care one way or the other.

I sat in the other chair while Mr. Friendly was doing the housekeeping chores around my box. The pain and itch around my eyes became uncontrollable. I could not take it anymore. I did not give a damn what they were going to do to me. I could not take it anymore. It itched so badly because the tape was eating my skin away. It was driving me nuts. It was unbearable. So I began prying the tape loose and with my fingers, massaging the area around my eyes. It didn't really help, but I could not stop.

Mr. Friendly went into total panic, I mean total panic, and

yelled, "What are you doing?" He could tell I was peeling the tape off my eyes. In reality, I was digging a tunnel beneath it to get to my eyes.

"I can't take this damn itch anymore. It's painful," I spat back.

Mr. Friendly was in full panic now and said, "You can't do that!"

Oh, really? Watch me. The next thing I said probably shocked him and made the floor underneath his feet tremble: "Go ahead and shoot me. It's better than having to withstand this itch. Go ahead. What are you waiting for?"

The next thing he said was totally illogical but might have been expected from this mental midget. "I don't care if you see me. What are you going to do? But the other guys are not going to like it."

I paid no heed and continued my burrowing and rubbing.

He finally said, "Hold on. I have an idea," and left the room.

When he came back, he stood behind me and started to take off the rolls of tape I had around my eyes. He said, "This will help."

After all the tape was off, he put a sanitary napkin on my eyes and re-taped my face with gusto.

"Better?" he asked, and in fact it did relieve some of the itch and pain.

After this full-blown earthquake, things calmed down, and he took me back to my clean box on the floor. Mr. Friendly regained his composure and acted as if nothing had occurred.

"You'll be going home soon. I just came from the office, and they are making preparations for your release. They have your reservations. In fact, I think I saw your ticket," he told me. The other night, he had told me he saw my ticket, but now he just thought he had seen it. It sounded to me as if my ticket was one-way and it was final, but not to Colombia. The office, what office? Oh, that's right, the FBI was holding me as part of their new Kidnapping and Extortion of US Citizens department.

"I heard that one before." I was no longer afraid to reveal my disbelief.

"Just hold on a little longer and it will be over," he promised. That was exactly what I was afraid of: *over.*

I was getting upset, something very rare for me. I've always been known for my even keel, always under control. But I'd had enough of this charade.

Mr. FBI entered the room at this point and said, "I told you we're the FBI. Like I told you before, I would not ask too many questions if you know what is good for you. It will be over soon." I still didn't like the way *over* sounded.

I sensed he was irritated by my questions and realized that I was wasting my time. I was not going to get a truthful answer from any of them. I didn't expect to, but I had nothing else to lose.

They returned me to my box, and I sat there staring into nothingness. Then, to my surprise, Lugo came in. Now I understood why the babysitters were not talking to me and had been so curt. They were terrified of him, and with good reason. A little while later, Lugo came back and told me that I had a telephone call from my wife. I didn't know whether they had told him about my little outbreak and that I was not a happy camper. He made no mention of it. The telephone call was not something I looked forward to, since I had to measure every word I said. They took me to the chair and gave me the phone, applying the gun to my head as usual.

"Hello, China. How are you, D. J. and Stephie?" I asked, always trying to sound as normal as I possibly could.

"Good, Chino. How are you doing?" she asked. She sounded calm.

"I'm okay. I'm wrapping up here so I can join you and the kids."

"Chino, tell me the truth. Who are you with? What's going on?" Her questions concerned me because I came to the realization that maybe she had still not caught on to what was happening. Was it possible she still had no clue?

"I'm alone, China, and I've almost got everything wrapped up," I said.

"Chino, your brother-in-law wants to go to Miami and hire a private detective," she said. *Oh, I wish you hadn't said that.* They got really nervous when she said that. My wife obviously did not know how to handle the situation, and she seemed lost. When she spoke to me, she didn't realize that whomever I was with might be listening to the conversation. Besides, she had always looked to me for guidance in any difficult situation, but this was different.

"No, China, tell him not to come." I wanted to tell her she should have done it already and ask her why she had waited so long. I responded with the only thing I did not want to say.

"Wait a minute," she said.

D. J., my son, came on the phone.

"Hi, Dad," he said cheerily.

133

"D. J., how are you doing? Are you behaving?" I always asked him if he was behaving. He was a quiet child that seldom caused any problems.

"Yes. I'm being good and listening to Mom. Bye, Dad. I love you."

"I love you, too. Bye, D. J."

This was a typical D. J. conversation. He didn't like being on the phone long or saying more than two sentences. In this particular circumstance, I was glad of it. Diana, my wife, came back on the phone. Lugo whispered in my ear to cut the call.

"Listen, China I have to go. The guy who cuts the grass is here, and I want to pay him. I love you." I gave them the phone and hung it up. I thought that she might realize what I had told her was ridiculous. The guy who cut the lawn never came by so late, since it's especially difficult to cut the grass when it's dark outside. I did not know if she would. They took me back to the box and chained me to the railing.

Lugo said, "If your brother-in-law comes here, we're going to have to kill him and anybody else he hires."

My wife had inadvertently had just made these thugs nervous and perhaps made things more difficult for me. I knew no one was coming, but I could not even begin to convince these criminals of that. It was no surprise to me that they would try to kill him and anybody he hired.

"He won't come," I responded, but I doubted they believed me.

"Well, if he does, he's dead meat. He's not leaving the airport alive," Lugo said. I knew this was his tough-guy act and a little show of bravado. That was pretty lame. Telling me they were going to kill him in the airport, but it also proved to me that they were genuinely concerned about the possibility. Things had just gotten much more complicated, and Lugo himself had started to doubt letting me go.

Lugo said, "We have a problem."

"And what is that?" I asked.

"If we let you go, how do we know you won't come back into the country?"

"I won't. All I want is to go and be with my family." I tried to reassure him, knowing it was useless.

"It's not that simple. We need to blame you for some crime like tax evasion or Medicare fraud so you won't think of coming back."

Again, I wanted to laugh. If the circumstances weren't so dire, I would have. I pictured smoke coming out of his brain as a result of the effort he had made to come up with that gem of an idea.

"I'm not coming back," I told him. What was the point? It was like talking to a brick wall.

"We'll have to look through your tax returns and see what we can find. If not, we are going to have to make you sign some confession," he said, trying to sound intellectual. I almost pissed in my pants. Look at my tax returns? I doubted very much that Lugo could read, much less be able to analyze a tax return. I wanted to tell him he was wasting his time, but I didn't. They wanted a confession under duress? Sure, I'd sign a few dozen if they wanted me to. It was apparent that this criminal enterprise lacked intellectual capacity. I didn't reply. I would just wait and see what happened. His statement was so stupid that it didn't deserve a reply.

I understood their intentions a little better now. They were actually going to send me to Colombia and hope that I would never come back. That was absurd, a ridiculous plan that was untenable, and they should have known it from the beginning. So now they had come up with the great idea to frame me for something so I'd be afraid to come back. It was clear they had no real plan. They were improvising as they went along. Bad theater. Their only objective was to clean me out, but they had unfortunately forgotten to plan or even think about the rest of the details, including what they were going to do with me after they got their booty.

The night watchman, Mr. Friendly, came in and gave me a cigarette. I was miserable and depressed and was glad he didn't hang around to talk to me. He just checked the tape and unbelievably added some more. The tape around my eyes was starting to eat away at my skin in spite of my sanitary napkin, and I started bleeding from both the areas around my eyes and ears. The wax balls in my ears became increasingly uncomfortable, and wax continued to drip from my ears.

I was crushed. For the first time, I realized that the cavalry was not coming, and whatever fate awaited me was in the hands of these criminals. I knew that once I had told my wife not to send anyone, it had shut off all possibility of someone coming to rescue me. There would be no SWAT team busting down the doors and arresting these criminals. The conversation with Lugo had made me realize that they now had second thoughts about releasing me. It had finally dawned on them that there was no foolproof way of guaranteeing that I would not come back and go to the authorities. So the only alternative was to kill me. No one was looking for me, and maybe they were right. They could kill me and dump my body somewhere, and no one would be the wiser. No one would care. I lay down to sleep and realized that for the first time since I was kidnapped, all hope seemed to be lost.

Chapter 16 — Acceptance

"EACH PLAYER MUST ACCEPT THE CARDS LIFE DEALS HIM OR
HER. BUT ONCE THEY ARE IN HAND, HE OR SHE ALONE MUST
DECIDE HOW TO PLAY THE CARDS IN ORDER TO WIN THE
GAME."
- VOLTAIRE -

"HOW A PERSON MASTERS HIS FATE IS MORE IMPORTANT
THAN WHAT HIS FATE IS."
- KARL WILHELM VON HUMBOLDT -

It was Thursday, and that day was Thanksgiving, one that I will never forget. Thanksgiving is a time to reminisce on memories of good moments with family, usually around a scrumptious feast. Those fortunate enough to have those things usually take them for granted and falsely believe that there are not many who go without. There would be no Macy's parade, football games, or sitting around with family and friends and enjoying their conversation. There would be none of that. It was a time of sadness and of accepting my ultimate fate in dealing with what life had dished out.

I received a cup of coffee and a cigarette for breakfast that day. I was hoping they would not chain me in the bathroom on this festive day. It was depressing enough. I did not want to sit uncomfortably in the heat. I did not get my wish. They took me to the bathroom and didn't even give me some dirty water to drink. I sat there in a stupor. I imagined what I looked like. It had been weeks since I had been able to shave and shower or even brush my teeth. The smell coming from my body must have been putrid, but surprisingly I could no longer detect it myself. I imagined that I smelled something akin to Roquefort cheese at this stage. I was still wearing the same clothes that I had been wearing that day at the deli. Actually, there were only tattered pieces of the shirt left. I could have been easily mistaken for a hobo or homeless person, if not worse. Personal hygiene, as well as the way I presented myself, had always been important to me. Obviously, those things were of little importance now.

Nonetheless, my dirty state added to my feeling of misery, along with my festering burns. I imagined that they were seriously infected by now, but the pain had subsided to a dull ache. The problem was the area around my eyes. The rolls of tape around my face had continued to eat into my skin, and my face, particularly around my eyes, had continued bleeding. I could feel the sticky liquid sitting in the pockets the tape afforded. My ears were dripping wax, and I started to get a dull ache in them. I had suffered from ear infections when I was a child, and this was the perfect recipe for a severe problem. My pants had been loose when I arrived at the warehouse, but I now had a hard time keeping them up. The small comfort that had been afforded by the sanitary napkin Mr. Friendly had placed over my eyes was gone. The item had disintegrated, and the itch and pain was as bad as it had been before. There was no lunch that day, not even a glass of water or a cigarette. I figured that they were merrily enjoying the day's festivities, eating and watching the games on TV while also celebrating their conquest and total destruction of their prey. They came to get me earlier than usual that day, and it was the night watchman, Mr. Friendly.

He took me to my cardboard box, which I never thought that I would be so thankful for, and said, "Would you like to hear the football game?"

"Sure," I replied. It would break the monotony I was immersed in and provide some sensory input other than the dreadful music loop all day every day.

He brought in the television and tuned in to the game. I was not even sure who was playing. I thought it was the Cowboys and someone else. Not that I cared, I just wanted a different kind of noise in my background.

Mr. Friendly said, "We are bringing you a home-cooked meal. It will be here in a little while."

"Thanks." I was thinking that one last good meal was what they give those waiting to be executed. Was that going to be my case?

Mr. FBI came to join Mr. Friendly, and they sat with me. We talked mostly about football, the Dolphins in particular. They watched the game while I listened. I found it interesting that they were stuck with me in the warehouse that day. Either they had no family or the pay for babysitting was very good. I couldn't imagine these thugs as the family type, anyway. They seemed to be in a jovial mood and were constantly trying to crack jokes. Perhaps they detected my somber mood and were trying to cheer me up. If so, it didn't work.

As we were talking, Mr. FBI told me that he wanted to retire from his current job and start a new career. Supposedly, I was to think that he worked for the FBI, CIA, or something like that. What I thought he was really referring to was his career as a petty criminal. Maybe it was because it was Thanksgiving and he was having second thoughts about a life of crime. Holidays sometimes can do that, but I bet tomorrow there would not even be a trace of those thoughts left in his mind. They gave me soda and a cigarette and were more attentive than they ever had been or would be.

I decided to get down to business. "Am I going to leave tomorrow?" I probed.

"I don't know. They haven't told me anything," Mr. FBI said, as if I had caught him off guard.

"Could you find out for me?" I pressed.

"Last I heard, they were having problems with one of the wire transfers and the transfer of the house," he said almost apologetically.

"Oh, I thought that was done already." I knew it was a lie, but I wanted to see what he said. They had changed their minds after the last conversation with my wife. Basically, they had come to the realization that there was no way to release me without me coming back and biting them. It was what I expected, and even though it was depressing, I was prepared for it.

Mr. FBI left me alone with Mr. Friendly, who said almost sadly, "They would not let me take your blindfold off for a few hours either. Do you want me to read to you?" I bet he had won some brownie points for suggesting that.

"I'd like to hear the news," I said.

He laughed and said, "Why? Do you think your story made it into the newspapers or TV?"

When had I asked him that had not even crossed my mind. It appeared no one was missing me.

"No, I just like keeping up with current events," I replied, which was true at the time.

He ignored me and just said, "I'll be back when the food arrives."

Why ask me what I want if he had no intentions of giving it to me? Par for the course. Later that evening, Lugo showed up, and he brought his dog along. Don't ask me why, but when I heard the leash and the bark, it threw me into a panic attack. I was defenseless, and if the dog wanted to snack on any part of my body, he would have had a free go at it. The dog came over and licked my face several times. He was the only one who showed some compassion for me. Dogs have great instincts, and I felt he sensed my position. It just goes to show you that some humans are lower in the totem pole than some animals. The humans who had kidnapped me could have learned a few things from that dog.

Later, both night watchmen came in and brought me food. It was turkey, stuffing, potatoes, and a soda. At least that was what it tasted like—without visual verification, it all boiled down to the taste buds. That was the last good meal I would receive, and I ate as if knew there would be no more.

Mr. Friendly asked me if it was good, to which I replied, very. I was famished, and it was a real meal for once. He gave me a cigarette and sat down beside me.

"What are you going to do when you leave here?" he asked me. Seeing that Lugo had just been in the warehouse, I felt he had been told to ask me the question.

"I don't know. I can't get a job in South America," I replied. There were not too many companies willing to hire ex-patriots in Colombia because of the political situation there. There was the possibility of going to another country on the continent, but thinking about such things was premature.

"Why don't you start your own business? You seem pretty smart, and it would be easy for you," he said. I felt that if I were so smart, I would not have been in the position I was.

"I'm cleaned out, remember? I have nothing to start a business with." I needed to remind myself that I was having a conversation with a mental giant.

"Well, you can sell what your wife took and use that," he said.

"There was not much, and besides, if I do sell it, it would be to feed my family," I replied. I was getting annoyed but reminded myself that maybe the conversation would yield some clues.

"I'll tell you something," he said. "You could come back and work in the States as long as it's out west," he said as if he was divulging a great secret.

"What do mean by west?" I said. This was getting more interesting.

"From Arizona and west, like that," he said.

"Why is that?" was my response.

"Because nobody would be looking for you out there. You come to the east and you're dead."

This was interesting. Now they were ceding the western states if I chose to come back. Did they really think that if I came back, no matter to what location, I would not go to the authorities? Could they possibly be so stupid? Did they really think I would make believe that nothing had happened? It was impossible to think along their lines, but it flabbergasted me that they even would consider taking that risk.

"Well, it's something to think about," I said.

"Don't mention it to anybody that I told you this, or we are both in trouble," he said quietly. So these great ideas belonged to Mr. Friendly, not the hierarchy of this criminal enterprise. He was different and, for some reason or other, felt sorry for me or wanted to help me out. Unfortunately for me, he didn't make the decisions, and what the other thugs chose for my fate was of ultimate importance.

I wasn't sure about Mr. Friendly. Maybe he had been sent to tell me these things to see my reaction and find out what I would answer. I'd have to have been pretty stupid to jeopardize any possibility of leaving that warehouse alive. Then again, they couldn't think much of me, and I was chained in the warehouse, after all. Nonetheless, I did not truly believe they were idiotic enough to take the risk of letting me go, but strange things happen, and I had to keep my hopes and mental fortitude up even in the darkest moment. I was not completely ready to throw in the towel.

The rest of the evening, the two night watchmen sat and talked to me. It was mostly about sports and other insignificant matters. Mr. FBI told me that I had grown quite a beard and that it looked good on me. What were they supposed to say? That I looked like something the cat dragged in or worse? It was this type of comment that really made me wonder about them. A few hours later, I lay down to sleep. Negotiating sleep had become difficult, and it seemed each night I slept less and less. I chalked that up to the inactivity and the fact that my internal clock had gone berserk. Most of the evening I either sat or lay down, and there was nothing I wished for more than to be able to sleep for a few hours to escape my surroundings.

Friday morning rolled around, and Lugo and one of his sidekicks came to my box. They had some papers for me to sign. I didn't know what they were and did not bother to ask. It would probably not do me any good. They put my hand on the spot where they wanted me to sign, and I tried to mess up the signature as much as possible without making it obvious. I sat for another hour or so and they came to take me to the bathroom, where they chained me once again.

It was obvious I would not be leaving today, and the entire thing had been one big lie. I was depressed and somewhat frightened because I realized the possibility of walking out of that warehouse alive diminished with each passing day. I knew no one was looking for me and that I could not expect or hope for someone to come storming through those doors to save me. I just had to wait and see what cards fate had dealt me. I had to maintain my self-control and keep my spirits high even as the situation grew increasingly more difficult. I had faith that I was not alone, and God or the Supreme Being would not abandon me.

That day, to add to my misery, happened to be the longest day I had to sit in the bathroom with no water and no food, not even a cigarette. It was late by the time the night watchmen came to get me, and their demeanor had changed from being jolly and communicative to grumpy and taciturn. I guessed they may have gotten their butts chewed out by the boss or received a stern warning. It did not matter. I didn't want to speak to them, either. They offered no information that was useful or valid, and I didn't want to hear lies just to get my hopes up. It was better that way.

I could not sleep at all that night, wondering if I had spoken to my wife and son for the last time. I didn't want to think and was exhausted by the emotional rollercoaster ride I was on. I told myself to just stop thinking but found that impossible. Under the circumstances, there was nothing else to do but think. I knew the whole story about letting me go that day had been bullshit. Nonetheless, I hoped I was wrong and there would be a positive surprise. I lay and sat awake all night with the music playing on the radio until it was Saturday morning and my second weekend in captivity. The fact that I could no longer sleep for any length of time had become torture in and of itself.

They brought me a cup of coffee and an apple for breakfast. I sat there for a while longer before they took me to the bathroom to spend another glorious day in the sweltering heat, dehydrating without water.

During that second weekend, something interesting began to happen. I don't know if it was a form of hallucinations or daydreams or something else that I had not heard of before. I learned that the mind is a perfect machine and it will give you escape routes so you will not go mad. It can turn itself off in order to protect itself and you when the stimulus (or lack thereof) becomes almost unbearable. Perhaps I was exploring some deep corner of my mind that I didn't know existed. Whatever the case, it was strange and at the same time fascinating to me. I will try to explain it, but the few times I have told people, I have received strange looks, as if they thought I had moments of insanity. But far from it, I never felt that I lost control or was insane.

Well, then again, who is crazy and willing to acknowledge it? Maybe I was on the brink of lunacy, but I like to think that my mind opened gateways to places that I did not know existed in order for me, at least temporarily, to find a refuge from my surroundings. This did not occur only in the bathroom, where one may theorize that, due to the heat, my circuit breakers went off. The experience was recurring both in the bathroom and in my cardboard box.

I will try to explain it, although putting the experiences into words and making it seem understandable is difficult. You are free to make any judgment about my mental state at the time as you wish.

While I was either sitting in the bathroom or in my box, I drifted off into a different reality. The bathroom in my mind's eye would totally disappear, and I was somewhere else. There were three common themes where I would go. One was some sort of house that I liked walking through. It appeared from my surroundings that it was the turn of the twentieth century, and my favorite place was a porch where I could sit and gaze at the stars. Now, mind you, I was there: I could smell the air, almost touch the walls, and everything was vividly, vividly clear. One of the times, they took me to the bathroom while I was walking instead of being in the warehouse. I was walking through this house and saw the rooms, the walls, everything in perfect clarity.

The second place I went to was scary. It reminded me of New York, with the elevated trains and old apartment buildings, but everything was completely dark and black, and there was no sign of life anywhere. I would just walk through the streets, not knowing where I was heading or why. The third one was probably the funniest. I was a caveman, and I was in my cave with someone who must have been my wife or partner. Again, the clarity and details of these places were amazing. It was all three dimensional, and I felt my presence there. I did not visit these places once but just about every day from the second weekend on. I would spend a considerable amount of time there, and there was no particular incident that ever triggered them. I would be just sitting there, and off I'd go. It was strange but at the same time wonderful, and I will not attempt to explain psychologically or otherwise what they were. To me, they were real.

I know that a psychologist would try to find a way to explain that, since I was under duress, my mind invented these places to escape. Maybe, maybe not. Even if we try, we cannot explain everything through science, even though we like to think we can by simply attaching a label or meaning to it. There is more than meets the eye and more than we are consciously aware of. I was not sure whether to write about this or not, but I felt that some people would appreciate the message while others would scoff at it and chalk it up to lunacy or some other mental abnormality as a result of my captivity. Let each reader make their own determinations and draw their own conclusions.

The night, the watchmen arrived and informed me that I would be cleaning up. I guess it got to the point where they could no longer stand the smell. At least I would be able to change my filthy clothes and maybe wash up a little. They gave me a hamburger, fries, and soda for dinner, my only meal that day. I was famished. It seemed they had a very limited menu, but who was I to complain? After I finished, they gave me a cigarette, and I waited for them to take me to the bathroom, which they did a few minutes later. They picked me up, and one of them grabbed me by the arm while the other guided me. Since we were not playing the circle game anymore, the distance was much shorter. Mr. FBI asked me to stick my hand out, and he put it on the barrel of the gun. He then jabbed my back with it and told me that if I made any unusual moves, he would kill me. I believed he would take great pleasure in shooting me. I believed he would neither hesitate nor show any remorse.

When we got to the bathroom, Mr. FBI said, "You are to face the direction we leave you. If you turn around, you're dead, you understand?" He liked to accentuate the "you're dead" phrase. It felt like the fifty-millionth time I had heard it in the last two weeks.

"Yes," I replied.

"There is no mirror in the bathroom, so you won't be able to look at yourself or behind you," he emphasized. I didn't want to look at myself. The shock would probably be too great.

"Fine," I replied.

"There is a bucket of water in there with some soap, a toothbrush, toothpaste, a towel, and a change of clothes," Mr. FBI told me.

"Okay," I said, hoping I could follow these complex instructions.

They started to peel off the miles of tape I had covering my eyes and face, and for a moment I wondered whether, when they finally took it all off, I would be able to see or not. I had not seen anything for over two weeks and was almost accustomed to a dark world. The final few layers were painful. The tape had started to eat at my skin, and it was raw and sensitive. They were not in the least delicate in removing it. With the final yank of the tape, they pulled out a chunk of my hair, which was now coated with grease from not washing. As he finished, he stuck his hand in front of me, and I saw that it was black. As I had suspected, one or both of my night watchmen were African American. Not that it made a difference to me. They could have been anyone. I did remember that one of the people who had grabbed me in the parking lot was a large African-American man.

Once it was completely off, he said, "Go ahead and wash up. Wash up everything real good, your face, arms, and balls." He accentuated "balls" for some reason.

They closed the door, and I was alone in the bathroom. I had a hard time adjusting my sight since my eyes were almost sealed together by the remnants of glue from the tape. At first, the light, even though it was dull, hurt my eyes. I was in a small bathroom that was approximately four by four feet. It had a sink, a toilet, white plaster walls, and a gray concrete floor. This was the bathroom I had spent most of my days in. The toilet had a handicap bar that I surmised had anchored my chain. The bathroom was filthy and didn't look as if it had ever been cleaned. In front of me was a small bucket with filthy water that was probably dirtier than I was. There was a bar of soap, a towel, a toothbrush, and toothpaste. They had obviously been rummaging through my closets, since they had also brought a change of my clothes.

The clothes I'd been wearing were beyond filthy. My shirt was ripped, and it was impossible to believe it had once been white. I looked at my arms. The burns were blistered and black. They looked infected and were painful to the touch. There was an obvious infection, but there was nothing I could do about it.

I felt my nose and ears and noticed both were bleeding. The tape had peeled off layers of skin. As I looked at the pail of dirty water, I realized this was the same water that they were giving me to drink while I was in this bathroom. Ergo, the bottle they gave me was also next to the sink. It was surprising that I hadn't gotten sick from it. I washed as best as I could and probably got dirtier by washing with that water. I tried to wash my hair a little bit with the little soap sliver. I couldn't shave and was now sporting a full beard. Brushing my teeth was not easy, either. I did the best I could, and any cleaning was welcomed, even with the limited items and the dirty water. I changed from my urinated pants and torn shirt into the pants they brought me and realized how much weight I had lost. My pants kept falling, and I had to hold them to keep them up. They gave me no belt, perhaps thinking I could use it as a weapon, or, even worse, I might hang myself before they got their loot. I actually felt a bit better, even though, by any standards, I was still filthy.

I called them when I finished, and I turned around as they opened the door. They immediately began to rewrap tape around my eyes and face. They must have used three rolls, and once they were satisfied that I looked like a poor man's version of a mummy, they stopped. They had another surprise for me. They put a hood over my face, one that came down to near my collarbone. It made breathing more difficult and was something else I needed to adjust to. I thought maybe they wouldn't feed me anymore, since eating with the hood on was impossible. It smelled like one of the bank bags used to carry coins. Fortunately, they didn't put more wax balls back in my ears. Perhaps they forgot, but I was grateful, because my ears hurt and I feared they were getting infected.

Mr. FBI asked, "Feel better?"

"Yes," I replied. *Just wonderful.* Actually, I did feel a little better than I had.

They took me back to my cardboard box and offered me a Danish. There were two kinds, and they asked me which variety I wanted. I told them it didn't matter, but they insisted, so I chose one. I had to lift my hood up so I could actually eat it, since my mouth was covered now. They said nothing when I did, so I guess that was what they expected of me. They gave me a soda and a cigarette, and after I finished, I just sat there trying to get used to the new hood that adorned my head. They seemed pretty obsessed with the fact that I might be able to see them. Maybe that was a good sign, then again, maybe not.

Mr. FBI informed me that they were tired of answering phone calls forwarded from my house and that they were no longer going to do so. Instead, they were installing an answering machine, and I would have to return the phone calls they thought were important. That was good for me; I didn't like answering phone calls here, and the less I had to do it, the better. A wrong word or slip of the tongue could have gotten me into trouble. Then again, it was hard to imagine more trouble than I was already in.

I lay back and tried to relax a bit. My little birdbath had helped. There was nothing I could do, nothing I could change. The rescuers were not coming, and these mentally unstable criminals would ultimately decide my fate. I didn't realize it then, but would later, that my fate was not in their hands. I lay down and drifted off into a troubled sleep, knowing it was now a waiting game.

Chapter 17 — The Waiting Game

"HOW MUCH OF HUMAN LIFE IS LOST IN WAITING?"
- RALPH WALDO EMERSON -

I woke up to Sunday morning, and all I had to look forward to was my third week in captivity, not an encouraging prospect. They were getting weary of having to look after me. I could tell, especially in the changed demeanor of Mr. Friendly and Mr. FBI. They wanted this thing over with as much as I did. It was not said explicitly, but I could tell they were losing interest in being stuck in the warehouse with me every night. Their formerly cheerful attitude was gone, replaced by annoyance and complacency. With what I assumed was less financial incentive than the others; the novelty of the situation had worn thin.

I was taken to the bathroom earlier than usual and given a bottle of water. I stayed there longer than I had on any other day. To me, this was a clear indication that my assumptions about them were true. They came in late that evening and took me back to the box. I was promptly informed that no one had gotten me anything to eat. Another day without a morsel to eat was further proof that they were tired of me. Things were deteriorating among the ranks and would probably get worse.

That evening, Mr. Friendly came in to tell me they would release me soon. That could mean tomorrow or in six months, longer or shorter or anywhere in between. The new plan they were hatching involved dropping me off in front of the deli, and from there I would be on my own. They planned to do this in the wee hours of the morning so no one would suspect foul play. He said they would leave me blindfolded in the parking lot, and once they left, I could take it off. Either they had no fear that I would go to the authorities, or they did not think about it. Later, it would be proven that this should not have been a concern for them.

I wanted to believe this plan was true but knew that how they were going to end this whole fiasco was posing a challenge for them. I asked myself if they could realistically take the risk of letting me loose in the streets of Miami. It seemed absurd and all too simple, but, then again, they were overconfident of themselves. Nevertheless, it was a large risk for them, and even if they seemed dumb, could they possibly be that stupid? I was hoping the answer was yes, but I had to maintain a level head and not get my hopes up unrealistically. It was probably a story they had given Mr. Friendly and Mr. FBI because, I had sensed, they were getting tired of babysitting for me and it had nothing to do with their real plans. That was a more logical explanation and sounded more plausible. Besides, they needed to keep my hopes up in order to keep bleeding me of my remaining assets. Maybe I was the stupid one.

The third week of captivity was the most uneventful. I spent the days tied in the bathroom and remained there until late at night. Then, Mr. Friendly or Mr. FBI would return me to the cardboard box. Conversation between us dwindled to a trickle. They were weary, and so was I. It was taxing on everyone, and there was nothing more to say. Their bosses had lied to them and to me.

I received sporadic meals that week, which consisted of mostly hamburgers. Some days, I would receive nothing at all, and on one particular day, I was given a hamburger for lunch and another one for dinner. There was no creativity at all with their menus. The night watchmen stopped giving me the nightly can of soda. Feeding me and supplying me with a beverage depended on whether they wanted to bother with it or not. Most of the time, they did not. I was a burden and an utterly worthless albatross every day to them.

By the end of the week, things started getting even stranger, if that was possible. I was taken to the bathroom in the morning. In the afternoon, they took me to my car and had me sit there for hours.

The first time, Lugo said, "Do you remember your car? Well, you're going to get familiar with it again."

To get me into the car, they pointed me backwards. Since I was blindfolded, I could not seem to get into the car. The way they were aiming me into it just wasn't working. This must have gone on for a good ten minutes. I could not figure out how to get into it. They knew it and burst out laughing uncontrollably. I was being used as entertainment again, and they just wanted to humiliate me some more. When they finished getting enough enjoyment at my expense, they pushed me into the car the right way. I was glad to provide them with some amusement. They sat me in the front seat and handcuffed me to the steering wheel. Then they secured me in the back seat. Strangest of all, they made me lie down in the trunk. I spent many hours at each location. What was their reasoning for this? Why the car, why the front seat, back seat, and trunk? I was so perplexed; the only thing I could think of was that they wanted to get my fingerprints all over the car. This must have been part of their final solution. It was too bizarre for me to comprehend their motivation.

During a couple of sit-in-the-car sessions, Lugo pulled me out and made me hold objects in the front and back of the car. I was posing for pictures! For what purpose, I don't know. I can't even begin to guess. Some items were bottles, others objects were unidentifiable. Why they did this still remains a mystery; their behavior was always strange, but this beat it all. They made me do this several times with no explanation as to what I was holding or why. I didn't bother to ask, because if they told me anything, it would most likely have been a lie. I still wonder what that was all about.

The car was presumably in the bay of the warehouse. It was not much better than the bathroom. The air was stuffy and hot, and by the time they came to get me out, I was usually slumped over the steering wheel, nearly unconscious. With no water, I felt as though I had trekked through the desert.

They took me to a table that week and made me sign some papers. They didn't tell me what they were, nor did I ask. However, there was one time that was different and stood out.

"This document is important. Don't mess it up," Lugo threatened. Without allowing me to say a word, he continued, "This is your death sentence." He laughed crazily. What a great way to get me to cooperate: Sign this and you're dead.

So it appeared we had reached the end of the road, and they no longer hid the fact they were going to kill me. It was not a shock. I was numb and void of emotions.

Lugo grabbed my hand and carefully placed it on the document.

He sternly repeated, "Don't mess it up."

I was thinking, *Game on. Let's play.* I purposefully twisted my hand and signed the document vertically.

Lugo went into a rage and said, "You motherfucker, you messed it up. That is the only one I had! What am I going to do? I should kill you right now."

I was trying to control my laughter. I had to have some fun, too. His tirade lasted for a while. I wished I had the tape off my eyes to see him go berserk.

Lugo was distraught, and I know he would have liked to beat me to a pulp right then and there, but he didn't, and I really had no idea why not. Perhaps it didn't fit into their brilliant plans.

What did he think? That he was going to tell me I was signing my death sentence and I would not offer any resistance? I guess he did. He really thought a lot of himself and that no one would defy him.

I was glad I had messed up his form, and if I could do it again, I would. My signature was degenerating more, and some of them must have looked pretty odd, especially vertical.

They boasted that the house was already transferred to their names, to which I thought, *Good, you fool.*

Lugo told me the forms were to get a loan from my insurance policy, which I knew they could not do. In fact, it was a change of beneficiary form to change the policy beneficiary to one of their accomplices.

At the end of the week, Lugo brought in my mail and asked me questions about it. They not only kidnapped me, tortured and robbed me and extorted all of my assets, but also were now taking my very identity and trying to live my life. I was disgusted with my weakness and the fact that I had let them do it. It was total identity theft, and I felt violated. I was now totally depressed. Even if I did get out alive, everything had changed. My existence was in doubt. I couldn't even be whom I had been before passing through the warehouse doors. They had stolen that from me.

They told me about the calls I had received and the messages on the answering machine. Fortunately, there were not too many calls. My mother had called me a couple of times, and they incorrectly told me it was my mother-in-law. My brother also called a few times, but they never told me he had called. They now knew I had lied to them about not talking to my brother, who really did care about me. My only concern was that he not leave contact information so they could track him down as they had threatened.

During that week, Lugo appeared to be on top of the world. He was singing and humming as he went about his activities. Why not? They had fleeced me of everything I owned, and no one had come to interfere with their plan. No one had posed any obstacle.

It was also during this week that I became convinced they were filming me as I sat in the bathroom. In fact, I was almost sure because of the flickering I perceived through my hood. Why would they do such a thing? Who knows? Nothing they did during that week made sense. Maybe they wanted to have a good movie to watch after they killed me. It would be a testament and lasting memory of their bravado, skill, audacity, and intellectual capacity, which they could play over and over while eating popcorn. I didn't understand but was sure it was not for any good purpose. I wasn't in the hands of choirboys. Maybe they were making a training film for their next audacious crime.

The way they were watching me also changed. Lugo and his sidekick were always there in the morning. It seemed their activity had increased and we were reaching a finale. Apparently, my perceptions were correct. Lugo had lost faith in the night watchmen, or else they had been complaining too much. Mr. FBI and Mr. Friendly no longer arrived together. Mr. FBI arrived early in the evening, and about four or five hours later, Mr. Friendly arrived and Mr. FBI left.

They paid less attention to my fundamental needs, so I was back to using the cups as my bathroom more frequently. They stopped talking to me completely. Mr. Friendly had a weird habit or maybe paranoia. He no longer sat in the room with me every night. Instead, he noisily burst into the room every half hour to hour. Did he think he was going to catch me misbehaving? Maybe he had just gone off the deep end as well. Maybe he was trying to catch me looking under the hood—I guess he forgot that I had ten pounds of tape under that. I was amused and had to laugh to myself every time he did it. At this point, they wouldn't hesitate to kill me, so giving them an excuse would have been simply stupid.

They let me change clothes again that week, but there was no birdbath. I did not get to even brush my teeth.

Lugo said to me, "I went shopping at a fine men's store to get you some clothing." He started to laugh.

"Really?" I replied, knowing full well that he had a sick sense of humor and that the clothes had obviously come from my house.

"Guess where?" he asked, and I could just imagine the huge smile on his face.

"I don't know," I said, playing stupid.

"7641 S.W. 148th Terrace. Have you heard of it?"

That was the address of my house. What a surprise. What a clever guy.

"Yes," I replied, bored with this little idiotic game he was playing. He was just sadistic and wanted me to suffer, typical Lugo.

Lugo asked me the code for the gate again. They had been rummaging, ransacking and God knows what else they were doing at my house, so why would he want to ask for the code again? He told me he was going to have some of my things, including the furniture, shipped to Colombia, so that was why he wanted the gate code. This was ludicrous. Did he really believe I was so gullible that he could pacify me with his idiotic lies? He obviously didn't think much of my intelligence. Perhaps he thought he was a genius. This was one unstable character. His mood swings were scary, to say the least. Sometimes it seemed as though he was trying to be compassionate, and the next minute he acted like the devil's best friend.

Lugo saw I was paying no attention to him and stayed in the room. He started playing the CDs I had in the car. He told me he did not like my taste in music. I never answered him, which probably angered him more, mostly because I could not care less if he approved of my taste in music. Like a child, he was looking for attention. He started throwing the CDs against the wall and yelling "Crap, crap!" Poor Lugo needed attention and was throwing a temper tantrum so that I would respond or show fear. It didn't work, and I continued to ignore him. He didn't get the response he was after and eventually had enough.

Before he left, he solemnly said, "I may be many things and have committed various crimes, but I'm not a murderer."

I remember that comment so well. To me, it meant that the boys had decided to kill me and he did not want that on his conscience. He had a conscience? Regardless, the outburst of anger I felt was related to the fact that they were currently deliberating my final outcome and he did not want blood on his hands. From the comment, it appeared that he had been outvoted.

I got the distinct feeling they were falling apart and becoming more disorganized. There appeared to be dissention among the ranks as to what they were going to do with me. The attitude change by the night watchmen, and now Lugo's little tantrum, indicated that things were coming to a head and there was going to be resolution, good or bad, sooner rather than later. It seemed those who wanted my death were in charge now.

On Thursday, Mr. FBI asked me if I wanted the same breakfast of eggs and sausage I had been given once before. I didn't have to think about it a nanosecond. I had hardly had anything to eat that week, and my mouth watered at the thought of the eggs and coffee. Next morning, they brought me breakfast, or what I thought it was, anyway. Lugo's sidekick stood right on top of me, standing in the box, straddling his legs on both sides of me. He bent down to give me the plate, which I eagerly took. The plate seemed light, but eggs didn't weight that much. I felt all around the plate: no eggs, no sausage, one—yes, one—potato, and half a piece of chewed toast. Apparently, someone had gotten to my breakfast before I did. No coffee, either.

They were laughing uncontrollably, and I sensed that a crowd had gathered to watch the spectacle. I felt like a lab animal that was under observation. I was humiliated and angry. I was angry with myself for being in this situation. I was not happy for my lack of awareness. I didn't say anything to them. There was nothing to say. Besides, that was what they expected me to do. I just chalked it up as another one of their humiliating games they enjoyed so much. It would not be the last, either.

During that third strange week, things continued to unravel. At the end of the week, while I was sitting in what I affectionately called my box, I started to hear loud banging and knew instinctively that it was coming from the bay where my car was kept. It was loud. It sounded as if they were banging away at some heavy metal object. It was loud enough that it drowned out the blaring music from the radio near me. I don't know why, but it occurred to me that it had something to do with my car. The banging lasted about two hours, and it nearly drove me bonkers. When the banging finally stopped, it got even weirder. I heard several gunshots coming from the same direction as the banging. I wondered if they were taking target practice so that when the time came to fire at a live target, me, they would be ready.

This all freaked me out, and I got very jittery. I wondered how these thugs could make such a racket and not raise any suspicion. The warehouse must have been in a pretty secluded area with little or no traffic. For a few moments, it sounded like a gun battle was going on. I thought maybe they were killing each other. Just wishful thinking on my part, but it was a happy thought.

Another curious development that week involved a change in taking me to the bathroom. Normally, whenever they came to take me to the bathroom, the attending thug would tell me to get up or to hold my hand out so they could unlock the handcuffs from the metal railing. But during that entire week, whoever was taking me did not say a word. It was obviously someone whose voice I would have recognized. I knew without a doubt that it was none other than Jorge Delgado.

I seldom recollect what I have dreamed the previous night upon waking up in the morning. There was, however, one dream during that week that seemed so real that I woke up in a state of total confusion. I dreamed that everything that was happening to me had been just that, a dream. In reality, I was home in bed, and everything that had happened was just a nightmare. When I woke up, I was so sure I would be sitting in my own bed, in my own house, and that everything would be normal. What a monumental disappointment. I woke up and went to rub my eyes. I couldn't because of the chains that bound me, and as I opened my eyes, my world was dark. I sat there in shock, refusing to accept that it was just a dream and I was really in the warehouse, chained to a wall.

So another week passed, and I was still in the same situation.

Another weekend went by, and both my resolve and my hope dwindled. It was getting harder and harder to be optimistic and keep my emotions in check. My energy level was getting lower and lower, and it became more difficult to concentrate and to think clearly about possible solutions and analyze what was going on around me.

And yet I was stubbornly unwilling to give up so easily, even though it seemed like a futile uphill battle. I kept reminding myself that I had to dig deep down inside and find those inner resources and willpower that I did had not known even existed or thought I would ever use. At times, I perceived the situation to be so hopeless that I wished they would just kill me and end the torture. But I shook those thoughts away as quickly as they came. I realized that any chance of survival depended on me, and I could not afford to think in those terms. I wondered how people who were held in captivity for years endured. I had only been there three weeks and was going crazy. Perhaps you reach a point of no return, where all hope is lost and you just exist. You stop fighting and become oblivious to your circumstances. I wasn't quite there yet.

From the onset of the ordeal, I had never really contemplated the possibility of being in that same position after three weeks. I really figured that once they got their money and all the other assets taken from my house, they would release me. At most, I thought a week would be the maximum they would hold me. Here I was, about to start my fourth week, and there were no signs that this was coming to an end. There was no mention from the night guards anymore about my imminent release, and I sensed that their plan for my ultimate fate had changed. Perhaps I was being too pessimistic, but I saw their choices as limited.

They could not be comfortable with just releasing me. There was no way to keep me from going straight to the authorities. But killing me also escalated their crime, though perhaps that did not matter to them. I believed there was considerable dissention among their ranks, and some wanted to kill me while others wanted no part of it. So I waited to see which faction would win.

And that weekend, I called my wife. It was a short call, and they just wanted me to tell her everything was going well and I was close to wrapping things up. They wanted me to tell her I was out of town. Maybe that was to prevent her from calling the house. This time, the story they had concocted was again less than plausible. Supposedly I was in Dallas, negotiating the sale of the deli. They probably wanted to ascertain her mental state in case she was taking any steps to find me. She would be forthcoming over the phone, and they could know what preemptive steps to take. There was none of that, so they could proceed with whatever plans they had. I was getting tired of these games of make believe, and each call was more difficult than the last.

Monday morning rolled in as I realized it was nearly a full month since this crazy nightmare had begun. Lugo and his sidekick entered the room, for some reason making as much noise as they possibly could.

"How much is the deli worth?" Lugo asked.

I was flabbergasted again at their greed and stupidity. I didn't know which was worse. This meant that I should get comfortable, because the sale of the deli was going to take a while, and I was not going anywhere.

"It all depends," I answered. I was being both evasive and truthful.

"If you wanted to sell it quickly," he prompted. He thought the sale was an easy task. In reality, it took time.

"I guess about a hundred and fifty," I replied.

"Who do you call when you want to sell it?" I could tell he smelled more money.

"Bob Cole. He is the area developer for Schlotzsky's in Miami," I said. I didn't care anymore.

"How long would it take to sell it?" He wanted instant gratification.

"Probably a while. First you have to find a buyer. Then you have to get approval from Schlotzsky's," I told him, sensing he didn't like my answer.

"But how long will that take?" He wanted it so badly.

"Probably a couple of months for the complete process," I replied. Lugo didn't believe me, and it did not deter him.

"I'm going to call this Cole guy and tell him I'm your cousin, Jim Schiller, and see if he can sell the deli fast," he said with arrogance. *Good luck*, I thought, but I did have to admit he was being creative.

"I don't think it can be done that fast," I told him, trying to burst his bubble.

"Well, I hope for your sake it can. We want the money from the deli, and if it takes a while, you are going be our guest for that whole time," he said, laughing.

This was devastating. I was looking at months of captivity; was I going to physically be able to last that long? I really despised being called a guest. I was not at liberty to decide if I wanted to be there or not.

His sidekick gave me a cigarette as a reward, and he and Lugo left the room. I sat there, pondering in disbelief their audacity and their insatiable greed. This meant that my captivity was just beginning and I had a long road ahead. I didn't know if I could deal with that at this juncture. Another two or three months seemed unfathomable. Then there was the physical part; food was scarce, and I had lost a considerable amount of weight. Uncertainty surrounded me, and there was nowhere to reach for some comfort. Again, I was frustrated by the fact that I could not do anything about it. What if I started being problematic for them? Would they kill me? Then again, they might do it anyway after they completely raped me financially. I tossed these thoughts over and over in my mind. What to do now was the main focus of my thoughts. There was no apparent winning strategy. I just had to minimize the suffering.

I was so bored, and I was forced to hear the same songs over and over again to the point of madness. The worst song was by Seal, "A Prayer for the Dying." It was very apropos, and I thought it was dedicated to me. Madonna's "Say Goodnight" was also in that category, and I changed Sheryl Crow's song's name from "All I Want To Do Is Have Some Fun" to "All I Want To Do Is Go Home." It's amazing what staring into empty space twenty-four hours a day will do to your mind. When Lugo was in the warehouse, he often put on some really strange music. I guess it fit his personality perfectly.

He seemed to enjoy it, and I wanted to barf.

Chapter 18 — The Greed Goes On

"GREED IS A FAT DEMON WITH A SMALL MOUTH, AND
WHATEVER YOU FEED IT IS NEVER ENOUGH."
- JAN WILLEM VAN DE WETERRING -

Monday evening arrived. The beehive had been stirred. There was an unusual amount of activity and quite a few people present. The night guards were there, and Lugo and his sidekick and some other fellow thugs were also present. I was given a hamburger for dinner. Food was so scarce that I was glad to receive it. They gave me a cigarette, and then all hell broke loose. Lugo came running in, a rabid dog with his crazy sidekick.

He yelled, "Get up, you piece of shit!"

I really thought the Grim Reaper was paying me a visit and Lugo had every intention of ending it right there and then.

"You lied to us," he snarled.

Maybe I did, maybe I didn't. Who cared?

Mr. Sidekick, or, as I fondly called him, Mr. Torture, stuck the barrel of the gun deep into my mouth. I tasted the silvery metal. I thought he was going to perform a tonsillectomy because he had the barrel so deep down my throat. It was revolting, to say the least, and I could not breathe. Well, it didn't seem like I had to worry about being in the warehouse much longer.

"What?" I mumbled. Saying anything was difficult.

"You have a house in North Miami Beach and never told us about it. I found it while going through your files," he said with bravado.

Now, if he had half a brain and could read, this could all have been avoided, but he didn't.

"That house was sold three years ago," I mumbled. It was the truth, and dimwit here could have verified it.

"Bullshit!" he yelled.

What could I say? *You should do have done your homework first? But then again, I'm willing to bet you weren't a good student.* It was amazing the madness and greed he exhibited.

Since the sidekick, Mr. Torture, was getting another opportunity to make me miserable, he took advantage of the opportunity. I could tell he really enjoyed it and lived for this. He shoved the gun further into my mouth to the point where my lips felt as if they were going to rip. Just to make me sweat and get a little kick, he cocked the hammer and laughed demonically.

"I'm going to find out, and if you're lying, you're dead!" he yelled. The threat had no affect on me by now. It served no purpose to threaten me anymore, and I shrugged it off.

But Mr. Torture was in a sadistic frenzy, and he was having too much fun to stop. He pulled the trigger of the gun, and I heard the click. He let out another of his evil laughs. He pulled the trigger again, another click. No bullet to the brain, just another sick laugh. He wasn't getting the response he wanted from me, so he stopped and pulled the gun out of my mouth. I think he was disappointed that I hadn't soiled my pants or tried to plead for mercy. I was rattled but refused to show it. That would only encourage them. The night watchman, Mr. Friendly, came in a little later and asked me if I was all right. I told him I was peachy and asked for a cigarette.

It had seemed these overt torture sessions were over. Once again, I was wrong. Greed blinded them and drove them into a state of fury, making them capable of anything. I refused to let them think they had crushed me, not after all this time.

Later that evening, Mr. Friendly came in and sat next to me. He was trying to act like some long-lost friend who was concerned for my wellbeing. I knew they had just had sent him to see if he could milk me for information. I knew the game well by now and welcomed the chance to play with him.

"Why didn't you tell them about the house?" he asked, trying to sound genuinely concerned.

"I sold it three years ago. Why would tell them about it?" I said, thinking, *Please ask me another stupid question.*

"I hope you're telling the truth," he said with concern. What if I wasn't? Were they going to kill me? What a joke. My fate was sealed anyway, it seemed.

"Absolutely," I said giddily, toying with him while I considered what an asshole he was. Though I was blindfolded, he had become transparent to me.

"I hope so. They were pretty pissed," he said. It seemed he did not like the way I responded.

"They can check it out. I told them the truth." He could tell it was irritating me. "The only thing I'm concerned about is when you plan on letting me go," I said. I thought I'd throw that out just to hear another lie.

"Soon," he said, trying to avoid the subject.

I pressed on. "They want the deli. That's going to take a long while," I said, trying to elicit a response.

"I think they got a buyer for it already," he said, almost mumbling.

Yeah, right. In less than twenty-four hours, they had found a buyer. I believed that, just like I believed that the moon was made of cheese.

"I hope so," I said, wanting to laugh, but instead I decided to continue to play games with this nitwit.

"How are you going to explain to your wife that you lost everything?" he said, changing the subject. This was his favorite question.

"I'll find something to tell her." I thought this guy must have been very low on the IQ scale. If I ever got out alive, I would tell her the truth. Why would I make up some wild story? This was certainly wild enough! I guess they managed their relationships differently. Why even try to understand where he was coming from?

"Just relax and get some rest. You want a cigarette?" he said, probably frustrated that he could not get any concrete information from me.

"Sure, thanks," I replied. He gave me the cigarette and left me alone. I just wanted to laugh. They thought I was not aware of their game. Using this low-intelligence messenger was so obvious.

Sleep was scarce and elusive, so I just lay there. If it came, that was fine. But by now it was harder to reconcile my days. Without a sleep period, the days all bled into one. The only escape I had found, sleep, was being taken from me. I just stared into the darkness, my mind blank, hoping that one way or another it would all end soon.

Tuesday morning arrived, and I was still sitting in the same cardboard box I had been in since day one, when this whole fiasco started. Lugo and his sidekick came in, bringing me an apple and coffee for breakfast. Lugo informed me that I would be leaving soon and he was making final preparations. Whether that meant I would be checking out permanently from this world or just the warehouse, I could not tell from his tone. His sidekick, Mr. Torture, had a weakness after all. I heard him argue with Lugo about it. He would not come near me because he said I smelled so bad. Well, one bath in dirty water in three weeks will do that to anyone. My hair could have caused an oil slick. It was plastered to my head. My body was also secreting an oily substance, and no one had to tell me I smelled ripe, even though I could not smell it myself. A hobo would probably look great next to me. In my misery I was happy that my state revolted them and that even if it was a little misery I could dish out, it was better than nothing.

That evening, Lugo and his sidekick brought me a present. They made me sit in the same place where I normally made the phone calls, although there were no phone calls to be made. In fact, those had disappeared almost completely. They brought me back to the cardboard box and made me lie down. They had placed a thin mattress on top of the concrete floor I had been lying on. They said that I would be more comfortable that way. They gave me an entire pack of cigarettes and a Zippo lighter. Sidekick was afraid I would burn my face or the warehouse trying to light a cigarette totally blind. I'm sure that if I burned my face, they would be very concerned and distraught. I did come close a couple of times. Lugo didn't seem too concerned about the possibility of me burning myself. In fact, he would probably have been pleased to witness it. It appeared that there was a rift forming between Lugo and his sidekick. They argued all the time now and didn't care if it was in front of me.

Maybe it was just me, but I thought these pleasantries had ominous connotations. Why would they make me comfortable after three weeks? The only reason I could think of was that they had arrived at the decision to kill me, and this was a way to make themselves feel better before they did it. What else could it have been? The other possibility was that they were nuts enough to intend on selling the deli and were trying to make the situation better so that if I had to be there several months, I would survive. I didn't believe that, because they were fighting among themselves and none of them appeared to want to be there any longer. I didn't jump for joy because I knew this was for them and not for my wellbeing.

Lugo warned me not to burn any holes in the mattress or there would be consequences. I found it funny that he was so petty and concerned about a cheap, disposable mattress. Unfortunately for them, being blind didn't help, and the first thing I did was burn a hole in the mattress. I tried to sit on top of the hole so madman Lugo wouldn't see it. But thinking about it, what did I care if he did? I was amazed that he considered this mattress a treasure after the booty they had gotten from me. Who could have figured them out, and who would have wanted to?

During those interminable days of captivity, one thing I learned to appreciate was the gift of my eyesight. Being a blind person those many weeks made me realize how fortunate I was in many respects. It was amazing that over time, mental images began to fade and I could no longer see them in my mind's eye. I learned to admire those who go blind through life and not only manage to survive but excel in some field. On one occasion, I joked with Mr. Friendly that if I ever saw a blind person needing help to cross a street, I would be the first one there to help. I wondered if I would I ever get that opportunity.

That same evening, Lugo came to talk to me. I was prepared to hear a doozy of a story from an individual who made lying his profession.

"We are making arrangements with the customs people for you to go to Colombia," he said. It sounded like I was going to be sent in a casket.

"I don't understand," I replied, which I didn't.

"You have to be taken out of the country without anybody knowing," he said confidently. *Okay, this guy has lost it.* That would be an impossible task.

"Why can't you just drop me off at the airport and watch me leave?" I asked, knowing it was a stupid question. I imagined taking that airplane with my appearance and odor of a skunk. I'm sure no one would have noticed, right?

"And walk you through the airport in handcuffs? What if you run into a business client or associate?" he said smartly. The real concern was if we were to run into the police. Lugo must have thought that my IQ was as low as his or that I was supremely gullible. I was going to play him.

[Note to the reader: This all occurred several years before 9/11 and the TSA crackdowns in airports.]

"I couldn't care less," I replied, trying to see what his response was.

"No, it wouldn't look good, and besides, you're going to see us," he continued. "You're going to have to get skunk drunk, and we are going to arrange it for somebody in customs put you on the plane." The part about not seeing them was believable. The rest of the story was ludicrous. Internally, I laughed. They had made their plans that were clear. But what he was telling me was a fairytale they had concocted, just a fairytale.

"I don't drink. I haven't in years," I replied. That was true. Maybe being drunk wouldn't be so bad, after all. At least I would be oblivious to my surroundings.

"Then we have a problem. We are going to have to find another way," he said.

"Fine, I'll drink," I responded, preferring alcohol to gambling with these thugs. Whatever, other drug they chose would likely be more dangerous. What I did wonder where all this was leading and what the real plan was. It couldn't be good for me, I was certain.

"Then we'll start giving you some this week so you don't puke all over yourself when the time comes," he said. I thought the vomit would add to the wonderful aroma I was already radiating. *Wonderful, I have something to look forward to.*

I did not say anything else, and neither did he. He left satisfied with his deception. Things were coming to a head, and this was all going to finish soon, good or bad. At least I would be drunk when the time came, and perhaps that would mitigate the pain or make me oblivious to it.

I felt I had to prepare myself to accept the reality that my days were numbered. But, nonetheless, I was going to go out with my spirits and head held high. Thinking of escape anymore seemed futile. My weakened state, combined with the fact that I was tethered with a thick chain to the wall, along with my lack of knowledge of my surroundings and the number of captors at any given time, made it hopeless to consider. If I did find some way to get out of the chains and tried to escape, they were probably waiting to shoot me. So what good would it have done me? There was the slimmest of possibilities that they might let me go after they got everything they wanted. It was by that slim thread of hope that I hung on. While I sat there, pondering my few options and grim future, Mr. Friendly came in and sat next to me and began to talk.

He said, "I hear you're going home soon."

Ah yes, the pine box. "We've both heard that one before," I replied. I kind of felt sorry for him, since his fellow thugs were probably misleading him. He was not the sharpest knife in the drawer, and he didn't realize he was being used.

"No, I think this time is for sure, just a few more days," he said eagerly.

"They are going to put me on a plane looking like this?" I replied with the intention of shaking some sense into his dim brain.

"No, they are going to rent a hotel room where you can shower and shave. They just need to find a secure one, that's all," he said convincingly. This story was getting better as it went along. The problem was that it made no sense and was contradictory. Was I going to get skunk drunk before or after the shower? Certainly this would occur sometime prior to handing me over to the paid-off customs official?

"Really? Sounds good," I said with a smile. I did this so he would go back to his friends and tell them I had bought the story hook, line, and sinker. Of course, I didn't believe a word of the story he had been sent to tell me.

"We need to wrap this up soon. We have another job in January, and I want to take a vacation in between," he said without any remorse in his voice. Another job? Were these guys serious? It sounded as though they were going to continue their criminal endeavors after they disposed of me. I guess this guy needed a vacation. Kidnapping and torture for a month can be very taxing on the system. This was ludicrous!

"So I will be out before Christmas," I said, trying to sense how much time I had left, not that I would get a worthwhile answer from him.

"Nobody wants to be here for Christmas," he continued. "By the way, I volunteered to take you to the airport." They wanted to be with their families and go to church so they could say thanks for all the pain and torture they inflicted, for the amount they stole, and for not getting caught. Sure, that made sense. Maybe by then they could also add to the list the thanks for being able to commit murder without remorse. Oh, yes, I found this very admirable.

"Hey, that would be great," I said as cheerily as I could. I was playing with him, and he didn't have the slightest inkling.

"I don't care if you see me or not. What are you going to do to me anyway?" he said.

Well, as I suspected, this guy was brain dead. I was not going to do anything. The authorities, on the other hand, were going to put him in jail.

"Nothing, I'm harmless. All I want to do is leave the country and be with my family," I said, trying to make this dope believe me. Everybody was lying to him, and he had no clue.

"Soon, I'll talk to the boss about taking you to the airport," he said proudly.

Sure, madman Lugo is going to go along with your plan. I decided that since I had nothing to lose, I'd throw something at him. I said, "How do you know that they're not planning to kill me?"

"I won't let that happen. If I know that they are planning something like that, then I'll help you escape," he continued. "I'll tell them you overpowered me and got away."

Maybe he was sincere in what he was saying, or maybe not. But it would be just my luck to have him of all people wanting to help me. I didn't believe he could pull it off even if he wanted to.

The obvious question was "What if you don't know?"

"Look, as long as I show up every night, you have nothing to worry about. If I don't show up, then you might have a problem."

That was exactly what happened; Mr. Friendly pulled a disappearing act. Perhaps he had shared one of his pearls of wisdom with Lugo and they decided he was a liability. Nevertheless, dumb as he was, he had been my only ray of hope and comfort. As ridiculous as the story was, I needed to pretend it was true.

"Okay, I hope you will be here every night," I said, knowing it may have been futile.

"Don't worry. I'm not going to let anything happen to you. I think you're a nice guy," he reassured me. I reached the bottom of the totem pole, a career criminal telling me I was a nice guy. Was that supposed to make me feel better?

"Just relax and get some rest," he said. I felt that his words were just that, words aimed to prevent me from causing any problems. I knew he wasn't in any position to help me, and I didn't really believe he wanted to.

"Sure," I replied as I sat back in my cardboard box.

He left, and I just sat there staring into the vast nothingness. I couldn't sleep. Sleep had become more and more of a challenge. There was no tossing and turning since the chains limited my mobility. So I just sat there and stared into the darkness. I had become melancholy and knew I had a limited time in which to accept my ultimate death and to make peace with myself. Perhaps it was these troubling thoughts, along with the inactivity, that was not allowing me to escape to the dream world.

Tuesday night turned into Wednesday morning, and Lugo and his sidekick returned. They brought me an apple and coffee for breakfast. Bizarre behavior from them was normal. They stood directly over me, one leg on each side of me, and dropped the apple. Then Lugo stood there for a few minutes without saying a word. What they were looking for or expected. I could not fathom. I felt like a laboratory rat again, the subject of some weird experiment beyond my comprehension. I think Freud himself would have been perplexed by their behavior. They left me to eat my hardy breakfast and returned when I was done.

Lugo was at his best—he snarled at me. "You have a big mouth," he said. At first, I didn't understand. Then it registered: Mr. Friendly had obviously told him about our conversation. That meant that Mr. Friendly had indeed been playing me all along as I suspected. That he would not allow his fellow thugs to kill me was a big joke. Either that or Mr. Friendly was so stupid he just blurted things out without thinking. Either one was possible. Regardless, it meant the small thread of hope had been cut and there truly was no one to save me. I must have been crazy, allowing myself to believe that the friendly thug was going to help me.

"Excuse me?" I replied, knowing full well what he was referring to.

"You keep your mouth shut or you are going to be in big trouble!" he yelled. Like I wasn't in big trouble already? What a joke. This guy had to be kidding.

"Fine," I said curtly. Arguing with this lunatic only meant physical punishment for me, and I wanted to avoid that. They welcomed the opportunity and enjoyed it too much.

"What are the keys in your keychain for?"

"The house and the deli," I said, bored.

"You don't have a safety deposit box?" he said. Unbelievable, these criminals' insatiable greed was demonic. They were still looking for more.

"No," I said in disbelief.

"We want to go to the deli. What is the alarm code?"

"Three-two-nine-nine," I said. *Have fun. I'm sure the employees cleaned it out already.*

"Which door has the keypad?" he demanded.

"The back."

"If the alarm goes off, what is the identification code?" he asked. Just for a moment, a brief image of the alarm going off and the police showing up with these clowns trying to explain why they were there crossed my mind. I could wish for that, even though it was unlikely.

"Seven-two-nine-six," I said, returning to reality.

"What is the combination of the safe?" he wanted to know.

"I can't remember. I think I wrote it in the notepad that was in my briefcase," I said, knowing that they were not going to believe me even though it was the truth.

"You can't remember or don't want to?" he said, trying to be intimidating and using a threatening voice.

"I always had a problem remembering that combination," I said. That's why I had written it down. Of course, I knew they didn't believe me.

He told his sidekick to go look in my briefcase and find the code. When he returned, he said, "It's not there."

"Then we have to call Freddy, the manager, to get it," I told them.

So they brought me over to the chair and had me call Freddy. The call was brief. Fortunately, Freddy did not ask me any questions and just gave me the code.

Lugo said, "How much money do you keep in the safe?"

"Four hundred, but I don't think there's that much, since they used it for payroll," I said. If they were looking for a lot of money, they were going to be disappointed.

"In the cash registers?" he asked.

"One hundred," I responded. I was sure it was all gone by now. I wanted to tell them that since they were greedy and hungry, why not cart off the spoiled meats in the refrigerator, as well?

"We are not after the money. We just want to see if you have any compromising papers in your safe," he said. Right, he probably thought I had hundreds of thousands of dollars in the safe. This was another Lugo fairytale that only he believed.

"There is nothing in there except the change box," I told him.

"We'll see," he said smartly.

"Fine," I replied. They were going to do whatever they wanted anyway, and so be it.

They left, and I would have laughed if it weren't for my deplorable situation. These guys were taking a huge risk for a small payoff. Going to the deli in broad daylight to look for more money was insane. With their limitless greed and low intelligence, they were unable to measure the risk. Even in movies and books, criminals never went this far, exposing themselves so carelessly. I didn't care that they were going to the deli; in fact, I thought it was stupid. They were not going to find anything there. I was sure that the employees had carted off anything of value, including the food.

They came to get me, and I was taken to my car and

handcuffed to the steering wheel. I spent most of the day there, as I had the previous days. No water, no food, and the only thing I had were the unbearable hot and muggy air that surrounded me. I was nearly unconscious by the time they came and got me in the evening.

Lugo came back and threw me an eggroll while I was still in the car. I could not pass it down, even though I had hardly eaten the last few days. He grabbed me by the arm, and I thought I was going to the cardboard box, but they took me to the bathroom instead.

While I sat there, he laughed. "The deli is a mess. What kind of employees do you have?"

I was sure that the deli had not been perfect when the last of the employees left, but I was sure these guys trashing the place in frustration when they had found nothing of value was what had caused the mess.

"Not very good ones," I replied, knowing it was what he wanted to hear.

"Who is your attorney?" he demanded.

"Gene Rosen has handled the few things I have had," I replied, not knowing where this was going.

"You're going to call him and tell him Jorge Delgado is to have power of attorney for the sale of the deli," he said.

That hit me like a pail of cold water. I just received my death sentence. There was no way they would reveal their identities unless they were going to kill me. I wanted to cry but did not even have the strength for that. Although I was in shock, I had known in the back of my mind that this was coming. Nevertheless, confronting it was another matter altogether. I wondered how much time I had left. A day,   a   week,   a   month,   did   it   matter? My hopes of ever seeing my family again had vanished. It was not to be. It was over. I had to accept the stark reality, no matter how difficult it was.

I could not respond and finally mumbled, "Fine."

"I talked to Jim Cole and told him I was your cousin, Jim Schiller, and was helping you with the sale of the deli if your attorney should ask," he said proudly.

"Okay" was all I could say. He continued speaking, but my mind was wandering, and nothing else he said was registering.

Finally, I heard him say, "You'll call your attorney tomorrow."

"Fine," I said, and for some unknown reason, I blurted, "How is Jorge?"

"He's fine. He's broke. He just had a little girl, and he is doing this job so he could make some money," he replied. He just had a baby and got involved in this mess. What in the world was Delgado thinking? This was unimaginable. How could his wife have let him get involved? I didn't understand.

"He always did like to spend everything he had," I said. Nothing mattered at this point.

"Look who's talking," Lugo said, defending his fellow thug and partner in crime.

"Yeah, well, I never had anything against Jorge. He's a good guy," I said, almost sensing that he was in the room with Lugo and perhaps my words would stir him and make him intercede on my behalf. I was wrong, very wrong.

"Yeah, yeah," Lugo said, not wanting to hear me because, in

order to manipulate Delgado, he had painted a very different picture.

Delgado's treason to both his family and me was unimaginable, unforgivable, and mind-boggling. But you had to understand Lugo's ability to manipulate. He was sending Delgado to see my attorney. If anything went wrong, Delgado would be the one identified and left holding the bag. Lugo was using him, and Delgado didn't even realize it. All Lugo cared about was saving his own skin and getting his loot.

That night, Mr. FBI came in as my night watchman/ babysitter. He promptly informed me that there was no food. He gave me a bottle of Gatorade and told me they were concerned that I was dehydrating. Who cared? They were going to kill me soon. Well, it was a nice bottle to use to urinate in, anyway. I reasoned that since my death sentence was handed down, food would be non-existent from now until that moment arrived.

In an unusual appearance, Lugo and his sidekick, Mr. Torture, returned that evening. They unchained me and took me to the desk to sign more papers. They sat me on a chair and told me there was a desk in front of me. I guess they were getting concerned with my deteriorating condition. They wanted my signature as good as possible and didn't want to risk the added difficulty I had when I was forced to sign while in the cardboard box. Either that or these documents were more important than some of the others I had signed most recently. Why I even signed them, I don't know. What was the point if they were going to kill me anyway? I refused to give up hope and perhaps foolishly thought that if I appeased them, my death sentence could be commuted.

While I sat there, Lugo commented, "If you ever franchise a service for signing documents blindfolded, remember who taught you the method."

That was something I would never forget. "Right, you get royalties, correct?" I said sarcastically.

"Of course, you got it!" Lugo said, and he laughed.

He was in a great mood, but his mood swung violently, and I could never tell what was coming next. Sidekick, Mr. Torture, hardly ever spoke. Maybe his IQ didn't permit him to say anything intelligible. Lugo seemed to get off on seeing me in the condition I was in, and the more miserable I was, the better he felt. He wanted me to call my wife to tell her I was in Dallas, finishing the sale of the deli, and everything was going well and as planned. I was also to tell her I'd be joining her and the children soon. I wondered if it would be the last call to her I was to make and whether, unknowingly, it was to be my final farewell.

I hung up the phone and waited to be taken to my box. Instead, Lugo said I needed some exercise. He wanted me to jog in place, so I did. He acted as if he was a drill instructor and barked orders: "Faster" and "Get your legs up." It wasn't easy, since I had to hold my pants to keep them from falling. I had lost a lot of weight. It was humiliating, but they needed some cheap entertainment, and I was it. They were laughing uncontrollably at seeing the blind man holding his pants up, trying to run in place. I admit I must have been a sight for sore eyes. After ten minutes, they had enough fun with me and took me to my cardboard box. One may wonder why I did as they told me and let myself be humiliated in such a manner. If I hadn't complied, they would have either beat me or burned me, and I think that was what they were hoping for. So instead of getting a beating, I allowed myself to be humiliated. It may have been difficult to recuperate from more physical torture given my condition at that time. Either way, it was irrelevant, and I was just looking to survive another hour.

So, back in my box, I sat and marveled at the fact that I had not gotten sick during my captivity. I had often been overheated and wet with sweat, followed by shivering from cold air conditioning, filthy and unsanitary. My place of confinement was equivalent to a pigpen. My nutrition ranged from inadequate to nonexistent. It appeared that my body had called on its extra defense system that prevented further misery. I was fortunate that my immune system was up to the task. Having to contend even with a cold would have inflicted further misery. The only real physical pain that I had to contend with constantly was my nose, ears, and eyes.

The tape had eaten away the skin on both my nose and ears, and they were constantly bleeding, but the pain on my nose was far worse. At one point, I had managed to get the tape over my ears to alleviate some of the discomfort. One of the night watchmen, Mr. Friendly, noticed but did not give me a hard time about it. I could not do that with the tape over my nose, so I had to grin and bear it. It was getting progressively worse and at times it drove me to the point of madness.

Yes, my mental state was another matter. It progressively deteriorated, as I had thought it would. I was riding an emotional rollercoaster that seem to be headed one direction now: down. I kept trying to keep my spirits up with a positive mental attitude, but after realizing that I had finally been given my death sentence, it was far more difficult. I kept lying to myself that I was going to leave that warehouse alive and pick up the pieces of my shattered life. That was also getting more difficult to do. You can only lie to yourself so long. By the end of the fourth week, I no longer believed myself.

I lay there in my total darkness and solitude. The night watchman no longer burst into the room to see if I was peeking or perhaps up to something else. He no longer offered me a soda during the evening, and now I had my own cigarettes, so he didn't have to bother with that, either. The bathroom necessities were resolved by the glasses and bottles I had collected. Once or twice during the evening, he would come in to make sure I had not escaped while he was busy watching television. He most probably slept in the evening while I was not fortunate enough to do so. At that point, I wished I had practiced magic during some point in my life. If I could find a way to free myself from the chains, it might have presented the best opportunity to escape. Mr. FBI had told me he wanted this to be over so he could get on with other things in his life, most likely criminal things. He referred to himself as nothing more than an expensive babysitter, which made me wonder how much they were paying him for his services. So I knew that whatever was going to occur, it would be soon. Fatigue was starting to set in for them, if only they could imagine how I felt.

Wednesday evening bled into Thursday morning. Lugo's pal, Mr. Torture, came in and gave me breakfast: an apple. There was no coffee this morning, and he said nothing when he dropped it on me. I ate the apple even though it was half rotten. Shortly after, I was taken to the bathroom. They still did not trust my inability to see and purposefully bounced me off the walls to make sure that it was so, or maybe just for fun. It was Mr. Torture taking me to the bathroom, and he was a pure sadist at heart and enjoyed inflicting pain, so the wall bouncing was to be expected from him.

Once I was in the bathroom, I waited for a few moments for Mr. Torture to leave. I slid over to the toilet to defecate. I was startled when Mr. Torture said, "So you had to take a shit, huh?" and started to laugh. He was weird beyond comprehension, and I knew he often watched me without saying a word.

Once again humiliated, I murmured, "Yes." I had lost all dignity by now, but this took the cake.

"Would you like some toilet paper?" he said, laughing.

"Sure," I replied. He threw it at me, and I was lucky to catch it on the bounce.

"How come you were walking so funny when I took you here?" he quizzed me. I had no idea what he was talking about.

"I don't know. I didn't realize it," I said. I was truly perplexed at whatever he meant or was referring to.

With that, I heard him leave the bathroom. At least I thought he did. All I could think of was that this was one weird guy and a dangerous one at that.

I sat there all morning, and in the early afternoon, Lugo and his sidekick took me to the car, where I stayed chained for the rest of the day. They came back later and gave me dinner: a bottle of Gatorade.

I decided that my time was short, so I seriously needed to make peace with myself. I did not know how much time I had left. I needed to retrace the steps and things I had done in my life, the good and bad, the people I may have helped and those that I may have inadvertently hurt. I wanted to be at peace with myself and pray for strength when the time came. The end could have come that day or in a few. But I knew time was getting shorter, and I wanted to be in the right mental state, if possible, when it arrived.

At times during my captivity, I felt a deep anger. You are not supposed to treat animals the way I had been treated. I had been put through all that humiliation just so they could steal my assets, but I feel that it may have been more than that. They were trying to steal who or what I represented by moving into my house and posing as me. I knew that in certain ways it had been my fault, for I had permitted them to do so, perhaps because I believed all those assets could be replaced, but lives could not. I naively believed that if I gave them what they wanted, they would let me go and let me be. But there was no end to their greed and thirst, and in some ways I felt that they would not be satisfied until they had taken both everything I owned and my life as well. To them it was the only appropriate finale to this whole affair, and everything pointed in that direction. I could choose to be blind to that because I did not want to see it. Or I could face it.

As difficult as it was, I needed to put all of that behind me and convince myself that whatever action I had taken was that which I thought was best. My anger was not going to resolve the dire circumstances and could perhaps prevent me from seeing more clearly. Besides, there was nothing that I could do. As hard as it was,

I needed to forgive myself for my errors and forgive those who had harmed me. It may seem ludicrous, but my prayers were more for them than for me. They desperately needed help, and I prayed that they would receive it or at least come to their senses and realize what atrocities they had committed upon another human being. I just wanted to go in peace, holding my head up high. Ultimately, I did not lose faith, nor did I let them take away my dignity, no matter how much humiliation they put me through. My spirits soared high knowing that I had done the best I could. At least I could find comfort in knowing that my family was safe and out of harm's way. I didn't want to be pessimistic, but I also had to be realistic if I was to confront what lay ahead.

That afternoon, Lugo and his sidekick came to get me and told me that I was to call my attorney, Gene Rose. They took me to the table and went through the usual procedure of hooking up the phone and dialing the number. I had to tell him that Delgado was going to his office for a power of attorney. Gene was friendly as usual. Before I could tell him the purpose of my call, he informed me that Delgado had just been there for the document. I was amazed at how brazen they were. They were not concerned about leaving a possible trail that might come back to haunt them. I quickly told him to go ahead with the document and handed the phone to them so they could hang it up.

I was perplexed. They either had a buyer for the deli already, or this was going to last a lot longer than I had thought. With Christmas right around the corner, I did not relish the thought of having to spend the holidays chained to the wall. But this made no sense, and what I perceived was that the end of this ordeal was much closer, and by Christmas I would not be there.

Back to the cardboard box I went instead of the bathroom, which puzzled me. They had me call my attorney to inform him that Delgado was going to see him, and by the time I called, he had already been there and gone. These were bumbling fools and had only been so successful in this crime because I had let them. Was it possible that they did not know he was already there when I called? I was still amazed that they were proceeding with the sale of the deli even though it might require substantial time. I guess no one was pressuring them, so they could take all the time they needed. Things had changed in the warehouse. It was full of thugs, and Lugo was there almost all the time. This told me that time was short, no matter what the sale of the deli indicated.

Lugo tried throwing me a curve and told me another lie. This seemed consistent with his psychotic personality. Either he thought I was completely stupid or that he was so brilliant no one could see through his poorly constructed lies. He definitely was an egomaniac and was so high on himself that he couldn't conceive of failure. Surely no one could possibly see through his lies. This time he told me he had "hired" Delgado for the power of attorney because people knew he used to be my friend. The problem was that Gene Rosen had never met Delgado and didn't know that Delgado had been my friend or business associate. The first time he met him was that day he went to his office. It appeared that Lugo was trying to cover up the screw-up he had made in blurting Delgado's name out. I'm sure Delgado had been there that day and had gotten angry with Lugo. This was

Lugo's way of appeasing him. I was insulted that they thought I was so stupid, but maybe that was an advantage.

I sat there that Thursday afternoon. The inactivity and lack of mental stimulation was torture in itself. I was an avid reader and normally devoured books and magazines. I not only lacked nutrition for my body but also for my brain. I was tired of thinking about the same things and frustrated at finding no solution that seemed feasible. I did not want to indulge in self-pity, which could only have been detrimental.

I lay down for a while, and Lugo and his sidekick came in and barked an order for me to sit up. Lugo wanted me to start drinking alcohol that afternoon so that when the time came for my release, I wouldn't puke all over myself. This was another of Lugo's bizarre ideas, and I kept wondering what his real intentions were. Did it matter? They gave me a drink and instructed me to drink it all in one shot. I managed to drink some of it—the rest of it spilled all over me. It burned as it went down, and I recognized the taste; it was tequila. I had not touched tequila since my college days. He handed me another, and I followed the same procedure. Lugo told me that he would be back later to give me some more. They left. The alcohol had an immediate effect, as I had consumed it on an empty stomach. I had to lie down since I was dizzy and lightheaded. In a way, the alcohol was a blessing in disguise. I could escape from my thoughts and the current reality, even if it was only for a short while.

They came in occasionally to check on me and see if I was acting like a lunatic. Fortunately, I had always handled my liquor well, and I didn't even get the motor mouth affect. I just lay there and stared into the darkness, as usual. Once again, I felt like a laboratory rat that was being measured as different dosages were given. I inferred that the liquor was not having the effect they desired. The liquor did have one positive side effect. It made me drowsy, and I was able to get a couple of hours of sleep after so many sleepless nights.

When I awoke from my short nap, Lugo and his sidekick came back and gave me a couple more drinks. They did not go down as harshly as the first, nor did they have a similar affect. Lugo told me that the next day, we would have a couple of drinks together. *Wow, something to look forward to.* I was fortunate to have a criminal and torturer as my drinking buddy. Maybe we could swap sad stories about our lives, maybe shed a tear or two and comfort each other. What a joke. I didn't say anything and just hoped he would go away.

That evening, Mr. FBI came to babysit. Mr. Friendly had pulled his disappearing act by that point. To my astonishment, Mr. FBI brought me a burger, fries, and a soda. I was famished and ate it as though I was eating some exotic French delicacy. The last few days' food had been nonexistent, unless you call Gatorade a meal.

In contemplating these latest events, I concluded that things had really gotten out of hand. They had to do something in the not-too-distant future. My physical condition had deteriorated drastically after nearly a full month of poor nutrition and inactivity. I was weak, and my legs were rubbery whenever they stood me up. I had lost a tremendous amount of weight, especially in the previous week. When they took me to the bathroom or elsewhere, I stumbled slowly, and I had to exert far more effort than normal to walk those few steps. My concentration span was shorter, and I didn't feel like talking anymore. I was just hanging on, hoping for resolution, whichever way that was to be, and hopefully soon.

It's funny how things sometimes appear to be bad when they happen but then turn out to be for the best, and the passage of time reveals exactly that. My brother was originally going to be my partner in the deli. Had he had been working with me at the deli that day. They would have kidnapped us both. Had that happened, we'd both have been long dead by now. My brother's personality was more confrontational, and he would without a doubt have refused all their orders and told them to go to hell. If he had recognized Lugo's voice, as I did, he would have told him that he knew who he was. He would not have had the patience and calmness that I tried to maintain. Perhaps his approach would have been the correct one. I might have contemplated his method if my life was the only one on the line. But I had to get my family to safety and could not have afforded to take the risk.

Sometimes I wondered if these thugs had watched too many action movies and were trying to duplicate what they saw. If not for my precarious situation, these creeps would have been laughable. They acted almost like caricatures of movie or cartoon bad guys. This was slapstick, and they were so full of themselves that it was almost certain the situation would end badly for them. It was just a matter of time; the writing was on the wall. They didn't know how to measure risk, and they were so oblivious to reality that it was scary. They actually felt that they could keep doing this in the same manner that any other business was run.

Friday morning rolled in, and there was no breakfast to be had, not that I expected any. I was quickly taken to the bathroom and from the bathroom to the car to spend another day in the sweltering heat. That afternoon, Lugo asked me about some company checks I'd written. He wanted to know about the recipients and if they had any money. I guess they were looking for another job or victim after they disposed of me.

He came and went every ten minutes or so, asking me the details of a check, and if he didn't get the response he wanted, he threatened to beat me to a pulp. Most of the time, I did not tell him the truth. I knew he could not verify what I said. I wanted no part in dragging anyone else into the grasp of these madmen. How could I ever want anyone else to endure this torture? This went on for several hours, and I was exhausted by the time he finally finished. It was amazing to me that they were looking for more victims with money. This endless greed was so outside of my prior experience that I remain stupefied by it to this day. Their future endeavors did not concern me; I just did not want to be the one who handed over their next victim. What concerned me was that they were so open in discussing their future plans in front of me. That was not a good omen.

Early evening, Lugo came back and took me to the cardboard box.

He said, "I want this thing to be over."

I did not respond.

"I'm tired of babysitting for Rolando," he continued.

"What does that mean?" I asked.

"You were not supposed to hear that," he responded.

But I'm sure I was, and it was another attempt by this goon to misdirect the blame. First he had mentioned Delgado's name, and now Rolando. Rolando was a friend of Delgado. It would certainly surprise me to find that he was involved in this mess. However, Lugo, in his egotistical blindness, didn't realize that I had known all along who he was. What I did not understand was why he was blurting out names if they were going to kill me anyway. Was it insurance?

He left and came back a little later with another alcoholic beverage. I didn't know what it was. It appeared that the tequila did not have the intended effect, and they were experimenting with other spirits. I finished the drink, and he gave me another and another. I held my liquor well, and all it did was help me relax. It sounded as though Lugo was taking a little nip with me.

"How are you feeling?" he asked.

"Fine," I replied, knowing that wasn't what he wanted to hear.

"Well, that's no good. It doesn't seem you're getting drunk enough, so we're going to have to try something new. You seem to hold your liquor well," he said, sounding frustrated. I didn't like the way *something new* sounded.

"I do" was my brief response. I was still thinking about what he had said. Well, it seemed that the liquor was having an effect on Lugo instead of me.

"You're an arrogant son of a bitch," he said, slurring his words.

"I don't think so. I'm quite down to earth. I'm introverted, and many people mistake that for being arrogant," I told him.

"You're an arrogant son of a bitch," he replied. His frustration for not having broken my spirit was showing, and he detested me for it. I wasn't going to argue with this madman, especially when he was drunk. What good would that do me?

"Yeah, it's too bad," he said almost remorsefully.

"What's too bad?" I inquired.

"That you stepped on too many toes," he said.

"Me, step on toes? All I ever have done is help people, especially those who have helped me," I responded, with the last comment aimed directly at Delgado.

"They don't feel that way," he said.

"That's unfortunate if they don't feel that way," I replied.

"Yeah, yeah, well, it doesn't matter anymore," he said. The tone of his voice was scary, not in a threatening way. It was as though, in his mind, he was trying to justify and reconcile something that he was about to do.

"While we were at your house, we were looking at pictures of the trip you and your wife took to London," he said, trying to goad me.

I did not respond.

"You didn't look too happy. Then again, you were with that bitch. How could you be?" he said, and he broke into morbid laughter.

I didn't respond, since I knew he was trying to rattle my cage. It would have only made him feel better if he got to me; that was what he wanted. He had the wrong city and the wrong country, but I didn't think geography or any other school subject was his forte. He gave me another drink and one after that. He then either left the room or just decided not to speak to me anymore. I lit a cigarette and sat back and contemplated his comments. Now I better understood why they had done this to me. Much of this was caused by my refusal to continue my business association with Delgado. Apparently, my disapproval of the friendship between Delgado and Lugo had added to the fire.

I knew there was a lot more to it than that: greed, as well as the fact that I made an easy target. But one has to be pretty warped to take things to this extreme. It wasn't really all that surprising that Lugo had manifested this behavior. On the other hand, Delgado was both a surprise and a disappointment. It amazed me that a human being could be manipulated into committing such hateful acts. But history has proven over and over that individuals and group minds can be corrupted to do anything, no matter how heinous. When you think of the atrocities of wars and then think in smaller, more individual terms, you realize that evil can be perpetrated at any scale, on any level.

About an hour later, Lugo returned and gave me another drink. He asked me how I was feeling, and, to his dismay, I responded that I was fine. Again, he said we had a problem, since the alcohol was not taking the effect he wanted. What were they hoping for? Was I supposed to act a complete fool? He gave me another drink, and by the taste I knew it was something different. He gave me a couple more drinks and finally satisfied himself that I had enough. What followed really perplexed me. Like most things that had occurred in that warehouse, I did not understand it.

"Hold this," he said, and he handed me a bottle. By its weight, I could tell it was full. "Hold that one in your right hand," he instructed.

So I held the bottle in my right hand. He came over and moved the bottle so I was holding it at a certain angle, as if I were posing.

"Hold this one in your left hand," he said as he gave me another full bottle.

He then came over and positioned the bottle as he wanted it. I held these bottles in my hand for about ten minutes. The only thing that ran across my mind was that I was posing for pictures again, but why? What was the purpose? Were they going to try to doctor these pictures and use them somehow against me? Anyone who knew me knew I didn't drink. He took the bottles away, and, without a word, he left, leaving me to ponder what they were up to. As with so many other things, there were questions, questions, questions, but no answers.

As he left, Lugo put on some strange music that fit his personality. I thought the music was going to make my head explode. Whatever they had given me did not sit well. It gave me a huge headache, and I felt nauseous. I sat back and concentrated on not vomiting. I had enough filth surrounding me and didn't want to add to it. I just hoped the nausea would soon pass.

Later that evening, my night babysitter came in. Good old Mr. FBI quickly informed me that there was no dinner. I wasn't surprised in the least. He gave me a large plastic bag in case I needed to vomit, which I thought was very thoughtful of him.

He said, "Use this if you're going to puke your brains out," and laughed.

"Gee, thanks," I said, and I rolled over to lie down.

By the end of that week, I was lying down more often than sitting up. When I sat up, I got tired easily. After a full day in the bathroom and car, by the time I got to the cardboard box, I was exhausted. This, combined with the lack of nutrition and inactivity, just made me want to lie down all the time. My physical energy was ebbing, and I felt drained all the time. Unlike the previous night, I was not blessed with easy sleep. The night watchman came to check if I had perhaps choked on my own vomit, and, without saying a word, he left just as quickly as he had come. I never did use the bag he gave me. I felt that the night watchmen didn't hold any animosity towards me. They were just paid henchmen doing their job for a wage. I lay there, admiring how baggy my clothes fit me now. I wondered how long I would last under the current circumstances. Saturday morning rolled in, and another weekend in captivity lay ahead. No reprieve, no escape from the hell I found myself in.

Chapter 19 — Finality

"MAN IS THE ONLY ANIMAL THAT CONTEMPLATES DEATH,
AND ALSO THE ONLY ANIMAL THAT SHOWS ANY SIGN OF
DOUBT OF ITS FINALITY."
- WILLIAM ERNEST HOCKING -

"IN THE DARKEST HOUR THE SOUL IS REPLENISHED AND
GIVEN STRENGTH TO CONTINUE AND ENDURE."
- HEART WARRIOR CHOSA -

The following days presented me with the same routine as the others, first the bathroom and then the car. I stopped wondering why they practiced this so religiously. Early evening brought Lugo and the cardboard box. I noticed that he was around more often and did many things himself. Perhaps he didn't trust others to perform tasks, or there was so much dissention among the ranks that others were not compliant. After he tightly chained me to the railing, he made me drink. Often, I did not know what I was drinking or the effect it would have. Then he gave me another, and it burned as it went down.

"We are going to have to take you out through the Bahamas," Lugo said, matter of fact.

"What am I supposed to do when I get there? You can't connect to Colombia from there," I remarked. In retrospect, it was something I regretting saying. If I were in the Bahamas, stranded, I would find a way to get help. Besides, I thought I was losing it. They had no such plans, and it was another of Lugo's bullshit stories to keep me off balance.

"You can't?" he said, surprised.

"No, there are no connecting flights from Bahamas," I said, again regretting having made them aware of it. I felt I had said something really stupid. Why was I playing into this liar's game? It was silly, but for some reason I could not stop. Maybe I wanted so badly to believe they were going to let me go that my mind refused to see how I was being toyed with.

"Well, I don't know what we are going to do. The customs people that we work with are not going to be there next week," he said, trying to sound convincing and serious.

Obviously I could not see, but if I could have, I would probably have seen a huge grin on his face. This made no sense. His whole story about the customs buddies was a crock. He was back- pedaling to save face. It was that or just changing the story again in his own sick and psychotic imagination. Wait, wasn't this the FBI, as one of his fellow goons had told me? Why would they have such a problem if they indeed were? These guys had all watched too many Miami Vice episodes.

"Okay, I'll go to the Bahamas. Are you going to give me some money so I can get to Colombia?" I said, trying to remedy my mistake. Besides, I thought, two can play the game. I just wanted to see his response.

"Are you crazy? We are not giving you anything," he responded as he gave me another drink.

Geez. It's not like you're giving me your money, just returning a very, very small fraction of mine.

"So how do I get there with no money?" I asked, being coy.

"We'll have to figure that out," he said, getting frustrated with the conversation. Once I cornered him, he did not want to talk about it anymore. Typical.

"Okay, just leave me in the Bahamas. I'll get to Colombia somehow," I said, trying to prod him along so he had to use his mental agility, or lack thereof, to spin a bigger and bigger lie. Of course I believed that the Bahamas story was also make believe, and they kept telling me different ones to keep my hopes up or confuse me or throw me off. Maybe they themselves still didn't know what they were going to do. But actually, they did, and I was not going on an airplane unless it was in a coffin. By now, I was sure of that.

"We shall see," he said, sounding as though he was in deep thought or simply caught off guard by my insistence.

"Why can't you just leave me at the airport and I won't cause any problems? I'll get on the plane, and you will never hear from me again," I said. It was worth a try. I certainly had nothing to lose. His response was one for the record books and the most creative so far.

"No, you are a wanted criminal, and we can't risk that. We have to get you out of the country without anybody knowing," he said, trying to sound serious.

Ha, ha, ha, I could barely contain my laughter. This is what psychologists call deflection. What he really meant was that he was a wanted criminal and that if he let me go, I might have turned around and went to the authorities. This guy's imagination had grown more ridiculous. Did he realize how stupid he sounded by telling me this?

I didn't respond because after the last one I couldn't say anything with a straight face. I truly believed that they had no intention of letting me go alive, thus risking me going to the authorities. Perhaps when the ordeal started out, they had simply thought of stealing my assets and not of murder. But things had changed, and this had dragged out longer than they anticipated, thus transforming them into killers of no resort. They most likely felt they'd been backed into a corner. Perhaps they could not agree on which method was best to kill me and how and where they would dispose of my lifeless body. The alcohol was probably going to be used to sedate me so that when the time came, I wouldn't put up much of a fight. I doubted it was for humanitarian reasons. They didn't care if I felt pain. On the contrary, they enjoyed it.

I sat back and stared into the nothingness that had become my world. The night watchman, Mr. FBI, came in and brought me food, a hamburger, of course. I devoured it in what seemed to be a single bite and wished I had ten more. I promised myself not to eat hamburgers again if I miraculously survived this ordeal. The night watchmen were the most consistent in bringing me food. If it had been left up to Lugo or his sidekick, there probably would not have been any.

Mr. FBI said, "You missed me?"

"Yes, of course I did. Where have you been?" I replied. Actually, this nut job was better than being around Lugo and his sidekick, Mr. Torture.

"Taking care of some business. I brought you some cigs also," he said, and he handed me the pack. "I will be back later," he said.

"Okay."

After I finished, he came back and offered to take me to the bathroom. I guess he was alone that day, because he poked the barrel of the gun into my back to make sure I knew it was there. He also made me touch the barrel to acknowledge it was real. For a fleeting moment, I thought of making a move. I didn't for various reasons. Firstly, I assumed he was alone, but there could have been others there. I had no way to know. Secondly, my physical condition was so weak I knew I didn't have the strength to fight and stood no chance of overpowering anyone. Thirdly, he had a gun and I didn't doubt that he'd use it if he saw himself threatened. So I was a coward and let the opportunity pass, not knowing what the outcome would have been—*c'est la vie*. He chained me to the wall and left until I finished. When I called him, he took me back to the cardboard box.

I lay there as time crawled on. I wished it would fly by so this ordeal would end one way or another. No more thinking, it was not getting me anywhere. That night I was able to sleep a little, a minor but welcome reprieve from the madness that surrounded me. Sunday morning arrived, and I was about to complete four full weeks in my cardboard box. Lugo, the madman, arrived in one of his hysterical moods and told me there was no breakfast, what a surprise. The day was as usual: first the bathroom, then the car. Today it was the trunk. Early evening back to the box where Lugo in a pissy mood and waited for me with a couple of drinks.

He handed me a drink and said, "We are not sending any of your furniture or personal stuff to Colombia. We are keeping it as evidence." What a surprise, they actually thought I believed their previous story about shipping it down there. These greedy little pigs wanted those things, also.

"Oh, really? What are you going to do with that stuff?" I said acting surprised when I was not. Trying to pass off pictures of my family as evidence, these thugs must have thought I was retarded. They were trying to keep evidence of the crime they committed? That was logical ... for them

"Can I have my family pictures, at least?" I said, trying to piss him off more. I was playing him. I needed some fun.

"No," he growled.

Guess who got up on the wrong side of the bed again? I guess it made sense; why would a dead man need pictures of his family? I guess they wanted to keep the furniture to furnish the house they had just stolen. I could not care less. Those things could be replaced. I didn't say anything to him. It was useless, anyway, especially in the mood he was in. He didn't say a word, handed me another drink, and left. These drinks did not have much of an effect on me. The night watchman, Mr. FBI, looked in on me. He didn't say anything, and he didn't return the rest of the evening. The way they were acting told me something was up and it would be only a matter of days, maybe hours, until things would resolve one way or another. The end was near, and I could smell it. My intuition told me it was show time.

Monday morning arrived along with Lugo and his sidekick, who brought me a badly bruised apple and a small bottle of Gatorade. Beggars could not be choosers, but the apple seemed to have gone through as bad a time as I had. They also gave me a fresh pack of smokes and left. I ate the apple, or what of it could be eaten, and put most of the Gatorade aside for later. Conservation and management of the few resources available was vital. Amazing. Tomorrow would mark four full weeks in that cardboard box. Four weeks before, I had never imagined this dragging out so long. But if we knew what life had in store for us sometimes, we might be able to avoid some of the bumps and bruises along the way.

Mid-morning, and Lugo and his inseparable sidekick trounced into the room.

Lugo now stood directly over me. "We have another problem holding back your release." It was story time, and I was about to be told another fairytale.

"One of the checks you signed was returned because of your signature. The bank called the house and left a message. Do you know someone at the bank?" Lugo asked. Well, up to that point, I had not been aware that I had signed checks. I thought some of the documents may have included checks, but I had never known for certain. The part about the signature was logical since signing checks blindfolded was no easy task. Besides, I had sometimes messed my signature up on purpose to make things more difficult for them with the remote chance that someone might notice.

"Yes."

"You're going to call them and tell them to pay that check, because we are going to re-deposit it."

For a moment, I felt like telling him to go to hell. I'd had enough. He could call and tell them. But I said, "Fine." My responses consisted of one word, but that was one word too many.

So they took me back to the desk and chair and went through the old procedure of hooking up the phone and dialing. I spoke to the bank representative and instructed her to pay the check, which, during the course of the conversation I learned was for forty-five thousand dollars. Once I finished, they took me back to the cardboard box and re-chained me to the railing.

"How many friends do you have?" he asked scornfully.

"Not many," I responded. Everyone knew that I was a homebody, and having friends and going out was not my style. It appeared that the only person who I considered a friend, Delgado, was one friend too many.

"That figures," he said.

"I spend my time at home with my family," I said curtly. Of course, I would not expect for him to understand that.

"Well, think of acquaintances and friends you have, because you're going to call them and tell them you're leaving," he said smugly.

Was I leaving permanently to somewhere they could not communicate with me? Checking out?

With that, he left, and my suspicions were confirmed. This whole episode was about to end very shortly. I feared that my time on this planet was now a matter of hours, not days. I was at peace with myself and asked for strength down the homestretch. These calls were to tell them I was leaving, yes, but in reality it meant I was leaving the living.

That was a rather unusual day. Hours passed, and no one took me to the bathroom or the car to spend the day. This was yet another indication that the final preparations were in process. In the afternoon, Lugo came to get me. He told me to call my wife and tell her things would be finalized soon. Of course, I could not convey how final things really were: permanent, dead as a doornail. They took me to the usual calling spot, and I talked to her and then to D. J., my son, who wanted to talk to me.

"Dad, when are you coming home? I miss you," he told me.

"Soon, D. J. Everything is almost finished," I said, choking back the tears.

"Yeah, I need your help with this computer game and homework," he added.

"I'll help you when I get there," I said.

"Dad, I love you and miss you so much," he said.

"I love you, too," I said, and I hung up.

I was taken back to the box, and that was one time I cried, because I realized I had just spoken to my son for the last time. I was blessed and cursed at once. That was the hardest call for me. His childish innocence could not outweigh the magnitude of the situation. At least I had gotten to talk to him one last time.

Lugo strolled in later and had a drink for me. After the phone call, I needed one. Lugo gave me another drink and said, "Where did you lease your car?"

"At Kendall Toyota on US 1," I said, not knowing what he was getting at.

"We are going to return it tomorrow," he said.

I was so tired of these lies and stories. What were they going to do? Walk into the dealer and say, "Here's your car back"? It just didn't work that way. I guess they were so stupid that they must have thought anyone they dealt with was on their same level. It was mind-boggling.

"Okay," I replied. What was I supposed to do? Argue with him and tell him he was a moron and to stop telling me bullshit stories?

"We are making arrangements with the customs people. You should be leaving soon," he said. His fairytales were annoying. Who believed him except himself?

"Okay," I replied. "Whatever, you say."

"I just have to see that the right people are on the night shift."

He misconstrued my lack of response, believing that I believed him. What a silly and erroneous assumption.

"Okay," I mumbled, thinking that I wanted him to just leave me alone.

"You're going have to get skunk drunk," he said as he handed me another drink.

"Why is that?" I said. Stupid stories deserved stupid questions.

"So you're almost unconscious and can't recognize any of us," he replied. He still believed I did not know who he was.

"Fine." I was bored to tears. What an idiot.

"So drink up so your system can get used to it," he said. I drank a little but did not finish it.

"All of it!" he ordered. I would be happy to drink it all if he stopped telling me fairytales and started telling me the truth.

So I drank the rest, then another and another. I was miserable and depressed after speaking to my son and wanted, rightly or wrongly, to drown my sorrows. I felt the full effect of the alcohol this time. I had no idea what I was drinking. It didn't matter. Lugo gave me one more and left. I sat there reviewing all the bullshit stories he had told me. How could he think that anyone could believe him? I was so sad after the brief conversation with my son. I was fatigued from thinking and always entertaining the nagging thought that if I'd done things differently, then the outcome might have been better or at least different.

But that was the beauty of life, with so many variables. Choosing to play them a certain way yields certain results. If I'd played those variables differently, the results would have been different, but no one could guarantee it would have been for the better. It remains an unknown. So I chose what I thought was best. I had to live and die with those consequences, good or bad. I knew it was a futile exercise, anyway. I could not change what had happened or where I was.

Wishful thinking and overanalyzing the situation were not going to change it. Ask anyone who has gone through a bad experience if they wish they could have changed things. The obvious answer is yes, of course. But we can and must deal with what is and not with what could have been. That was where I found myself: accepting. Negative experiences always offer something positive and many times can propel us into new directions that we would not have gone if it were not for those challenges. The saying that there is always something good in the bad is true. Unfortunately, it did not look like I would be alive to benefit from those lessons.

The night watchman, Mr. FBI, came in and brought me the usual hamburger and fries. I was grateful for the food but made a mental note. *If I get out alive, no more hamburgers.* I sat back and ate, hoping it would bring me down from the alcohol-induced stupor. It had the affect I hoped for, and I felt much better after finishing.

My intuition was deep, indescribably so. I felt it, literally in my bones, a certainty that my life was reaching its end; the curtain was going to drop on this whole fiasco that had lasted four full weeks. I did not know how they planned to kill me. I did not care to guess. I was tired of their constantly changing stories that were aimed at distracting and placating me. I was tired of being considered a fool who bought their lies, pinning my hopes on them. Lugo was a pathological liar, and making up his stories came as easily as breathing for him. His ego blinded him into believing he was clever and invincible and that everyone catered to his whim. The simple truth was that he was a manipulator who used violence, threats, and brute force, not his charm, to get his way.

There had been a lot of commotion that day in the warehouse. It seemed Lugo had called a meeting of the thugs or the board of directors of what I fondly referred to now as Insane Criminals Inc., and all were present. Final preparations needed to be made. Early in the evening, Lugo came in and said he wanted me to sign some documents, probably the last ones. When I finished, he left without a word. I was relieved that he did not give me any more to drink. I sat back and stared into nothingness, as usual. No one came by for most of the night. I could not reconcile sleep with the feeling that I had a very short time left. So I alternately sat and lay down, waiting to see if my intuition was right.

Tuesday, December 14, 1994, rolled in like a lamb but was to leave like a lion. It was a day that changed my life and almost ended it. This day marked four weeks since my world had been totally thrown upside down. Four weeks of misery chained to a wall. Four weeks of humiliation and torture that no one should have to endure. Four weeks that not only changed my life but how I saw the world and the people inhabiting it. But these four weeks also fostered some good. I gained greater belief in myself, in my faith, and in the power of my spirit and resilience and mental tenacity to survive.

I sat there for a good while that morning, hoping I would receive my rotten apple and Gatorade. I got the Gatorade but no apple from Lugo's sidekick, Mr. Torture. A few minutes later, they came to get me. Today, instead of taking me to the bathroom, they took me to the car. I spent my day chained to the steering wheel until I was almost unconscious from the fatigue and dehydration caused by the humidity and heat.

Early evening, they returned me to my cardboard box. Lugo was mad at me because he realized I had burned a hole in his five-dollar mattress. I ignored him. He went on one of his tirades. I ignored him. He yelled, cursed, and screamed. I ignored him. While I sat there, I tried to estimate how much they had stolen from me. I figured they had cleaned out all my accounts, clients' accounts, IRAs and so forth, which would come to approximately 1.2 million. With the house and furnishings as another four hundred thousand, I figured they had netted at least 1.6 million. (I was wrong, and my figures were too low.) But I really didn't care about his cheap mattress or if he was upset that I had ruined it. The pettiness was typical of him.

I lay in the box for a while and, to my surprise, Mr. Friendly showed up and said, "Get up, you're going home. I'm going to take you to wash up and change clothes." I didn't know if "home" meant going to see God or what, but I obviously didn't believe him.

"What happened to the hotel and real shower I was supposed to get?" I inquired, prodding him. You figure for the princely sum of 1.6 million that was the least I could ask for. Besides, I was beyond filthy, and I wanted to die clean if I could. Silly, I know.

"We couldn't find a secure hotel, but you're going home to your family," he said enthusiastically. Translation, we didn't want to risk getting caught by taking you to a hotel and what's the difference if you die clean or dirty. By "family," I thought he might mean my deceased relatives.

"Great," I answered unenthusiastically. I know I should have been thrilled at that point, but I had a nagging feeling that this was all a show and I was going to die that evening. I was certain, I can't explain why.

He released the chains from the railing, and my last walk to the bathroom began. He gave me the same instructions as he had the previous time. He was going to take the blindfold off, and I was to wash up and change and call when I finished. The same bucket of dirty water, soap, toothbrush, and toothpaste was before me, and the bonus was that they had deodorant. When they took the tape off, it was very painful as they pulled skin and hair away with it. The tape had eaten the skin off my nose almost to the bone, and both my nose and ears were bloody. A lot of my hair was yanked away. It hurt, but I didn't care how it looked anymore. And they certainly didn't care. My hair was one greasy lump pasted to my scalp.

From somewhere in the background, Lugo shouted out, "You're probably going to have some problems with your eyes at first and may not see well." I knew he was not concerned about me, I think just curious about the effect this was having for possible future reference.

I didn't respond to him, so again he asked, "Can you see okay?"

I knew the correct answer and the one they wanted to hear, so I replied, "No, not very well. Everything is blurry." This was not true, but I knew better. The problem was not my vision but opening my eyes, because the glue from the tape had shut them tight.

Once I was able to open my eyes sufficiently, the first thing that impacted me was how skinny I was. I never imagined I had lost so much weight. Too bad I could not sell this secret diet and make millions. The bruises on my arm from the burns were infected and were an ugly black but, for some reason, didn't hurt much to the touch any longer. I proceeded to wash as best as I could. I was told that if I needed more water, I could get it from the sink. That was when I realized how weak I had become. I could hardly lift the pail of water to pour it in the toilet and had just as hard a time filling up the pail and putting it on the floor. The captivity had taken such a toll, not only psychologically but also physically. I did the best I could, given the scarce implements. Again, the best word for this was "birdbath." But I was filthy and had not even brushed my teeth in a long while, so anything was welcomed.

After I finished washing up, I changed into the clothes they had brought from my house. They were all far too large on my emaciated body. I was unable to shave since they still hadn't brought a razor. Perhaps they thought I would try to use the plastic razor as a weapon. I had a full beard and knew I still looked like a hobo even though I had no mirror. Perhaps the lack of a mirror was a good idea. It was better that I didn't see what I looked like. Once I finished, I faced the wall and called out to them. One of them came from behind me and said, "Keep your eyes closed."

"I'm going to guide you back towards a chair. Don't open your eyes. If you do, you're dead, understand?" he said.

Well, well, we were back to the "you're dead" threat, so nothing had changed. I thought I was dead anyway. If I opened my eyes, did I die one way, and if I didn't, a different way? Good question.

"Yes," I replied. My boredom was nearly as great as their greed.

Lugo yelled from somewhere in the background. "How are his eyes?" Maybe Lugo was not as stupid as I thought. He kept his distance from me so that if I happened to disobey and open my eyes, I wouldn't see him. How foolish. With his distinctive voice, I had identified him from day one in the warehouse. This meant he was willing to let the other thugs take the fall if things went wrong, real nice guy. Did his "staff" not realize how they were being manipulated and used?

"He looks like he has a bad sunburn, that's all," Mr. Friendly yelled out. Well, I wouldn't have wanted him as my doctor. He would have said that a bullet hole was a small scratch. My skin was eaten away around my eyes and bleeding. I wondered what beach he went to where people got this kind of sunburn?

"Don't open your eyes or you're dead," he said. I felt like a child whose parents tell him not to do something over and over again. I wanted to open my eyes just to disobey them, but I didn't. I was very obedient.

He put some cream on my eyes, which relieved the itching somewhat, but I doubted it was going to make it heal as fast as they wanted. With each rub around my eyes, he kept saying, "Don't open your eyes, or you're dead." I wondered why they were even bothering to do this. Did they want to make me pretty before they killed me? At the time, I was baffled, but later I understood their motive. For a fleeting moment, the thought occurred that maybe they were not going to kill me after all, that I had misread the situation. But just as quickly, I realized this was similar to the last breaths a drowning man takes, holding on to an illusion in order not to face reality.

Mr. Friendly joked around and asked if I preferred to wait for release until my eyes had healed. I didn't acknowledge his smart-ass silliness, and he just kept doing his job.

When he had finished applying the cream, he began wrapping my eyes again. This time, they put bubble wrap first. The kind used for packing boxes, creative. On top of that, he wrapped the same gray duct tape that I had worn for four weeks. When he finished, he asked me if any light was coming in. I told him no, but he added more for good measure until he was satisfied that I was in a dark void.

Mr. Torture came by and patted me on the back and said, "You're not such a bad guy."

I almost vomited when he said that. Was he referring to the fact that I had accepted my torture with dignity, or perhaps that I didn't fight back? Maybe he needed to make his conscience feel better before he killed me. Besides, what other fool just hands over his assets as easily as I did, with nobody concerned enough to investigate his disappearance? No one.

I was taken back to the room where I lived in my cardboard box, but instead of throwing me in it, they sat me in a chair and chained me to it. So I knew that whatever was going to happen was going to happen sooner rather than later. I had hours, if that, to live. Lugo arrived in a good mood. It wasn't every day he got to kill someone.

"It doesn't look like we have a very good menu in this hotel. You lost some weight," he said, and he laughed uncontrollably.

"Your house was transferred to D & J International, by the way," he said. He was offering me information that I did not need to know. It was obvious that they thought I was not going to be around to use it. D & J, I surmised, meant Danny and Jorge.

"Okay," I answered. Did I care anymore? No.

"We couldn't sell the deli, and I'm tired of this whole thing. So we're going to sell the equipment in the deli for whatever price we can get," Lugo said. If he was tired of it, imagine how I felt. What a surprise that they couldn't sell a deli in three days. Selling the equipment could get them a few dollars more. Endless greed. Someone could write a song about that.

"The equipment is worthless when sold secondhand. You aren't going to get much," I told him, trying to deflate his ambition.

In fact, I was telling him the truth.

"We'll see," he said disbelievingly.

Right, since you're Lugo, they're going give you more. Well, perhaps so, because you will con someone.

They were being very open right then and not trying to hide anything from me, since dead men tell no tales. So why would they have been concerned with all this information coming back to haunt them? Lugo and his parade of other thugs came and went as though they were paying their last respects. Mr. FBI came in and actually started a conversation.

"You're going home. Isn't that great?" he said enthusiastically.

Well, it would be if it were true. "Yes," I replied without emotion.

"Everything is set with the customs people," he said.

Oh, I bet it is, any other good stories to tell me? "Good," I replied.

"We just have to wait until their shift," he said.

Or wait until it's dark enough and there's less traffic before you take my lifeless body out of the warehouse.

In the midst of this personal hurricane, I found myself at peace. I accepted what was coming and knew that I had done the best I could. At least I had done what I considered to be right. I was comforted by the fact that my family was safe and sound, although the thought of my children growing up without their father saddened me. Life was not fair. I didn't pretend it was. I believed everything happened for a reason, and perhaps the circumstances I found myself in did not allow for me to see it clearly. I was not afraid. I was not going to lower myself and beg for mercy when the time came. I wanted to go out with dignity. I did not fear death. I felt a peace and calmness that I cannot describe. I felt I was not alone and had great faith that God would not desert me in my hour of need. I had run out of options and would just let my faith carry me to whatever outcome awaited me.

I was startled out my thought process by Lugo.

"You're going to call your friends and tell them you're leaving and never coming back," Lugo said.

You mean I'm checking out permanently. This is the end of the line? A one-way ticket? "Fine," I replied. I couldn't care less about these outlandish stories anymore.

"You tell them that you don't know where you're going, that you have marital problems and you have a new girlfriend. You can say her name is Lillian Torres," he instructed me. This was another good one, a Pulitzer Prize–winning story. Did he actually expect people to believe this? Where did he come up with these gems? I didn't know it at the time, but Lillian Torres was a real person and another member of the gang.

"Do you understand?" he said again, forcefully.

"Yes," I finally responded. I was trying to digest the whopper of a story he wanted me to tell.

"You are to tell them that you're depressed and suicidal and don't know what to do," he said. This was going to be hard to do, but now I understood. He had stressed the suicidal part, interesting.

"Fine," I replied. Then everything clicked into place. That was how they were going to justify my death. I committed suicide over a failing marriage and a new love. I underestimated them, and the story was a fairly clever concoction. Anyone who knew me knew this was ridiculous, but stranger things happened in real life, and people can be so gullible.

This was the final nail in the coffin confirming that I was within hours of my death. Death was knocking at the door, and soon it was to be opened. I didn't believe this was what they had planned all along, but this story should not have surprised me. I hung on even though it seemed hopeless. I hung on until there was nothing left. I had just reached that point.

These were the most peculiar phone calls I had ever made in my life.

"You better sound real depressed, you understand?" Lugo said with his threatening voice, a useless tactic at this point.

"Fine," I said. *Why bother arguing with madmen? The depressed part should come naturally, anyway.*

"Okay, have you thought who you are going to call to say goodbye?"

"Just Kathy Leal and Gene Rosen, my attorney and friend." Kathy Leal was my realtor, and she barely knew Gene Rosen and me. I thought of these two because perhaps they would think the call was suspicious and act on it. Maybe they would think I was crazy and simply ignore it.

"Who are you going to call first?" Lugo barked. A picture of him with a hyena's head, salivating, came to my mind for some reason.

"Kathy Leal."

They dialed the number, and I spoke to Kathy, trying to sound depressed and desperate while at the same time trying not to laugh. Her reaction to the phone call was total confusion. I told her the story of my failing marriage, the girlfriend and forthcoming disappearance and that I had gone over the deep end.

There was barely any reaction at all, just "Okay," but then what did I expect?

Then they dialed Gene Rosen and passed me the phone when he answered. Before I could begin telling my sad story, he informed me that Delgado had just been there and didn't want the power of attorney any longer. I knew that they heard what he told me because they always listened in on an extension. So, without letting Gene speak anymore, I told him the same sad story. While I was speaking to Gene, Lugo whispered in my ear to tell him that he was losing a client but he would have a new one in D & J International. I imagined that if Gene had known that his new client was a criminal enterprise comprising psychopaths whose main business was kidnapping and extortion, he would have been so thrilled and forever thankful. I think Gene did not know what to say when I told him the story and was confused, but I'm sure he'd heard crazier stories.

Lugo thinking that Gene was going to be their attorney was typical of him. No one refused to do what he ordered, and he saw nothing wrong with his criminal ventures. As soon as I hung up, Lugo went ballistic.

"That was no good; do you want me to beat the pulp out of you? Well, do you?" Lugo screamed. I imagined smoke coming out his nostrils and ears. This whole idea was stupid. What did he expect?

It was not clear to me what had pissed Lugo off about this call.

No response from me. *Screw you. Do it if you want. I'm tired of these games.* Lugo was looking for a pretext to finish things and wanted me to hand it to him on a silver platter. In retrospect, it didn't matter, because he wanted to beat me to oblivion anyway. Lugo was mentally deranged with a violent temper he could not control. He was itching to kill me, and the smell of blood drove him mad to the point he would not control himself any longer.

"You really didn't sound depressed!" he yelled.

Mr. Einstein, what is that supposed to sound like? I said nothing—there was no point.

"You're going to call him back and tell him the same story, and this time, sound depressed, or I'm going to beat you to a pulp," he screamed. He was working himself into an uncontrollable frenzy. He could not control or put off his desire to kill me any longer.

"Fine," I replied. I thought calling him back was really stupid. Calling the same person to tell him the same story seemed weird. Could you imagine what the person at the other end would be thinking? *Hi, I needed to sound more depressed the first time I called you, and since the goons that have me tied up didn't think I passed the audition, they're having me repeat the performance.* This was stupid beyond belief. They didn't consider that it would raise suspicion if I called him again.

So they called him back and handed me the phone, and I went through the same story. It was hard to sound depressed because I thought this was so stupid. Gene was trying to tell me he understood and wished me the best. In the back of his mind, he had to think I had gone over the edge. They yanked the phone from my hand and hung up in mid sentence. They were brilliant.

"That's better," Lugo said. I thought it was the same as the first time, with no emotion. But Lugo heard it differently and left me alone. For now, that was what mattered. All I could feel was total disbelief at this craziness.

It was show time. They gave me something to drink in a small bottle about the size of a Gatorade. I drank some; it had a fruity taste. He also gave me another pack of cigarettes. I guess they were giving me my last cigs. I drank a little and sensed that someone, probably Lugo, was standing near me, watching.

"Drink it all, but slow. We have time. The customs people won't be on duty until two in the morning," he said. I wished he would stop with the ridiculous customs story. There were no planes leaving for the Bahamas or anywhere else at that hour. They were just waiting until the streets were deserted so they could take my lifeless body out.

"Okay." Why I even replied, I don't know.

"We need you to be totally drunk so we can drop you off at the airport," he told me. Fairytale time once again, so I played along.

"What's going to happen to me then?" I asked, thinking this was going to be a good story.

"Our contacts at customs are going to put you in a type of jail, and in the morning they will put you on a plane to Colombia," he said confidently. Too bad he did not do his homework: The only planes to Colombia left in the afternoon.

"What about a passport and money?" I asked, trying to make him slip up.

"We are going to leave all that in a duffel bag with you when we drop you off," he said, noticeably getting irritated by my questions. But I wanted to goad him and play with him. See how fast he could spin his web of lies.

"Fine," I said.

"Don't freak out on us if something goes wrong and we have to pull out of there in a hurry," Lugo told me. This meant this whole story was crap.

"Sure," I replied. I just played along, letting Lugo tell this fabrication.

I guess he forgot he had told me a different story last time that I was leaving through the Bahamas because they could not get me on a plane to Colombia. He probably didn't know which version he had told me last, since it was all made up anyway. I guess it's hard to keep your story straight and recall all the minute details when you're making things up as you go along.

Perhaps they thought I had a poor memory. They kept changing their story. None of them made any sense. None were consistent. First they were "the family," then the FBI. In the end, I had no clue who they were claiming to be. To me, the reality was that they were just greedy criminals with a thirst and lust for blood. In the beginning, they were going to let me go in a few days, and then they did not know. I was going straight to Colombia, then to the Bahamas, and now we were back to going straight to Colombia through customs.

They were improvising as they went along and told me the most convenient tale at any given moment. Did they figure my desire to leave the warehouse would cloud my memory and I wouldn't recall previous stories? Or perhaps it may have been a result of the disorganization of the group. No real plans existed. They did not know what to do or how to do it. But it looked like they had finally decided. Neither going to Colombia nor continuing to live were future prospects for me

I sat there, sipping on my bottle of whatever it was, when Mr. Friendly came in.

"Goodbye, Marc. I'm sorry for everything that's happened to you," he apologized.

Give me a break. A little late for that now. "Yeah," I answered, feeling no sincerity in what he was telling me.

"Marc, please understand that you have to disappear and never come back. If you do, you're dead," he said with emphasis. I understood now. They had sent him in to give me this little speech. But it also appeared that he wasn't in the loop, because he still believed they were really going to let me go.

"No problem. You will never see or hear from me again, I promise," I said, trying to make him believe me, even though it was futile.

"Many people say they understand, but they don't. You and your family are dead if you ever come back and go to the police," he said convincingly.

"I understand," I replied, but I felt this whole exercise was a waste of time.

Whatever they gave me to drink was certainly not alcohol alone. I only drank a little, and it hit me like a semi truck. My head was spinning, and I could barely stay awake. They had drugged me. I guess all my drinking these previous days did not satisfy their need for me to be totally out of it.

Lugo came in and said, "Drink up. You have to drink another one."

"Another one?" I questioned. There was no way I was going to finish this one before passing out.

"Yeah, another one," he snorted.

Mr. FBI came in and put something in my hand. "Here's a hundred and eighty dollars. That's all we could come up with," he said.

Out of 1.2 million dollars, all you can come up with is 180 bucks? You guys spent it all already.

I had no idea what I was doing by now, I was so disoriented. I think I put it in my pocket. This was a good show, anyway. My head started wobbling like one of those dolls that people sometimes put in their rear windows. Lugo came over and took the bottle from my hand before I dropped it on the floor. This was some serious and powerful stuff they had given me.

"Do you want to lie down?" he asked.

"Yes," I murmured. I could hardly open my mouth to speak, and saying yes took a considerable amount of effort. I felt as though my body were paralyzed.

He unchained me and took me over to the cardboard box and threw me on the mattress. He chained me to the railing, although, in my state, that was utterly useless. He handed me the bottle and ordered me to drink the rest of it. Good luck, I thought. I lit a cigarette but could not smoke it because I could not feel my lips. Then, all of a sudden, the world swam away, and I lost all consciousness, not knowing if it was for the last time.

Chapter 20 — Miracles

"MIRACLES, IN THE SENSE OF PHENOMENA WE CANNOT EXPLAIN, SURROUND US ON EVERY HAND: LIFE ITSELF IS THE MIRACLE OF MIRACLES."
- GEORGE BERNARD SHAW -

"IMPOSSIBLE SITUATIONS CAN BECOME POSSIBLE MIRACLES."
- ROBERT H. SCHULLER -

I'm alive! I'm alive! I could not open my eyes completely and was still utterly disoriented. I suddenly realized that I was in a hospital. I was alive! I cannot describe what I felt in that moment. The happiness was fleeting as the pain ripped through my body. From the little I could see, I was tied down to a board on top of a hospital bed. The first thing I murmured was for the nurse. I needed to vomit. She and another nurse tilted the board on its side, and I proceeded to vomit a gush of blood.

Let's back up and allow me to replay to you what occurred after I passed out in the warehouse and how I got to the hospital ICU. This comes from testimony in the trial and other public documents, for I obviously could not have known it in any other manner. To this day, I have no recollection of these events, and I have a memory lapse between the last recollections of being in the warehouse and waking up in the hospital.

Around two in the morning, they loaded me into my car, and Lugo, his sidekick, Delgado, and one of the night watchmen, Mr. Friendly, went for a ride. Mr. Friendly was the driver. (So much for his assurances that he would not let anything bad happen to me. He was psycho.) They drove my car to a spot near where the deli was located, at Thirty-Fourth Street and Seventy-Ninth Avenue, in the Doral area of Miami. This was a perfect spot for what they intended to do, since that area had hardly any traffic at all, especially in the wee hours of the morning. It was an area mostly surrounded by warehouses and, strangely enough, only about a mile from Metro-Dade police headquarters.

They crashed my car, a new 1994 Toyota 4-Runner, into a utility pole to simulate an accident at a velocity of about five to ten miles an hour. The banging I had heard in the warehouse was them trying to damage the car prior to taking it out there in order to give the impression the accident was with greater force than what would be achieved at slow speed, striking the utility pole. They hauled my unconscious body into the driver's seat to make it look as if I had been driving. They doused the car and me with gasoline and placed a propane tank in the trunk. They lit the car on fire and retreated to their car to watch the spectacle. They were about to witness a human barbecue and the fireworks of the car as it burned and blew up.

Somehow (mind you, I don't remember a single second of that night, and as far as I knew, I was unconscious) I managed to get out of the car. I supposedly staggered like a drunk with no direction, completely disoriented. They were totally aghast when I appeared on the road, moving away from the burning vehicle. They went ballistic and decided to remedy the situation. Lugo, in a typical lunatic tirade, starting yelling, "Run him over! Run him over!" So then they decided to run me over.

They ran me over once, and I was completely helpless to even try to move out of the way. Lugo then kept yelling. Now it was "Run him over again! Run him over again!" They backed the car up and ran me over again. They wanted to make sure I was dead. They backed up the car again for a third run, but for me, miraculously, a car was approaching, and they decided to take off rather than risk being seen. They figured I had to be dead anyway, and the third time would have just been insurance.

Someone saw the burning car and called the fire department and paramedics. By the time they got there, my car was a burned-out frame and I lay nearby in a coma. I was first transported to the nearby Parkland Memorial Hospital in Hialeah, but my condition was too grave, and they could not treat me, so I was taken to Jackson Memorial Hospital, where they had a trauma center.

The reason why they decided to make my death look like an accident was simple. One of the documents I had signed in the warehouse was a change of beneficiary form for my insurance policy. It changed from my wife to Lillian Torres, Lugo's ex-wife. By making it look like I went nuts, got drunk, and drove my car into a utility pole, they stood to collect two million dollars from the insurance policies. I'm sure they were jubilant and celebrated that night. There was no way that I could have survived. Unfortunately for them, they had begun counting their eggs before they hatched.

I lay in the post-operating room at the hospital. I gazed down at my body and noticed that I had a zipper on my belly from my chest down to my pubic hair, formed by the staples used to close me up, fifty-four in all. I had tubes sticking out from just about every part of my body, including a catheter sticking out of my penis. It seemed I could not get away from urinating in one kind of container or another. The pain I felt those first few minutes I cannot describe. I really don't want to remember it. The nurse kept coming over and wiping the sticky substance from my eyes and moistening my lips, which felt like cardboard.

She went to the end of the bed and said, "Wiggle your toes for me."

This was one of the scariest moments of my life. I could not move my toes of either foot.

"You've been in a bad car accident. Your spine was twisted, and you lost a lot of spinal fluid. The doctor is concerned about paralysis," she said dryly.

I wanted to cry, but I couldn't even muster the strength for that. Great, I had survived and now I was paralyzed. Cut me some slack! Was it just going to go from one thing to the next?

"What else happened to me?" I managed to whisper.

"The roof of your bladder was blown off, you have spleen damage, and your pelvis is fractured," she said.

I also had large bruises, cuts and burns all over my body, including my arms, legs and buttocks, but those were so minor when compared to the other injuries that they almost seemed irrelevant. I had undergone six hours of surgery. They had split me open like a cantaloupe to explore and see how many vital organs were damaged or malfunctioning. Now, when I reflect on it, I realize I was very fortunate. At the time, I didn't know what had happened and just felt I had gone through a meat grinder.

"It was no car accident. It was attempted murder. I was kidnapped," I whispered to the nurse. So began my journey to have someone listen and believe. It did not prove to be an easy task.

I guess she must have thought I was delirious from the morphine being pumped into my body. She just walked away and ignored me.

I arrived at the hospital as a John Doe and had no identification or money. Yes, they took back the one hundred and eighty dollars before they tried to toast me in my car, if it had been that much to begin with. I never really knew what had been given to me. Just this alone should have raised curiosity. Who gets into a car accident and has absolutely no identification? Somehow, this didn't seem strange to anyone, either. I wondered who in that hospital was doing the morphine, the staff or me. I knew strange things happened in Miami, but how strange do things have to get before someone notices? There were bright red flags, yet no one paid attention or cared enough to do something about it.

She came back and made me wiggle my toes again, and eventually I was able to wiggle the left side. What a relief I felt when I was able to do so. The toes on my right side would not budge, but I knew with a little prodding they would. She kept wiping my eyes with a wet towel. I must have looked like a raccoon, except with cut and bloody eyes. None of these unusual things attracted her attention. Perhaps she had seen too much or just did her job by rote and avoided making any observations or questioning what she saw.

"I need to talk to my lawyer, I'm a victim of a kidnapping," I whispered to her. *Hello, call the police.* No one home, and no one cared.

I must have repeated my request to talk to my attorney several times before it finally yielded results. I talked to Gene and told him what had happened. I imagined he was a little bewildered and confused. Not more than twenty-four hours ago, I had called him twice to tell him about my so-called marital problems and that I was eloping with this new girlfriend. Now I was calling him and telling him I had been kidnapped and they had tried to kill me. Nonetheless, he said he would come down to the hospital. I asked him to call my sister and tell her what happened and where I was. I had no idea what time of day it was or even what day it was. The nurse took the phone from me and told me that they were waiting for a CAT scan to determine the extent of my spinal injury. Afterwards, they would take me to a regular hospital room.

Gene came to visit me while I was still in post-op. I told him in general terms what had happened. I don't blame him, but he must have thought I was delirious from the drugs. He called both my wife and sister and told them where I was and what had occurred. My sister later told me that Gene called her and said, "Your brother is in the hospital and is telling this crazy story about being kidnapped." I can't blame anyone for thinking I had gone over the edge, because what I was describing just doesn't happen every day. I knew it was going to be an uphill battle to have anyone believe and help me. But one would have thought that, as a precautionary measure, they would have called the police anyway. Still, no one did.

They performed the CAT scan, and I was finally taken to a regular room. I was in a lot of pain and kept moaning. The morphine was not taking the edge off the pain. The nurse came in and told me that if I didn't stop the moaning, they were going to kick me out of the hospital. That would have been interesting. What were they going to do? Roll my bed into the parking lot and leave me there, or roll it to a bus stop and have me take a bus home? I did not have a home anymore, anyway. I could not help the moaning; I was in pain, serious pain. I did not know what pain was until then.

I was in and out of consciousness, and when I was awake, I expected the police to be there to hear my story. No one came, and it seemed that I would not be able to make anyone believe me. I know the staff at the hospital must have wondered about me. I did not smell like roses, and my hair was an oil slick pasted to my scalp. In other words, I appeared to be a hobo. Perhaps that was why they did not take my story seriously. Many homeless people have schizophrenia or other mental disorders, and I looked like a street beggar.

The next day, my sister, Michelle, and my brother, Alex, arrived. I will never forget my brother's first words when he saw me: "Holy shit, were you put in a blender and spit out?" he remarked.

The look on their faces said it all. I didn't need a mirror. Oh yes, I must have been a miserable sight. My sister told me that I looked like a raccoon and asked me what had happened to my eyes? I was glad they were there and I was no longer alone. I was still scared and felt exposed and vulnerable. I was supposed to be dead and I wasn't. When the goons found out, I was sure they would try to remedy that. My sister talked to Gene Rosen, and together they informed the hospital personnel that they should not give out any information relating to me to anyone who might inquire. The hospital promised to abide by our wishes. They did not keep their promise.

The first couple of days, I wasn't able to do anything except to deal with the pain. After a couple of days, I started calling to cancel my credit cards. I was shocked by the unprecedented shopping spree they had enjoyed. They had managed to charge over a hundred and sixty thousand dollars. I tried to explain the circumstances to the credit card companies, which proved to be extremely difficult and in some cases nearly impossible. No one seemed to believe what I was saying. I called Freddy, the deli manager to change the locks at the deli to stop them from carting anything else out. I was trying to save anything I possibly could, since most everything was gone. Freddy was able to obey my order and came by the hospital to tell me that everything was there except my computer. At least they did not have a chance to clean out the deli completely.

I called the bank and was pleasantly surprised that there was still a balance of forty thousand dollars in one of my accounts. Apparently this amount was still in the account because of my signature. I could not understand how the bank had questioned a signature on a forty-thousand-dollar check but passed checks for five hundred thousand and seven hundred thousand dollars without any reluctance whatsoever. I blocked the account but didn't try to explain what had happened to me. At this point, they would not believe it, anyway. I knew that blocking access to whatever was left of my assets would alert my abductors to the fact that I was still alive, if they hadn't already figured that out. I called the brokerage and mutual fund accounts. It was too late. They had all been cleaned out, even my IRAs.

I was amazed at how people will take advantage of you when you need their help the most or when they see you are down and vulnerable. Freddy saw me in the hospital, but he did not have the locks changed at the deli. He also went shopping to the tune of a thousand dollars for personal items using the deli credit card. What a great guy. Thanks a lot. I was astonished that even he would stoop to such a low level, but then again, at that point, nothing should have surprised me.

When I became more coherent, I started to panic. My sister did not help the situation, either. Her intuition told her she needed to get me out of that hospital as soon as possible. A positive characteristic of my sister was that she took action without procrastinating. Her reasoning was simple: If I were released from the hospital, where would I go? I had no home or relatives and was not in any condition to travel to Colombia. Everything that I had a month ago, including a life, was gone. But it went further than that. She had an uneasy feeling about the whole situation. Her intuition proved to be right. My brother was jittery and paced the hospital room with his "be good" stick (a small Billie club). We were all on a razor's edge and expected those goons to come flying through the door with guns blazing at any moment.

One of the ideas we tossed around was hiring a private detective to stay with us while I was at the hospital. We called Gene Rosen, and he recommended Ed Du Bois. We called Du Bois, and I wonder what he thought when we told him my story. Nonetheless he came to the hospital, and after seeing me, he started believing me. He told us what it would cost to have someone stand guard in front of the door around the clock. The cost was so prohibitive that we discarded the idea almost immediately. Ed suggested that we get out of town. It was not safe staying in Miami. Ed would play a very important role throughout the coming ordeal.

While we were discussing the alternatives, Michele asked for my clothing and personal possessions from the hospital staff. They brought her my boots and a pair of ripped underwear. That was all that I had left. By the looks of it, I would have to walk out of the hospital naked, with just a pair of boots on.

My sister decided that she would airlift me to a New York hospital near where she lived so she could keep an eye on me. When the doctor came to check on me, she told him what she had decided.

He objected and told her that I was in no condition to go anywhere, that he would not go along with it or sign the release. My sister, true to her nature, told him flat out that she did not care what he thought and that she was taking me on Friday to New York whether he liked it or not, and to make sure I was prepared to go. The doctor, most assuredly, had never had anyone speak to him so bluntly. He turned to me and said that I had been in a bad car accident and needed to take it slow. I told him that I was not in any car accident and that it had been attempted murder. I explained that I had been kidnapped and to please call the police.

My brother and sister were standing by me as the doctor's facial expression contorted. He was shocked and could not believe

241

what he had just heard. What happened next will always be etched in my mind. The only way to describe it was unreal. He just smiled a weird smile and left the room. We all knew we were screwed and that no one was going to help us. It was definitely time to evacuate. I guess the doctor thought the drugs were good, huh.

The next day, my sister made arrangements with a local air ambulance company to transport me to New York. We were set to leave paradise and all its glorious memories at eight the following morning.

Friday morning arrived, and I was looking forward to getting away from the place that had caused me so much pain the previous month. That morning, I overheard two doctors speaking just outside my room. They commented on how strange the entire situation appeared to them. I had arrived at the hospital as a John Doe, with no papers or any clue as to my identity. I wondered why, if they found it so strange, they did not bother to call the police?

The doctor finally came in and removed the entanglement of tubes that crisscrossed my body. To me, it all seemed surreal, and I was well aware that the second chapter of this story was about to begin. My sister was good at making arrangements and obtained the services of a nurse to accompany us to New York.

I was put on a board and then transferred to a gurney and finally placed into the ambulance. When we arrived at the airport, my gurney was loaded into the plane. I said goodbye to my brother, who would not be accompanying us, instead returning to his home in Tampa. My sister boarded, and the plane door was shut. As we taxied onto the runway, tears flowed from my eyes. Tears of sadness for what I had endured the previous month, and tears of joy for having both survived and for finally going somewhere I could feel more secure, far away from those who wanted to kill me.

At approximately ten that morning, Lugo, his sidekick, Delgado, and one of their henchmen arrived at the hospital. They'd been calling frantically, trying to find me. The first and most obvious calls were to the morgues, where they expected to find me. The calls left them in shock; I was not at any of them. That meant only one thing that I had survived. They called all the area hospitals and finally tracked me down at Jackson Memorial Hospital, who was kind enough to give them my room number. Remember how they had promised to reveal nothing?

They went to the hospital to finish the job. They armed themselves with pistols with silencers, determined to kill anyone who was with me and who might get in their way. Their plan was to suffocate me with my pillow. They could not leave any loose ends. When they entered my room, they couldn't understand. Perhaps I'd been taken for an exam. Lugo asked a nurse where his friend was. He was informed that he had left earlier that morning. Lugo and friends were shocked. Their prey had escaped.

Chapter 21 — The Long Road Back

"REVENGE IS THE ACT OF COMPASSION, VENGEANCE IS AN
ACT OF JUSTICE."
- *SAMUEL JOHNSON* -

We landed in New York City, and an ambulance was waiting
for us. The cold winter air, which at another time may have bothered
me, felt great. The ambulance attendees that took me from the plane
and carried me to the ambulance nearly dropped me. Good thing I
was strapped in or I would have kissed the pavement. But I took it in
stride and actually chuckled. There was nothing like being free, and
all those events that put me in that position seemed far away, for that
instant, anyway.

We went to the Staten Island Community Hospital near where
my sister lived. Even though I knew that Lugo and company would
be desperately looking for me, I felt that for now, at least, I could
have a little peace so I could try to begin to mend. I felt a great
urgency to inventory what I had left, if anything. With the help of
Gene Rosen, who took care of most of the inquiries that needed to be
made, all my accounts were researched. There was not much left, but
whatever there was I needed to protect and put away somewhere
safe. I didn't want to think about it, but knew I had to deal with the
issue of the criminals that were still running around loose. They were
not going to take the risk of having me go to the authorities. But

gathering from the reactions I had received thus far, it was likely to be difficult to convince the police of my story. This was extremely frustrating after what I had been through. I decided to put that aside now and concentrate on regaining my strength, both physical and mental, so that I would able to confront the challenges that lay ahead.

My sister was always by my side when she did not have to work. My parents came to see me and brought me shaving cream and a razor, so I was able to shave for the first time in five weeks. I almost felt normal, if that was possible. I did not tell them what had really happened and just told them I was in a car accident. I was not ready to talk to them about my experience, and my parents would not understand. I thought it would be best that I tell them in different circumstances, when the time was right. When I did finally tell them, they didn't understand it, anyway. But then again, I don't think I understood it, either.

There was a circumstance that occurred at the hospital that really rattled me. The doctor came in while my sister was visiting and asked me about my condition. I asked him what condition he was referring to. He said the hospital in Miami had reported that I was HIV positive and that I was a drug addict who injected drugs intravenously. My sister and I told him that this was impossible and that there must have been a mistake.

So I had a test for HIV performed. I was in shock. A million things went through my mind. Had those criminals injected me with something while I was unconscious? Did the hospital in Miami give me tainted blood when they gave me the transfusion? The part about the drugs I understood, because I was certain I had been drugged the night that the accident was staged. It made sense why no one at the hospital had taken my story seriously or called the police. They probably thought they were doing me a favor. I had to live with that uncertainty for almost five weeks until the results came back. There was no reprieve or peace to be found anywhere, just one thing after another. When the results finally came back, they were negative, a simple mistake. I wondered when the test to see how much I could withstand would finally end. I unfortunately found out it was going to be much longer than I expected.

The doctors in New York were a little more curious and questioned the injuries I had sustained. The doctor told my sister that he was confused because the injuries I had were not consistent with a car accident, based on his experience and the specific type of accident I had. He smelled that something was amiss and kept asking my sister questions. She told him to keep it to himself and leave it at that. If the attending Miami doctors had been a little bit curious as this doctor was, perhaps they would have called the police and the thugs could have been quickly apprehended.

The joy of being alive and free was quickly lost. I felt melancholy because not only had I lost my home and personal belongings, I had lost my identity as well. It seemed that the old me had died that night of the staged accident, the person who now lay on that hospital bed was someone else. The emotional toll was finally settling in, and the realization of what I had been through flooded my thoughts. I had always been an individual who thrived on challenges. Now I wondered whether I had the will to face what lay ahead. I was emotionally and physically exhausted but could not take the luxury of procrastinating. The thugs were still out there looking for me and were not going to stop until they finished what they had started.

I just wanted to sit in a hot shower for ten hours and let all my worries go down the drain. It had now been five weeks since I had been able to indulge in that creature comfort and I knew that it would do a lot for me physically and emotionally. Of course I was overjoyed to be alive and to be able to thwart their sinister plans. I was given a second chance, and I could not take that for granted. But I just wanted it to be over, and the end did not seem anywhere near.

As I lay there in the hospital bed, I could not help but wonder what my life would be once I left the hospital. I had no life to go back to. Perhaps a new start was for the best, and it was God's gift to me.

The order of things was simple. I needed, for both myself and for the safety of others, to have the criminals who had hurt me locked up. From what they had told me in the warehouse, I may not have been the first, and I was certain that I would not be the last. This criminal enterprise would certainly be encouraged by how easily they were able to take my assets without any opposition. They had told me they felt they could run their kidnapping and extortion business with impunity and no one would be able to stop them or even care. They felt invincible. I knew that I had actually been very lucky and that their next victim might not be so blessed, since they had doubtless learned from their mistakes and would not likely repeat them.

The hospital dietitian came in to visit me and wanted to know why I was so gaunt and underweight. If she had known about my nutrition the previous month, she probably would have marveled that I still had some meat on my bones. At times it was frustrating because no one believed or understood what I had just gone through. But I had to learn to live with that and stop expecting anyone to understand the trials and tribulations I had just experienced. It was not possible, and words could not paint an adequate picture of what it had been like.

On December 24, 1994, Christmas Eve, the doctor came in and told me that if I could manage to walk on crutches, I could go home that very same day. He proceeded to take out the fifty-four staples closing my abdomen from the six-hour operation. I thought I had left the torture behind in that warehouse in Miami; I guess I was wrong. That process, combined with pulling the tube from my penis, was more torture. It made me wonder if the pain and torture was ever going to stop, or had I signed up for a lifetime membership without knowing? I hadn't been out of a bed for ten days and did not know if I could walk or not. The orderly came to take me to physical therapy. Getting out of bed for the first time was another dreadfully painful experience. I almost fell getting out of bed, but the orderly caught me. I was determined to leave the hospital that night and was dammed if anything was going to stop me. With grit and determination, I was able to walk enough steps with crutches to satisfy the doctor, and he ordered my release.

The first problem was clothing. I had arrived at the hospital basically naked. My sister was able to borrow some clothing that fit me, but no shoes. At around six o'clock a wheelchair was brought in to take me to the waiting car downstairs.

This was my first time out in the open in almost six weeks, except for the brief time I traveled from the hospital in Miami to New York, which I hardly remembered. As the doors opened and the cool evening air caressed my face tears streamed from my eyes. I had thought for so long that I would never experience that precious moment. That made me realize how valuable one's freedom is and how fortunate and blessed I was to receive another chance. I was able to feel like a human being again and determine my own destiny, the freedom of mind, body and soul. As I rode in the car and marveled at the city lights, it seemed as though I had just woken up from a bad nightmare. In that short ride, I found new fortitude, and I promised myself that I would continue fighting and would bring those criminals to justice.

Fifteen minutes later, I arrived at my sister's house. I asked my brother-in-law to help me into the shower. I must have sat in that shower for two hours and could never recall water feeling so good. After the shower, I almost felt human again. The simple pleasures and privileges we have in life that we take for granted, I thought.

My sister bent over backwards to take care of me, offering me food every fifteen minutes, but my appetite was puny. She wheeled me outside to get some sun because she said that my skin color was a sickly yellow. The first few nights were difficult, and I could not sleep much. When I did, I had the recurring nightmare of being chained in the warehouse, and I woke up sweating and yanking my arm, expecting resistance from the chains.

Two days later, my wife and children, whom I never thought I would see again, arrived. The reunion was tearful and emotional, and my children were too young to realize what was going on. Little by little, I told my wife what had happened in the warehouse. The biggest shock to her was that Delgado was involved. I would have reacted the same way.

Almost immediately, we started discussing what we should do. I did not want to stay in New York and perhaps put my sister and her family in harm's way. These madmen were still out there, and I was sure they were looking for me, leaving no rock unturned in the process. I had become paranoid, actually very paranoid, and many times I sat by the window and just looked out. I looked for any suspicious movement or cars that parked too long in front of the house.

On December 31, I asked Gene to call Metro-Dade police to report the crime. They told him that I had to come to Miami if I wanted to report it. I told Gene that was not possible for a couple of reasons: Firstly, I still could not walk properly, and I was not going there hobbling on crutches. Secondly, those criminals were still on the loose, and I didn't know what most of them looked like. I was not going to take the chance of running into one of them or being spotted by them. I knew the probabilities were small since Miami was such a large and populous city. But, even as small as they were, it was too large a risk, and I did not feel like rolling the dice. I also needed to be mentally prepared for the task, and I wasn't. So the idea was discarded for the moment to come up with a better plan and for me to be in better condition.

Gene helped me in other areas, also. We needed to resolve the credit cards and the deli issue, and my wife's car was still missing.

Gene gave me ideas, and I discussed them with my wife and sister. One of the ideas involved negotiating with the perpetrators for the return of the money, something that, I thought, was fraught with risk. I didn't want any contact with these individuals and thought that idea might backfire and put more people in danger.

The New Year came and went, and I still had no plans as to what to do. We did decide that as soon as I was fit to travel, I would leave the country and go to Colombia to recuperate away from all possible dangers.

I finally came to a decision that seemed to be my only course of action to get these individuals off the street. Through the years, many have criticized me and questioned it. But it is always easier for others looking at it from a different perspective to arrive at a different decision. Even looking at things from hindsight, I might see things differently. I did not have that luxury and did what I thought was best and safest at that juncture. Even after, it was proven that this did not persuade the authorities to believe me, and the criticism continued. It's easy to judge and give opinions based on faulty or incomplete information. It was another thing to be in my shoes.

I decided to try to negotiate with them through an independent third party. Why? First, anyone outside my family who was told my story scoffed at the idea that I had been kidnapped and believed it was a figment of my imagination for some unknown reason that I chose to create. I had no evidence to back up my story. I could not get the police or anyone else to go to the house and see that they were living there or to go where this individual lived to find items belonging to me. From my days in the warehouse, I knew they were not exceptionally bright. So I knew that they would probably be stupid enough to negotiate and, in the process, confess their crimes. In the worst-case scenario, we could get compromising evidence to convince the police to initiate an investigation.

In addition, I also felt that if the story was out in the open, then they might slow down their efforts to find me or another victim to perpetrate another similar crime. They would have to feel extremely uncomfortable to know someone was looking into my story. I was going to the police. There was no doubt about that. It was just matter of waiting until I had enough evidence so there could be no doubt about what had occurred. The least I could hope for was to keep them on the defensive and off balance. Not for a moment did I contemplate that those thugs would return my assets, but that was not my ultimate objective, either.

Gene recommended a well-known group that handled kidnapping negotiations. When I called, they informed me that they did not handle situations such as mine and recommended I call the FBI. They probably would have laughed at me, so why should I have done it? So I called Ed Du Bois, who had visited me in the hospital. I filled him in on what I wanted to do and asked him whether he would be interested in helping me. He said he was and asked me to send him certain information in writing, including the names of the individuals involved and any other information I felt was pertinent. I did just that, and our working relationship started in January of 1995.

I had much of the information Ed wanted already written. Gene had suggested that I write down everything that happened in the warehouse in the event I should need it later on. He also thought it would be therapeutically beneficial to get it out of my system. I followed his advice and wrote almost two hundred pages the first week of January 1995, most of which is the basis for this book. I continued to add to it as the events warranted and new information came to light.

In the meantime, my ability to move around was improving and the pain subsiding. I didn't have a single document that identified me, since they had taken both my wallet and all the documents in the house. In a moment of lunacy, I decided to go to Tampa and visit my brother and get a duplicate driver's license. One day during the third week of January, I hobbled on my crutches onto a plane, and off to Florida I went. There was another objective to my trip: to convince my brother that he needed to keep a low profile and take maximum precautions, because he was the most likely one they would be looking for in order to find me. This turned out to be true. Much later, I learned that my paranoia was well placed and that Lugo and his henchmen had driven to Tampa to look for him. Fortunately for both of us, they had not found him.

I landed mid-morning in Tampa, and my brother was there to greet me. He took me to the licensing office and back to the airport with my new driver's license. We didn't even go to lunch, and the time I spent there was less than two hours. For some unknown reason, I felt that document gave me my identity again. It's silly, but those were strange times. I warned my brother again to be on the lookout for any individuals who were acting strangely or appeared to be following him.

When I returned, my sister and wife insisted that I accompany them on errands. They wanted me to get fresh air and start living a somewhat normal life again. Up to that point, I had rarely ventured out. I agreed and was paranoid, constantly looking around for any signs of them. I felt that they would be waiting for me around every corner. I had become a prisoner within the confines of my sister's house and realized that I needed to break free from those thoughts that chained me.

Ed Du Bois, in the meantime, was diligently performing his research. During that process, he came up with an interesting fact. John Mese, a certified public accountant, had notarized all the papers. It just so happened that Ed had known Mr. Mese for twenty-five years. Mese was a former bodybuilder who owned Sun Gym, a gym for steroid-crazed bodybuilders. He had access to someone who could give more information and possible contact to the other criminals.

The plot thickened. I remember that it was at Sun Gym that Delgado had initially connected with Lugo. In my mind, some things began to come together.

Initially, Mese denied knowing both Delgado and Lugo and told Ed that he didn't know what he was talking about. Ed also reached Delgado through his beeper, the number that I happened to remember, and told him they needed to get together to straighten things out. Delgado, the genius he was, told Ed he needed to get in touch with Lugo and would get back to him, something that he did not do.

The game of cat and mouse had begun. It was Delgado trying to avoid Ed and Ed trying to pin Delgado down. Ed made several trips to Delgado's house, but Jorge would not come out to talk to him. Maybe Delgado thought naively that if he ignored Ed, the problem would go away. Wrong. So Ed decided to pressure Mese instead and make him pass on the word to the others and hopefully arrange a meeting.

Gene was busy negotiating the sale of the deli and preparing the quitclaim title action to regain ownership of the house. He also hired an individual to go to the house and repossess my wife's car. He later told Gene that upon arriving at the house, he was met by several individuals who claimed they lived there. They told him that the car had been there but now was gone and they didn't know where. It magically disappeared right before them. That was their story. He also mentioned that the characters who were there looked dangerous and not to be messed with. He left rather quickly.

It was crushing to know for certain that other people were living in my house, even though I had suspected it. It disturbed my wife to imagine these thugs sleeping in our bed and going through our children's personal possessions. But I insisted that we had to stop thinking about those things. That would only cloud our judgment, and we needed clarity to act swiftly and decisively. I was pleased that we were putting pressure on them from all directions. At the same time, I was wary, because when you corner a rabid animal, its instinct is to lash out violently, and these individuals were worse than that.

The frying pan was getting hot, and I was concerned about my sister's family's safety. I applied for a new passport through the mail, and when it arrived, our plans were to leave the country for a while.

There was nothing I could contribute by being there.

Because all of these things happened six years prior to 9/11, obtaining my fresh identification papers was a simpler process than it is now, as I finish writing these words in 2012.

The nightmares continued, and I often woke up sweating and shaking my left arm to release myself from the chains that were attached to the railing. At other times, in my dreams, I relived getting burned and tortured. My sleep, instead of being a refuge of peace, had become a place where I would re-experience hell.

On February 10, 1995, just a couple of days after my new passport arrived. We left the country and went to Colombia to stay with my wife's family. I found it ironic that about five years earlier, I had fled that country as a result of a kidnapping, and now I was fleeing there as a result of another. There was not much for me to do. Ed and Gene were handling most of what could be done. I hoped that by being somewhere far away from the events, I could heal faster both physically and mentally. I also wanted to put my brother, sister, and parents out of harm's way. I was not leaving defeated, for I had just begun to fight, and it was only the first round.

Chapter 22 — Refuge in Colombia

"IN NATURAL HEALING, THE DOCTOR IS PEACE AND THE
NURSE IS LOVE."

- UNKNOWN -

When I arrived in Colombia, I felt a strong sense of relief. I was in a country that was in turmoil and had many of its own problems, but I felt safe since I was far away from the reach of those who had tried and still were trying to take my life. While I was there, life became mundane. I became reclusive and hardly ever wandered outside the walls of the apartment where I was residing. I shut the outside world off completely and hardly spoke to anyone, especially about what I had been through. It was a period of introspection and evaluating my life and what had led me to those events and the miracle of my survival. I did not want pity from others, and I knew that most could not understand what I had been through. Words seemed shallow and could never describe what I had felt. So I turned within.

Most days, I sat in a chair by the window and marveled at the beauty of nature. I did not know or want to deal with what would happen with my life. That could wait. I knew whatever lay ahead would unfold as it was supposed to and I need not be concerned in trying to change the course of my destiny. As I sat by the window, I always had a telephone beside me and waited anxiously for a call from either Gene or Ed. I knew that they were trying to do everything that was possible to restore order in my life and bring the criminals to justice. I had faith in them and knew that the situation was in good hands. There was nothing I could do.

At the same time, my sister was going through her own tribulations in fighting her cancer. I tried to speak to her every day to find out how she felt and what her doctors had told her. That, to me, became more important than what I had gone through. I felt that it was important not to succumb to feeling self-pity and needed to be there for her in the limited way I could. The daytime and being awake became my friend and the nighttime and sleep my enemy. In the first few months, I had nightmares of still being in the warehouse. With time, they faded, but in the beginning it was another demon I had to fight.

Slowly but surely, time healed my physical wounds. The scars started to fade, although they still exist and remind me of my ordeal. Though the physical scars fade, the invisible ones inside of you persist for a lifetime. While I was in Colombia, I chose to let them heal, let them fade and move on. This was a period when I got to spend a lot of time with my children. When they got home from school, I would either play computer games with my son or invent some other game. The nights were also spent with them, helping them do their homework. This permitted me not only to spend quality time with them but gave me an important escape from thinking about my troubles. It was a good time, even amidst all the turmoil that surrounded me, a refuge from all the madness. I felt very fortunate to have survived and to be able to savor those moments.

Unfortunately, I was in the eye of the hurricane, and turbulent times would soon appear again.

Chapter 23 — The Negotiations

"LET US NEVER NEGOTIATE OUT OF FEAR, BUT LET US NEVER
FEAR TO NEGOTIATE."
- JOHN FITZGERALD KENNEDY -

While I was recuperating in Colombia, Ed continued his pressure on Mese in order to get a meeting with Lugo and Delgado. Gene was able to negotiate the sale of the deli to the Schlotzsky's area developer for one third of what I had invested in it. To me, it was a blessing to receive anything at all, and it relieved me of the burden of the rent and other expenses, since even contemplating re-opening it was out of the question. It was the best possible and only solution to that dilemma.

While in Colombia, I spoke on an almost daily basis with Gene and Ed, and they kept me informed of any new developments. I sat by the phone and waited as things began to come together.

I was amazed that "Criminal Inc." thought they could continue to act with impunity even though they knew I was alive. I canceled nearly all of my credit cards, keeping only two in case of emergencies. For these two credit cards, I changed the mailing address to Gene's office. It didn't take very long for them to call the credit card company and change the address to one of their PO boxes, which gave me more proof of their criminal ventures. But they felt that I was no threat or they were too overconfident to think otherwise. Finally, I had to cancel the cards, because if I changed the address one more time, they would probably change it back again.

Ed also made several trips to the house. He informed me that the furniture all appeared to be there but that he did not see any people. He spoke to a few neighbors, and they confirmed that, in fact, someone was living there. From the descriptions they gave him, it sounded as though Lugo and Delgado were there often. They told the neighbors they had bought the house so they could throw corporate parties. It sounded as if their future victims would be chained there and it was going to be used for their criminal enterprise. They described them as nice and courteous. What would they think if they had known who these new neighbors actually were?

I started receiving the credit card statements and saw they had gone totally berserk. They had purchased everything imaginable and not one or two but large quantities of the same item. The items they bought included electronics, clothes, baby clothes (for Delgado's daughter), kitchen items, videos, music, china, personalized stationary and thousands of condoms and pornographic movies. Some things they bought from the catalogs my wife received at home. It was all mail-order merchandise, and they showed no fear of getting caught. I guess I may have earned a new reputation as the world's largest consumer of pornographic movies and condoms, since everything had been bought under my name. I wondered what the credit card companies or these vendors thought. As I said, these criminals were sick in many ways, and their selection of items purchased was just another indication.

Ed arranged to meet with Mese during the first week of

February at the latter's office in their Miami Shores neighborhood. He took the transfer documents, along with the history I had written of my ordeal, including the identification of Lugo as the perpetrator, and a description of my imprisonment and torture.

Mese greeted Ed heartily and led him into his office, where he pointed at a chair in front of his cluttered desk, piled high with files and papers. Upon seeing Mese, Ed realized it must have been a while since the two men had socialized. Du Bois noticed that Mese had lost much of the muscle he'd once carried as a long-time weightlifter and body builder. His formerly impressive build had been replaced by an equally impressive girth. The man was clearly not a patron of his own Sun Gym property, and these days he just promoted bodybuilding shows but certainly didn't participate.

"John," Ed began the conversation, and he stared earnestly at Mese, "I have something I want you to take a look at because it concerns you and my client, Marc Schiller." He handed Mese the initial pages of my history, withholding the last page that identified Lugo.

"The name of your client doesn't ring a bell," Mese said as he began reading. When he finished, he observed, "It sounds like this guy has had a rough time."

Ed retrieved my memo. "Yeah, he has. Do you know a Dan Lugo or Jorge Delgado?"

Mese stared into the middle distance for a few seconds before responding, "I know Lugo from my gym. He works there. I also did some work for both him and Delgado on an IRS matter. But how do I fit into all this?"

Ed shuffled through his papers and handed Mese two additional documents. "These include your name and notary stamp, and I'd like to know what you know about them."

"My name?" Mese responded, surprised.

"Yes, your name, and," Ed tapped the bottom of the page Mese held in his hand, "your wife's name is there as a witness."

Mese scanned the papers and handed them back to Ed. "Ed, I handle stuff like this every day. I don't remember all the details, but I think Lugo brought a Latin man in here, and," Mese nodded at the documents, "that's what this is all about."

Ed leaned across the desk and pointed at the date of November 23 on the quitclaim deed for my house. "This was notarized on November twenty-third."

Mese nodded his assent.

"The problem here, John, is that Schiller's wife was out of the country and had been for five days." He showed Mese my wife's passport with the stamped date of November 18, indicating when she had left the country, and then held his finger on the return date in late January. "What the hell is that all about?"

Mese shook his head in bewilderment.

"I want to talk to Lugo. Can you arrange that?"

"Sure. I'll take care of it and call you with the details."

"Soon, okay?"

"Sure," Mese answered confidently. "We'll get this straightened out when we meet with Dan."

Ed tried to contact Delgado, even going to his house to confront him, but Delgado avoided every attempt the private investigator made to connect. On most occasions, Ed knew Delgado was hiding in his house when he showed up and knocked on the door for several minutes. This told Ed that this man had something to hide. And that he was a coward.

Ed heard from Mese a few days after their initial meeting and agreed to meet with Lugo and Delgado on Monday, February 13, in Mese's Miami Shores office. The morning of the meeting, Du Bois got together with his lawyer and best friend, Ed O'Donnell, to let him know about the case and who he would be meeting with later that morning. Given what I told him about Lugo and the gang, the private investigator decided that he should take these precautions. He also enlisted the help of another friend who would accompany him to the meeting, Ed Seibert. Seibert had a long and distinguished career in law enforcement as a homicide cop in Washington, DC, and in the security field, with stints as an agent for the Bureau of Alcohol, Tobacco, and Firearms (ATF) and as a ballistics and weapons instructor for various clients in Central America. He was a man Ed knew would have his back if the need arose. To be doubly safe, Ed positioned two men outside and across the street from Mese's office, ready to provide reinforcements.

As Ed and Seibert drove to the meeting, Seibert reviewed various documents to brief himself on the purpose of the meeting and on the background of the characters he would be dealing with. "You know," Seibert said after reading through the file, "no one ever made a ransom demand."

Ed nodded.

"That tells me they never intended to let this guy live. He was dead the minute they grabbed him."

"That's what I think," Ed agreed. "These are some really bad guys."

"Dangerous guys," Seibert added, and was happy he had decided to conceal two handguns, one at the small of his back and another strapped to his ankle.

Mese met Ed and Seibert in the reception area and offered them coffee or water, which both visitors turned down. He asked them to have a seat, explaining that Lugo and Delgado were running a few minutes late. As Mese turned to leave, Ed stopped him and handed him a photo of me, asking, "Was this the person you notarized the documents for?"

Mese took a moment to study the photo, and then shook his head. "Can't be sure." He laughed as he handed the photo back to Ed. "All Latins look alike to me."

Two hours later, Mese reappeared in the reception area. "Come on back." As he led the private investigators down the hallway, he told them Lugo couldn't make it but Jorge Delgado could provide them with all the information they needed. This was typical of Lugo; he wanted Delgado left holding the bag. Great friend he was.

Entering the office, Ed was surprised by the unassuming appearance of the person sitting behind the small, gunmetal gray steel desk. Thin to the point of looking emaciated, a dour expression on his face, the man gave off an impression of meekness as he avoided eye contact and shifted in his chair, clearly uncomfortable. Ed had prepared himself for a more imposing, even intimidating presence, and he was looking at a very unimposing figure. Mesa directed Ed and Seibert to two wooden chairs positioned in front of the desk, made the introductions, and left the room.

Ed began the conversation by explaining, "I represent Marc Schiller. I think you know something about his being kidnapped and having his assets stolen. It's all here in a memo," he said, lowering his chin toward the file folder in his lap.

"Can I see what information you have?" Delgado asked, and Ed handed him my memo, the house deed, and the change-of-beneficiary form for my life insurance. Delgado read the summary of my ordeal, glanced very briefly at the other pages, and handed everything back to Ed. "This is over a business deal," Delgado said flatly, dismissing the matter.

Ed stared at Delgado. "Really, nothing more than a business deal?" He shifted to the front edge of his chair, bringing his large body closer to the desk. "This is how you do business? Kidnap someone? Torture them? Steal their assets and then try to murder them? An unusual way to work, don't you think?"

Delgado blinked nervously and cleared his throat. "I'm not going to comment on that." He tried for assertive but only managed to whine.

Ed lifted off his chair and leaned on the desk, bringing his face close to Delgado's. "I've got this whole thing figured out, Jorge."

Delgado pulled back slightly and made another effort to come across as confident and self-assured. "What do you have figured out?"

"If you had killed Marc Schiller, as you intended to, this would have been the perfect crime. You had all his cash, all his property, his home, his cars, and then you had a two-million-dollar bonus. You had it all set up properly, and all the calls were diverted from his house to the warehouse. You had a script for him to play that he was going through a mid-life crisis, was wild and crazy, met a young girl, was liquidating, and was going to drive off into the sunset, in love. So, had he died, you would have been successful. Only one thing, asshole: He lived, and you and your friends left a paper trail that's easy to follow. I followed it right to your doorstep. I'm going to put you in jail."

Mese walked into the room at this point in the conversation. Delgado was glad for the interruption and suggested they all meet again the following morning. Mese offered his second office in Miami Lakes, a location more accommodating to Lugo and Delgado, the unspoken promise being that Lugo would attend this second meeting. The men agreed to reconvene there at nine o'clock the next morning.

Ed and Seibert arrived in the lobby of Mese's office at nine and studied the building directory. Du Bois noticed that JoMar Properties, a company in which Delgado and I were once partners, shared the address with Mese. The men walked into Mese's suite and approached a receptionist, who was surprised to see them. She explained that there were no appointments on the book and she wasn't expecting her boss until later that morning. Hiding their annoyance, Ed and Seibert told the young woman they would wait.

Two hours later, Mese walked in and expressed surprise at seeing Ed and Seibert. Ed was not happy and let Mese know it. "Look, John, you were the one who suggested we meet here, and we all agreed on nine this morning." He pointed at his watch. "We've been waiting two damn hours. Now, where the hell are Lugo and Delgado?"

"Let me call them," Mese said. Ed noticed the man was sweating profusely. "Just give me a few minutes," he said, and he hustled to the rear of the office.

He returned and assured Ed and Seibert that his clients were on their way. "Here is the information on the work I've done for these guys," Mese said, handing Ed a file folder. "Please read everything, take notes, and we can make copies of anything you want." Mese then led them into a small office, again promising that Lugo and Delgado were on their way.

Du Bois cleared space on the top of the desk, which was littered with the remnants of a busy working session, including an ashtray overflowing with cigarette butts, and two champagne glasses smelling of sweet liquor.

As any experienced detective would do, Seibert started to comb through the contents of the trash can, which was filled to the brim with crumpled pieces of paper. He straightened out a couple of pages on the desktop and then went quickly back for another handful. His eyes widened. "Jesus Christ, Ed," he said, and slid the pages in front of Du Bois. Then he got up and locked the door to the office.

Du Bois was looking at a treasure trove of information that included bank statements, deposit slips, and paychecks made out to Mese that tied the CPA to the laundering of my money. When arranged in order of dates and check numbers, the money trail guided Ed and Seibert from my accounts to Sun Fitness Consultants and Sun

Gym. Ed helped himself to another handful from the wastebasket and discovered canceled checks made out to Lillian Torres and JoMar Property Investments from both the Sun Fitness and Sun Gym accounts.

Seibert gestured toward the ashtray and glasses. "Someone was here trying to purge their files of everything that tied them to the case," he said, and he continued to study the papers he had taken from the trash. "What morons. They left the stuff right here for the taking."

"They must have thought the cleaning people would get rid of it," Ed said, going back to the wastebasket. "Thank God for this kind of stupidity or we might never get any of the bad guys off the streets."

Ed and Seibert looked at each other and, without a word, began stuffing the find in their pockets and briefcases. When they had what they knew would help them build their case, Seibert unlocked the office door.

Not much later, Mese came into the small office and said that Delgado had arrived but Lugo couldn't make it, what a surprise. He led Ed and Seibert to his office, where Delgado was leaning against a bookcase, trying to affect a casual, almost dismissive, pose. It didn't work. It was clear the man wasn't sitting down because he was too nervous to do so. As it was, he was shifting his feet and crossing and uncrossing his arms as Ed and Seibert settled into chairs facing a large wooden desk, where Mese sat.

Ed didn't waste any time. He began ticking off a list of accusations on his fingers and had gotten from kidnapping and torture to extortion when Delgado stopped him.

"We're not going to talk about this anymore," the man declared.

Ed glanced at Mese, who remained passive. "Then what the hell are we doing here?"

"We're going to give the money back."

Du Bois jumped on this, quickly realizing that what the man was offering was as good as a confession. "How much?"

"All of it, one million two hundred and sixty thousand. But we're going to need a contract signed by you and Schiller agreeing that this is connected to a business deal that went sour and that neither you nor your client will ever discuss this matter with anyone, and neither will you go to the police."

Du Bois grabbed a pen and a blank sheet of paper from the desk and wrote out the agreement right there. He wanted to get these men on record as soon as possible, knowing that whatever he and I signed would not be binding in a court of law. It read as follows:

"Jorge Delgado agrees to pay Marc Schiller the sum of $1,260,000 as return of proceeds from a sour business deal. Further, Schiller agrees that the incident allegedly occurring between November 15, 1994, and December 15, 1994, as described to his attorney and investigator, did not happen."

As they left the office, Seibert leavened the situation with a dose of reality, though the meeting had ended well for the investigators and me. "You know, if these guys get away with this, they'll kill whoever they get their hands on next."

"They aren't going to get away with anything," Du Bois said.

"We're going after them no matter what bullshit agreement they sign."

Ed contacted Gene and me, notifying us of what Delgado had proposed and recommending that we pursue this with the understanding that the goal remained the same—to put the bad guys away for a long, long time. While there was only a faint hope that anything would materialize in the way of getting my money repaid, the finalization of an agreement like the one proposed by Delgado would be as good as a confession that the kidnapping and extortion had indeed happened. It was something solid we could take to the police when, at present, there was little to conclusively substantiate the crime.

The day Ed met with Delgado, one of thugs had tried to go shopping with one of the credit cards that I had changed addresses on. So I wondered what their real motivation in meeting Ed was. It didn't appear that they were serious in trying to reach an agreement. Then again, Ed met with Delgado, whom I considered to have no say in what went on. His function was to take orders from Lugo and to be used by him.

After Ed met with Delgado, he received a call from someone who said he was an "informant." This individual, whose identity I still do not know, told Ed that he wanted to meet him. They met at a Miami Lakes diner, and the individual stressed that they wanted to get the matter resolved. Whether he represented the rest of the thugs or was trying to save his own skin was unclear. The meeting was short and the message clear. He gave Ed his beeper number and assured him that he would call Ed back whenever he needed him.

Who it was and his motivation remain a mystery.

Prior to drafting the agreement, I consulted with Gene, and he told me the agreement was not enforceable because a crime had been committed. I wanted a piece of paper or a confession that I could go to the police with. Did I actually believe that Lugo and his company were going to return the money? No. Lugo had shown his greed in the warehouse, and I did not believe for a minute that he would. There were two possibilities: One, they would sign the agreement and give me no money, which did not matter, for what interested me was their signature on the agreement. The other possibility was that this was just posturing for something else that they were planning, and they had no intention of signing it anyway.

Ed also consulted with his attorney, Ed O'Donnell, on the recent developments. O'Donnell was stunned that Delgado and his cronies had proposed an agreement that not only wasn't enforceable but was essentially evidence of a crime. "What idiots," he observed. "They'll never get a lawyer to work with them on this."

But Delgado and Lugo did find a lawyer through a stockbroker with whom they were trying to invest their stolen funds. Joel Greenberg was in his first year of practice and apparently eager for the business. Lugo suggested that the character for the Italian lira be inserted in place of the dollar sign, thereby effectively reducing the payment from $1.2 million to $1,200. This was passing for clever negotiating skills within the group, but Greenberg refused to go along with this approach. There were revisions requested by Lugo and crew, including one that read: "Marc Schiller agrees that neither nor any member of his family will ever threaten or attempt to blackmail Jorge Delgado, Danny Lugo, or John Mese." The irony dripped heavily from this wording. I agreed to these and other demands for changes that trickled in over the next several weeks.

At the end of February, Ed sent a fax to Mese noting that there had been no progress toward restitution. He accused Mese of taking all this time to destroy incriminating evidence and demanded that the matter be settled by the following day, February 23, at twelve-thirty in the afternoon, or he would seek state and federal prosecution, criminal and civil. Mese shot a response right back to Ed, denying any culpability and promising legal action if anyone alleged otherwise. Du Bois had had enough and sent a lengthy demand to Lugo, Delgado, and Mese via Joel Greenberg:

We have tried to negotiate in good faith for the return of the items that do not belong to you, and you have stalled and continued to perpetrate criminal acts during these negotiations. It would appear that you prefer to explain your acts to the authorities instead of settling this matter.

We will no longer stand by idly, and we will no longer negotiate with those who continue to act defiantly. These are non-negotiable terms and conditions for settling this matter:

Return all of the money taken from Mr. Schiller.

Return all personal documents taken from him.

Return payment for vehicles stolen from his house.

Repay all fraudulent credit card purchases made from his and his wife's cards.

Pay for all items stolen from Mr. Schiller's house and all damages to it.

This is non-negotiable. No more documents signed, no more negotiation. Unless these items are returned by Friday, March 24, 1995, before 11:59 AM, we will refer this matter to the federal and state authorities and seek all remedies, civil and criminal, permitted by law.

You decide to settle now or go to jail. This is our last intention of settling this matter. If we do not hear from you by this date and time, we will assume that you prefer to explain your actions to the authorities.

While this back-and-forth was going on throughout February and March, Gene successfully arranged for the quitclaim deed on the house. A court date was set to allow parties to contest the motion, but there was no contention, and ownership reverted back to me. A few days later, Ed and my realtor, Kathy Leal, went to the house to inventory the contents. They arrived to an empty shell. Their footsteps echoed against the tile floors as they went from one barren room to the next. The house had been stripped of everything. Every stick of furniture, all family pictures and documents, my clothing, my wife's clothing, and the children's clothing, all of the children's toys, and a ten-person Jacuzzi were gone. Six ceiling fans had been ripped from their mountings. Even the decorative light switch covers had been taken. I didn't have to worry about the items in the house anymore. There was nothing left. I was surprised that hadn't tried to take the walls, since that was the only thing left. Du Bois did find a single piece of paper blowing around the floor, propelled by the air conditioning, which hadn't been turned off. Written on it were the telephone numbers for the Palmetto and Miami Jackson Hospitals.

When he showed it to me, I knew right away that it was Delgado's handwriting. This confirmed that my brother and sister's decision to take me away from the hospital was a wise one and most likely saved our lives. They were not careful in leaving incriminating evidence behind. It seemed they thought they were invincible.

Ed kept in contact with the informant, who kept reassuring him that they wanted to resolve the issue and get everything settled. By the way they were acting it didn't appear to be true. It was more like a ploy to stall for time, and this guy, whoever he was, was part of it.

I was getting antsy and began to push Ed with the idea that we had enough evidence and should go to the police. Ed wanted to make sure that we didn't miss anything and had a concrete case to present.

I was beginning to think that the entire purpose of negotiating was to distract me while they made plans to leave the country or put some other nefarious plan into action. In fact, I thought they had already done so. But they couldn't be that smart, could they? Eventually, somehow, Ed got their attorney to draw up another agreement. I promptly returned it to him, as I had before, but told him I was tired of the games and that we were being toyed with. He quickly sent it back to their attorney, who supposedly was going to have them sign it. It never did happen. Not surprising.

On March 24, O'Donnell received a reply from Greenberg addressed to Ed. This was the month-old list of non-negotiable demands. This was the final date for compliance. Rather than address the points made by the private investigator, the reply from Greenberg went on the offensive and accused Ed of threatening his clients and thereby committing extortion. The young lawyer claimed that Ed was acting beyond his purview as a private investigator, and he demanded that his involvement in the case end immediately. In the meantime, the lawyer said, his clients were requesting additional changes to the original agreement, which he would provide soon.

Angrily, Ed responded immediately:

Dear Mr. Greenberg,

The purpose of these delays is finally becoming quite clear: Your clients need time to continue their criminal acts against Mr. Schiller, and fraudulent charges against his credit cards continue to mount.

A recent visit to his home found it to be cleaned out. His 1993 BMW 525 station wagon has been stolen. The household furnishings totaling over $75,000 have been stolen, and these include oriental rugs valued in excess of $15,000, a stereo system and television valued at $11,000, a computer and printer system valued at $4,000, and a Jacuzzi valued at $10,000. To get the Jacuzzi out of the pool area, they ripped out a section of the screen and aluminum support for the pool screen system.

Ed's letter went on to promise that unless my demands were satisfied, he would deliver complaints against Greenberg's clients to the authorities and that it would be "a RICO complaint so large that it may have to be delivered in a U-Haul truck."

The informant, as mysteriously as he had appeared, disappeared. There were no more return calls when Ed dialed his beeper. Delgado and Lugo's unidentified informant, just like a ghost, had vanished into thin air.

It was the first week of April, and our patience had run its course. I told Ed again that we were being played for fools and that they never had any intention of signing. They wanted more time. One of the reasons I thought they might be delaying was that they had spent a considerable amount of the money and simply did not have it available to return. The way they had been purchasing useless items in bulk, it would have made perfect sense. Perhaps, I surmised, they were planning their next criminal endeavor and were looking for their next victim, anyone they could clean out, which would allow them to return the full amount to me. It was all speculation, and perhaps Lugo and pals just simply did not want to return the money because, in his twisted way, he thought it was his now.

This case was getting very personal for Ed also. His wife and children reported seeing men parked near their house for days at a time when Ed was at work. The men appeared to be keeping a close watch on the comings and goings of the family and visitors. Ed also received a call from a contact with the phone company, letting him know that someone had been trying to access his phone records for information on calls he was making to South America.

Concern for the safety of his family increased when Du Bois discovered that Lugo and his band of cutthroats had spent more than $12,000 on sophisticated surveillance equipment in The Spy Shop, including technology that would allow phones to be tapped and conversations to be heard over distances. Ed called me, very distraught. He told me he was afraid for his family and his own safety. I could not blame him.

I told Ed that I had decided to give them a short period of time, and if we did not get a satisfactory signed agreement, I would go to the police. I really had no choice with or without a signed agreement—I had to go to the police. I did not want to live my life hiding or always looking behind to see if someone was coming. I knew that going to the police was going to be a big challenge, but we had evidence and Ed to back me up, right?

Ed's communications with the criminals had ended. No matter how many calls Ed made, it always yielded no response. Ed put in a call to Al Harper, a Miami-Dade Police captain and veteran homicide detective. The second week of April 1995, I boarded a plane to Miami. Ed was going to prearrange a meeting with the appropriate people, and I was going to stay one night in the airport hotel. The next day, we would go to the police, and in the afternoon I would catch my return flight to Columbia. Disbelief enfolded me as I sat on the plane. I was going back to the place that had so recently been the site of so much misery and pain. Bitter memories raced through my mind. I knew it was the right thing to do and prayed that everything would unfold as planned. I landed in Miami on a sunny afternoon in April, and all the memories came flooding back.

Chapter 24 — Houdini

"FOR WHAT WE CALL ILLUSIONS ARE OFTEN, IN TRUTH, A WIDER VISION OF PAST AND PRESENT REALITIES."

- GEORGE ELIOT -

I landed in the sunshine state, and as I disembarked the plane, my heart was beating so hard I thought it was going to jump out of my chest. I kept thinking, what if I ran into one of those lunatics? I did not know many of them and might run into one of them unknowingly. At least I was not walking on my crutches anymore and could limp a little faster now. When I arrived at customs, I know I caught their attention: A man coming from Colombia, looking terrified and sweating, I surely must have been carrying drugs or something of that nature.

I was scared, very scared, and both my body and face did not hide it. In no time, they pulled me over to the side. If they had not, I would have wondered about them not doing their jobs. I was taken to a room for interrogation. I was glad because I felt safer there. Naturally, they asked me where I was coming from, although I knew they were aware I had been in Colombia. So they peppered me with all the usual questions: why I was there, how long I would stay, and so on and so forth. I did not let them finish and told them the story from beginning to end and why I had come back, the short version, anyway. They showed genuine concern and had a guard wait with me by the door for Ed. I was truly impressed with them and forever thankful that they not only believed me but also protected me while I waited.

Ed was prompt and met me just outside of the customs area, and I left with him to the airport hotel. There he showed me several of the documents he had retrieved from Mese's wastepaper basket and others he had compiled through his research. I was very impressed and thought we had irrefutable evidence of the crime committed and at least enough for the police to launch an investigation. Ed left, and I hid in the hotel room until next morning; sleep was out of the question. I sat in a chair and waited. I felt like a prisoner again, unable to venture out. This was getting old, and I needed to put an end to it so I could start trying to put my life back together again. That was why I was there, I kept reassuring myself. I told myself that it would all be over in a few hours when the police organized their manhunt to apprehend those lunatic criminals. Once again, I was wrong.

The following morning, Ed picked me up promptly, and we drove to Metro-Dade police headquarters, which was less than a mile from where they had tried to kill me. The trip seemed surreal, and I had to pinch myself to make sure I wasn't dreaming. As I talked to Ed, I thanked him for the great job he had done and told him I felt confident everything would go well, considering the amount of evidence he had gathered. I really believed this would mark the end of this nightmare and I could turn the page and begin a new chapter in my life.

We arrived at police headquarters, and I was in good spirits and ready to tell my story. Ed had prearranged a meeting with someone he had contacted, whom he knew. We proceeded to the small office where Captain Porterfield was located. Upon arriving, we were instructed to sit in a small reception area until the captain could meet with us.

Captain Porterfield came out to greet us and showed us into his office. It was apparent that he and Ed knew each other as they exchanged some jokes and small talk. The captain asked me to tell my story. I was a little nervous and apprehensive at first but proceeded to tell him, in as much detail as I thought he needed, what had occurred in November and December of the previous year. The captain sat patiently listening to the story and waited for me to finish before making any comments. He had some questions that were superficial and did not ask for more detail.

Once I finished, Ed continued, and he spoke of his meetings with the various thugs, the informant, and showed him the various documents he had gathered. In fact, by now, Ed had a very thick folder that consisted of many documents. My first impression was that Captain Porterfield genuinely believed my story and was going to follow up on it and begin an investigation. What did concern me was that he did not ask many questions. He didn't ask for more details or clarification of anything. That seemed rather odd, but I did not pay too much attention to it. I sort of figured that would come later.

Captain Porterfield appeared concerned and explained that he had to present the case to his superiors. This also struck me as strange, but I figured that they had their protocol to follow. He asked us to return the following day, and, reluctantly, I agreed. This meant I had to stay another day in Miami, something I definitely did not want to do. Du Bois took me back to the hotel, and I sat there, wondering how it was all going and how it was going to end.

Since I had nothing to do for an entire day, Gene came by the hotel to pick me up. We returned to his office. It was a gamble going out, but I simply could not stand to sit in that hotel room, staring at the walls, and thinking about these problems. We discussed the problem I was still having with my wife's missing car. When we arrived at his office, he made several calls to find out the procedure for reporting it stolen, as there was no other choice. We finally resolved to have a Metro-Dade patrolman come to the office to take the report. The officer arrived shortly, and we completed the report. I told him the story about my kidnapping, although a very truncated version. His first remark was that it sounded as if it was out of some movie. He was visibly startled by the story and forgot the report in Gene's office, only to come back later to retrieve it. He did not doubt my story nor insinuate that I would make it up for some unknown reason. Gene took me back to the hotel, and again I sat and waited to see what Metro-Dade's course of action would be.

The next morning, Ed arrived, and we headed to our appointment with Captain Porterfield. This time, we did not have to wait. Instead, he was waiting for our arrival. I thought that this was a good sign and that they were eager to proceed with my case. He was curt and to the point. He informed us that he and his supervisor felt that my injuries were consistent with a car accident. What they were dealing with was a robbery, since my chain had been stolen.

Therefore, I should go to the robbery unit and report it. My mouth dropped open. Was this really happening? A robbery? I showed him my burns from the torture. Both Ed and I tried to argue with him and told him that they were making a mistake. He would have none of it. I asked him how and why I would make up such a story and in such vivid detail. He did not respond. I told him that I had a doctor who would testify that my injuries were in fact not consistent with an accident. When does a new car blow up because it hit a utility pole, I asked him? How about irrefutable documents that Ed had gathered? How about the fact that Ed used to be an FBI agent—did his word not mean anything?

Nothing. He did not respond. Go to robbery, case closed. I was a lunatic who, for some unknown reason, had decided to enlist a well-respected professional to come vouch for me while I told the police a crazy story that I had made up. This was insane. They could not be brushing it off so lightly. Never did I expect this. This was beyond comprehension. The police would not even look into my allegations. I was shocked and revolted to learn that the thugs were right all along when they told me that the police would not care and not believe me. I had reached a dead end and felt that these criminals would continue their mayhem and there was nothing I could do about it. I understood that they might not believe me, since they did not know me. But Ed was well known and respected. How could they not possibly believe him?

What would I do now? Where should I turn? I thought they might be a little skeptical since it was such an outlandish story. Nevertheless, I had Ed, who was respected and had compiled a mass of incriminating evidence. At least they could have done a preliminary investigation to verify if I was making it all up. Ed wanted to go to the robbery unit. I saw no reason for doing so. It was a waste of time. He insisted, and I finally agreed. We headed upstairs, where the robbery unit was located. This unit was located in a large room filled with cubicles. We were to see a Sergeant Deegan, whose cubicle was located at the far end of the room. As soon as we walked in, I noticed that all eyes were on us and many had smirks on their faces. Their entertainment in an otherwise boring, routine day had arrived. As we approached Sergeant Deegan's desk, she and her partner, Sergeant Myers, got up and gave me a standing ovation with huge smirks on their faces. I was humiliated again and could not believe what was happening. I kept thinking the criminals were right—no one cared.

As I went into Deegan's cubicle, Ed walked back to the waiting room, where he asked the receptionist if she knew anything about the strange demonstration that had greeted us. The young woman looked around carefully and, confirming they were alone, whispered, "Please don't let anyone know I told you, but we got a call from SID saying we should expect an Academy Award performance from your client."

Sergeant Deegan showed no interest in my story since she presumed it was all a lie. She thanked me for putting on such a good show and asked me if I thought I was Houdini because no one could have survived the story I had spun. Then they proceeded to tell me that I was most likely a drug dealer and that what had been done was done for revenge. They thought they had cornered me by asking me to take a polygraph. They were disappointed when I eagerly agreed. I told her that I would take one, two, as many as they wanted right there and then. They told me to come back in a week. I explained to them that I lived out of the country and was leaving that very same day.

They responded, "Oh, too bad."

Then she told me that I was lying and did not know what was going on. She continued by asking me if I was aware that it was a crime to file a false police report. I was angry but maintained my poise and asked them calmly to ignore me and just follow up on what Ed had compiled, and that way they could dispel my story. She laughed and refused, insisting I was making it all up. She said that I had a vivid imagination. Mockingly, she asked if I wanted to file a report for the chain that had been stolen. I replied no thanks. Ed tried to intercede and pleaded with them. They told him that I was lying and did not want to speak with him or waste resources on such a wild story.

When we left, I was both irate and distraught. In my own sarcastic way, I mumbled to no one in particular that going there had made me feel so much safer as a citizen, since the police department could, without error, determine what was true or not and choose to investigate accordingly.

I now faced a life of constantly hiding and looking over my shoulder. Ed had no words. What could the man have possibly said? He had not foreseen this outcome, either. It was inconceivable that such a crime could be perpetrated and there was no one to investigate or intercede. I kept thinking back to what they had told me in the warehouse, that they could do this over and over again and run it like any other business and no one would care. At the time, I had thought it was ludicrous. Now I realized that what they had said appeared to be true.

We returned to Ed's office, and he made several calls to friends in the FBI. He was trying to arrange a polygraph test that afternoon before I left. He was not able to arrange it and took me to the airport to catch my flight.

As I sat there in the airport, my depression deepened. Nothing had turned out as I hoped. So I reasoned I had to reorganize my life according to the cards I had been dealt. The road to going to the police to have the criminals arrested had led to a dead end. I refused to give up. I was not going to hide. There had to be a solution, and that solution would eventually appear. I determined to keep my spirits high and my faith solid. I was not alive to throw away my life in self-pity. I decided that somehow, I was going to keep fighting.

As I waited for the plane, Delgado came to mind. I wanted to have some fun. I had some time to burn. I remembered Delgado's beeper number, so why not call him? I went to a remote part of the airport and found a pay phone. I didn't know if he had changed his beeper number, but it was worth a shot. It was time to put some fear into this old friend, to make him feel a little of what I had been experiencing these past five months. I dialed Delgado's beeper and left the number of the pay phone I was calling from. I paced in front of the phone, entertaining a jumble of emotions. When the phone rang, I picked it up.

"Hello."

There was a split second of hesitation before the voice asked, "Did you call my beeper and leave this number?"

"This isn't over," I spat into the receiver.

"I don't know what you're talking about."

"This isn't going to work, Jorge. You can't hide. I've been to the police and gave them a file folder full of information that tells all about what you and your friends have done, and the evidence that proves you're involved."

"I still don't know what you're talking about," Delgado insisted calmly.

"I'm not going to stop until you and Lugo are rotting in jail. You are a piece of shit, and you deserve everything that's coming your way."

Almost in a whisper, Delgado said, "We have an agreement."

I laughed. "No, we don't. You're going to jail, and I'm going to put you there. Better keep an eye out for me. Make sure you're looking over your shoulder every minute of every day, because I might be right behind you."

I slammed the phone down and looked around to see if this animated conversation had attracted any attention, but the area was largely deserted.

I felt better, even though it hadn't achieved anything. I'm sure that he was not feeling the same way. His worst nightmare had just come back to haunt him. I imagined the first call he made was to his master, Lugo. Did my call achieve anything? No. But shaking him up and making him uncomfortable was worth it. Besides, the added benefit was that he called me at a local number and perhaps thought I was back in town, and they would concentrate their efforts looking for me in Florida rather than where I really was. Okay, it was a little psychological terrorism, but I had received my fair share from them.

I called Mese next, determined to put the fear of God in him as well. Mese hung up on me, but I didn't let it drop and sent a fax to him on April 25.

This problem will not be solved by hanging up on me. I will not rest until you and your cronies are in jail and until this problem is resolved one way or the other. You are neck deep in shit. You have to first understand that. You notarized and prepared documents that almost cost me my life.

The evidence against you and your pals is enormous. It's an open and shut case. You cannot win.

I followed up the next day with another fax to Mese:

How can you be so complacent about the mess you are in? I called you Friday, Monday, and Tuesday, and you still have not contacted your attorney. Are you stupid or naive enough to think this problem is going to go away?

You decide, return what is not yours now! Or face the music.

Tick, tick, tick...

I was only trying to give them some of their own medicine even though I knew it would lead nowhere. Making them uncomfortable and hopefully causing them to squirm had some entertainment value. I also wanted them to learn what it was like receiving instead of giving mental torture. It was the only tool I had left.

Detective Deegan was also busy on April 26. She went to my

home, which she found empty. She toured the neighborhood and questioned neighbors who confirmed that I had lived in the house but left suddenly for Colombia, or so they had been told. Indeed, some men had moved in, and when Deegan showed them a lineup of photos, all identified Lugo as one of those who was living in the house. Now convinced that something was up, Deegan filed a report on the matter and subpoenaed my financial records and information on the credit card purchases.

Ed called shortly after Deegan's visit to my home to get an update. The detective filled him in on what she had found and told him she was waiting for some financial information on me. Ed was nonplussed about this continuing attention being focused on me, but he kept his composure. He pointed out that everything he and I had told her was being confirmed by her own inquiry and asked why she was continuing to waste time investigating his client. Ed pointed out that the MDPD was spending thousands of hours going after the victims of a serial killer operating in the Tamiami Trail area of the city when all the victims had lengthy criminal histories for drugs, prostitution and larceny.

"What's your point?" Deegan asked.

"You're not investigating Lugo and company because you think their victim is a criminal. If Schiller is a criminal and the worst criminal that ever came to Miami, isn't it still illegal to kidnap him, take his assets, and try to murder him?"

"Of course."

"Then get out there and investigate Schiller's assailants before they strike again. Show your badge and ask a few questions before they hurt anyone else."

"I know how to do my job. I don't need you telling me how to work this case."

"Next time I'll bring you a body or a signed confession to hurry things along," Ed concluded.

The private investigator had no better luck with the FBI. He made contact with Art Wells at the Miami office.

After being fully briefed, Wells commented that my story seemed like a made-for-TV movie. He declined to move forward despite the mountain of evidence Ed had provided to him, the same mountain Ed had given to the MDPD police.

In the future, I would have to defend, over and over again, the reason for not going to the police earlier. This is the question people always ask, both then and now. Those who ask this obviously don't understand. What difference would it have made? Would have they believed me if I had done it ten days, a month, or two days after I was out of the warehouse? I don't think so. I went with an ex-FBI agent who had compiled irrefutable incriminating evidence, and what was the result? I reported it from a position of strength to no avail.

So those who still criticize me fail to comprehend the situation. It would have most likely been worse, not better, if I had gone earlier. But then again, in hindsight and from a different perspective, it is easy to criticize and judge. Besides, I told hospital staff repeatedly to call the police and had Gene report the crime ten days after it occurred. No one was listening or cared; it was simply too wild a story and I could not possibly have been alive to tell it. For those who are wondering, no, I never recovered any of the money taken. We can put that to rest once and for all as a motivational factor. My credit cards were mostly forgiven because they were unauthorized charges, but of course I lost use of them.

The remainder of April and much of May I did not do much and left the situation on the back burner. I continued to talk to Ed, though not as often. We could not come up with another strategy and even contemplated trying to go to the police again. There was absolutely no contact between Ed and Mese, Lugo, Delgado, or the informant. We entered into a vacuum of information. The telephone call I had made to Delgado did not seem to have any impact. They did not react. So the days went by, and it seemed that my case would go unpunished and I would find no remedy or justice for what had been done to me.

At the end of May, I received a call from Ed informing me that the police wanted to talk to me. A young and wealthy Hungarian couple had been kidnapped and was now missing. There were many similarities to my case, and they suspected that some, if not all the same individuals, were involved. They were desperately looking for the couple and wanted my assistance. It appeared that the criminals had found new victims and were at it again. Why not, no one cared, right?

Seeing the urgency of the matter, I flew to Miami the next day. Gene met me at the airport, and together we went to Metro-Dade police headquarters, where I had been just two months earlier. Upon our arrival, we were directed to the homicide division, not robbery. There, detectives Nick Fabregas, Sal Garafalo, and Sergeant Felix Jimenez met us. State prosecutor Gail Levine and an FBI agent were also present.

My first thought was, where were these people when I needed them? This was an interesting turn of events. Didn't they say I had a vivid imagination and made everything up? I noticed that Sergeants Deegan and Meyers were absent from that meeting. It did not matter to me. The couple was in grave danger, and I wanted to help in any way I could. These bloodthirsty, greedy criminals were not going to make the same mistake as they had with me. When it was finally over, this young couple wouldn't stand a chance of being alive. So time was of the essence, and the quicker they found them, the better the chances of saving them.

Detective Garafalo filled me in on what was happening. The young couple, Kristina Furton, age twenty-three, and Frank Griga, twenty-eight, had last been seen in the company of Lugo and his fellow steroid-crazed weightlifter friend Noel Doorbal, who was also the cousin of Lugo's ex-wife. Doorbal was the one I referred to as Lugo's sidekick, Mr. Torture. The couple's car, a yellow Lamborghini, had been found ditched in Dade County, far to the west of the metro area. There was no trace of the couple.

The police thought that these individuals were involved and feared the worst. I sat there for hours, recounting my story in detail and answering their barrage of questions. They showed me mug shots, and I identified both Lugo and Delgado. They had the evidence Ed had given them and asked me questions concerning the documents. I did not feel vindicated, only sad that they had not listened to me the first time I had gone there. This young couple would then have been in this situation.

They took photographs of the scars I had received from the torture and injuries. They showed sincerity and were almost apologetic in their behavior. There was no joy in the midst of the uncertainty regarding the missing couple. In the afternoon, Gene took me to the airport so I could return to Columbia. It appeared that this chapter was about to end for me. As the plane took off from Miami, my prayers were with the young couple, and I hoped that they would be found safe and sound. But I knew too well. I knew who had kidnapped them. I knew what they were capable of.

The next day, Gene called me and told me that the story had made the Miami Herald. Great, this was just what I wanted, publicity. The police effort concentrated on searching for the missing couple. The police wanted to know if I knew the location of the warehouse. Through Gene, the message was relayed that I suspected it might be the same one where Delgado kept his jet skis, in Hialeah, Florida. They found the warehouse and conducted a search and found an ominous sign, a chain saw. The media reported that the police feared the worst and hopes for finding the couple were diminishing. I hung on to every piece of information that I received. There was no one better to understand the couple's plight than me.

The next day, the news reports said that Delgado and Doorbal had been arrested. Doorbal quickly admitted taking part in my kidnapping, but Delgado did not say anything. They also searched Lugo's apartment, but he was nowhere to be found. In Doorbal's apartment, they found most of my furniture and other personal items. They also found certain items pertaining to the couple. There were also personal items belonging to me in Lugo's apartment and in

293

Delgado's, where they found my wallet in his safe.

They were so cocky and arrogant and stupid that Doorbal had furnished his apartment with my furniture. All three had kept my personal items as mementos and did not fear that one day it could all be used as evidence against them. Lugo's apartment yielded another interesting find: various passports under different aliases.

A week passed, and there were no new leads on the couple's disappearance. At the end of the week, I learned that Lugo had been arrested in the Bahamas and quickly brought back to Miami. Upon his arrival back in the States, he gave the police the location of where the couple's lifeless bodies had been dumped. He was hoping that his cooperation would mean a reduced sentence. Only a short while later, he denied what he had said. The police recovered the bodies. They had been stuffed into fifty-five-gallon drums and dumped into a southwest Dade canal.

Upon hearing the news, I was distraught, revolted, and very sad. The nightmare the young couple had gone through was obviously worse than what I had experienced. Now more than ever I realized how fortunate I was and what a miracle it had been that I was alive.

Gene began receiving a barrage of telephone calls from the news media and television programs. It had become a circus. Gene and I agreed it was best not to concede to those interviews, although we finally decided to give one interview so that my story was clear and out before they started their fabrications, especially in regards to Lugo. So we agreed to give the Miami Herald an interview through the telephone. I spent two hours recounting the story of torture and humiliation. It resulted in a two-page story being published.

The police did an extensive investigation and were able to piece together what had occurred between the criminals and the young couple. Lugo and Doorbal had approached Frank Griga about a possible business venture. The night that they were kidnapped, May 24, 1995, Lugo and Doorbal met Furton and Griga at a Miami Lakes restaurant. After they left the restaurant, they all decided to go to Doorbal's nearby apartment, also located in Miami Lakes. When Doorbal and Lugo tried to get the alarm code for Griga's residence, a scuffle ensued in which Doorbal bludgeoned Griga to death with a hammer. They placed Griga's body in the bathtub to bleed out before they disposed of it. According to the police, there was blood everywhere where the scuffle had occurred.

In the meantime, Kristina Furton was downstairs in another room. When she heard the scuffling, she began to scream. In order to subdue her, they injected her with a horse tranquilizer called Rompun. It appears Griga at one point was also injected with the same tranquilizer. She continued to scream, and they injected her again. They were trying to get the alarm code for the house from her now, and she gave them one. Lugo and his girlfriend, Petrescu, went to Griga's house to try the code they were given while Delgado and Doorbal stayed behind with Furton. She continued screaming, so they injected additional amounts of Rompun. When Lugo and his girlfriend arrived at the house, they discovered that the code did not function. They called Doorbal to get the correct one from Furton. Doorbal informed Lugo that she was cold or perhaps dead.

The next day, Lugo, Doorbal, and Delgado rented a truck to

take the bodies to the same warehouse where they had held me. They used what used to be my black leather sofa to stuff the bodies in and carry them out. In the warehouse, they proceeded to dismember the bodies so they would fit into the fifty-five-gallon drums. They burned the bodies with acid in order to thwart recognition. The headless body parts were stuffed into the drums; these were disposed of in the southwest Dade canal. The heads and fingers were disposed of in the Everglades. Their teeth had also been pulled with pliers and scattered along a Miami freeway. Lugo and Doorbal were unsuccessful in extorting any assets or money from Griga and Furton. They had not survived their ordeal for even twenty-four hours. I guess I had my answer as to what would have happened to me if I had also refused to give them all my assets.

There is one bit of information that has continued to intrigue me. No answer has been discovered or provided. The question was posed by one of the detectives during the investigation. He asked me who attempted to travel to Colombia with my passport on December 5, 1994 and why? I responded it was obviously not I, since I was chained to a wall at that time. Were they going to Colombia to find my family? Or was it a ploy to make it look like I had left the country so that, in case I disappeared, no one would question it or look for me? I was told that whomever it was had not been allowed to travel. So they were unsuccessful in whatever they were trying to accomplish. Who tried to travel that day, and why, remains a mystery that has never been answered.

In the beginning of June, at the request of the police department, I returned to Miami. Detective Garafalo wanted me to identify pictures of my furniture and personal belongings that had been found in Lugo's and Doorbal's apartment. They asked me to hear a tape recording of a voice and asked me if I could identify it. I recognized it immediately. It was that of Mr. Friendly, one of the night watchmen. His real name was Carl Weeks, a small-time criminal who had been offered almost nothing for his babysitting services. Mr. Friendly, the same guy who promised that he would not allow them to kill me. Of course, I knew it was the same Mr. Friendly who had been behind the wheel when they ran me over, twice.

Soon after I traveled to Miami, the police searched Mese's office, and he was also arrested. The police recovered my wife's car, which had been painted from green to black, and they had tried to change the VIN number, as well. The car was in the possession of Lugo's girlfriend, who was also arrested. The magnanimous Daniel Lugo had given it to her as a present. The investigation was moving now at light speed. The police also arrested Steven St. Pierre, the other night watchman, and the one I referred to as Mr. FBI. So much for his story of being an FBI agent that he liked to boast about—I wondered if he had told that story to the arresting police.

The prosecutor, Gail Levine, had become paranoid that I would no longer collaborate with them. I could not understand why, since I had never given them any indication to that effect, and it was in my best interest that these maniacs would no longer be roaming the streets, looking for prey or revenge.

After Delgado was arrested, Linda Delgado called Gene to ask me to intercede for her husband. That was a joke, right? It was

Delgado and Doorbal who had talked Lugo into killing me because they correctly guessed that I knew some of their identities. I could not understand the thinking or the gall of Delgado's wife in asking for my help. Didn't she realize her husband had tried to kill me? I guess in life you eventually see and hear just about everything. But this one beat them all.

In June 1996, I flew to Miami to speak with the prosecutor, Gail Levine, and to attend Mese's bond hearing. To my surprise, Delgado was sitting in that courtroom, dressed in his jail orange. I know he saw me but was too far away to say anything to me.

The prosecutor also reached a plea agreement with Lillian Torres, who would testify that she never met me but had been paid by Lugo to pretend to be my girlfriend in order to collect on my insurance policy.

Carl Weeks decided to plead guilty also and was given a two-year sentence. If he lied during the investigation or trial, it would be raised to forty years. This was big challenge for him, since telling the truth was not his forte. His credibility, though, was going to be tough to overcome. He admitted to the prosecutor that he used to steal from drug dealers and felt that it was okay since they were criminals. It was amazing he was alive.

Mario Sanchez, another individual involved, was also arrested. It had been Sanchez, Weeks, and Doorbal who kidnapped me from the parking lot at the deli.

Upon arrival at the warehouse, once Sanchez saw what was being planned and what they were going to do, he decided not to get involved. Surprisingly, Lugo had told him a lie, saying that they were only going to shake me up and let me go. Interesting to note that Sanchez was also afraid Lugo might get him for pulling out of their joint venture. Sanchez pleaded guilty and received a little over a year for his involvement.

I already knew most of the information that started coming out. Then there were other revelations that sent chills through my spine. They had tried to nab me a few times. Once they came to my house dressed as ninjas and waited for me to come out to get the newspaper. It was not Halloween. This would explain the reason why our alarm had been going off so often. Another time, they tried to intercept me while I was going to the deli. With Miami drivers, who would have noticed? This will give you an idea of how observant I was.

Then again, I think you need to believe that someone wants to hurt you in order to be on the lookout for these things. What was more troubling and revolting to me was that they contemplated kidnapping my six-year-old son as he came out of school. They also contemplated kidnapping my wife as she went to buy the groceries. Fortunately, none of those things came to fruition, or the ending might have been much different.

I began to shuttle from Colombia to Miami on a monthly basis for different reasons related to the case. My sister and wife also went on a couple of occasions. The case grew in size, and so did the number of defendants and witnesses. Before long, Stephen St. Pierre, Mr. FBI, decided to plead guilty so he could work out a deal. He cooperated fully and gave a full account to the police. His testimony was severely damaging to Delgado, Lugo, and Doorbal, more so than that of Weeks. Because he had no prior criminal record, his testimony was seen as more credible.

It came out that the reason why I had been put in the bathroom each day, besides torturing me, was because Delgado was watching me, and they wanted to avoid any contact between us. If he saw the need to speak to me, I would have recognized his voice easily. If only he had known from the very beginning that I knew he was involved. St. Pierre also gave a detailed account of the homicides of Griga and Furton.

In February 1996, the prosecutor called me and told me that she was negotiating a deal with Delgado in return for his testifying against Lugo and Doorbal. I objected and reminded her that there were sufficient witnesses and evidence that Delgado's testimony would not be critical. Nonetheless, she brokered a deal with him. In return for his testimony, the prosecutor gave him a sweet deal of fifteen years. He had been looking at life in prison if he had gone to trial and was found guilty, which would have been inevitable. I was not pleased that someone who committed such heinous crimes as kidnapping, attempted murder, murder, and robbery, among other things, was receiving such a lenient sentence. But I had no say, and for some reason or other, the prosecutor pushed extremely hard for this.

Delgado gave a 204-page detailed statement on both my case and the case of the young couple. This statement put a nail in the coffin of Lugo and Doorbal's chances for a victory in court.

The state also decided that both cases, the murder of the couple and mine, would be tried at the same time. There would be two separate juries, one for Doorbal and one for Lugo. Mese was also offered a deal of nine years, which he turned down. He would be tried separately. The trial was originally set for February 1996. It was pushed back for three months due to the volume of evidence and witnesses.

I spent the second half of 1995 and most of 1996 either traveling to Miami for the case or to New York to be with my sister, who was dying of cancer. Everything was happening at once, and I forgot about my problems and concentrated on being there for my sister and collaborating in the trial. The trial kept getting postponed. That year, 1996, I was spending more time in New York than anywhere else, as my sister's condition kept deteriorating. She passed away on February 21, 1997, at the age of forty-four. I was distraught at losing an ally and a friend who I could always count on and had been instrumental in saving me. My life was on hold because of those two events.

The rest of that year, I waited for the trial to finally end. I could not move in any direction until the case was resolved and finally closed. It seemed my life had revolved around being with my sister and the never-ending nightmare of my kidnapping case. Between June 1995 and December 1997, I went to Miami twelve times to give depositions and provide information.

In January 1998, almost two and a half years from the first time I went to Miami to help the police and three years after my kidnapping, two juries were finally selected. The trial began on February 24, 1998, and lasted for ten weeks. There were more than one thousand two hundred pieces of evidence and ninety-eight witnesses. It was the longest and most expensive criminal trial in Dade County history.

I was one of those witnesses. I testified for two days and nearly twelve hours. I arrived nervous, not because I had to finally confront my tormentors but because of the crowd of spectators and all the television cameras and reporters. I was not afraid of my torturers, who had humiliated me and tried to rape me of my dignity, my identity, and my life. They could not do me any more harm—it was over, and I answered every question posed by both the prosecutors and defense attorneys calmly and serenely while I looked directly into the defendants' eyes. My message was clear: I'm a survivor, and my spirit shall not be broken. I'm a survivor, and my spirit soars high.

Chapter 25 — Closure

"I DO NOT BELIEVE THAT SHEER SUFFERING TEACHES. IF
SUFFERING ALONE TAUGHT, ALL THE WORLD WOULD BE
WISE, SINCE EVERYONE SUFFERS. TO SUFFERING MUST BE
ADDED MOURNING, UNDERSTANDING, PATIENCE, LOVE,
OPENNESS AND THE WILLINGNESS TO REMAIN VULNERABLE."
- JOSEPH ADDISON -

"LIFE IS NOT SEPARATE FROM DEATH. IT ONLY LOOKS THAT
WAY."
- AMERICAN INDIAN PROVERB -

On May 4, 1998, a jury found Lugo guilty of two murders and
sixteen other charges, including kidnapping, attempted murder,
extortion, theft, and a host of others. On June 1, 1998, Doorbal's jury
came to a similar conclusion and found him guilty on all the same
charges. On July 7, 1998, the juries recommended the death sentence
for both Lugo and Doorbal. They are now sitting on death row,
appealing their respective cases. Lugo is delusional and maintains he
had nothing to do with the murders and my kidnapping. The Mese
jury also found him guilty on all counts and sentenced him to fifty-
six years. He died in prison in 2006 from a heart attack. The trial was
over, and so were the three and a half years of my life that had been
devoted to getting justice.

Judge Alex Ferrer, who presided over the case, wrote, "This case was very emotional to sit through. It still bothers me to some extent. I don't think it could have been worse if he had been a prisoner of war. Schiller was obviously emotionally bothered by it. It's hard to imagine that anybody would not be emotionally distraught about what happened to him. He tried to keep very cool composure but … I think even just relaying it in court was traumatic to the people that were hearing it."

The obvious question most asks is how I could have possibly survived. There is only one answer I can think of: divine intervention. Someone was looking after me that night. It is that simple. I have something to complete in my life. If I had died, that would have been left unfinished. There is no reason to search for complex answers, because they don't exist.

If you ask me what I learned from the experience, I would answer that in a succinct manner: Love and cherish life and those around you. Tell those you love how much you appreciate them every day. Live every day of your life like it's the last day and there's no tomorrow. If you find yourself in a difficult situation and there appears to be no solution, have faith that one will appear. Remember, miracles happen—miracles happen all the time. Grow, learn, and love, and laugh. Those are the gifts; don't waste them only to realize it when it's too late. Always reach for new heights and let your spirit soar.

Many times, unfortunate and difficult circumstances in our lives turn out to be positive. They transform us to be a better person and to appreciate those things we once took for granted. They inspire us to reach heights that we could not imagine before. They instill a sense of urgency to address and correct things that we have ignored. They make us understand who we truly are and solidify and increase our faith in a higher power and in ourselves.

Some say I cheated death. I don't believe so. I believe no one cheats the Grim Reaper, and when our journey is complete and our time is up, there is no escape from death's grip. It was not time for me to die, and there are other things for me to do in this life before the final chapter is written. These things may be so subtle that I may be completing them without realizing it. There is no neon sign that points me in the direction I must go or to what I must do. My survival may be for the benefit of another whom I now know or will find further on down the road of life. It may be that my mission is unimportant in this life, but I will help another complete their mission that will make a difference and is important for the human race.

My sister was informed that she had breast cancer the very same day I was kidnapped. No matter how hard she tried and fought the deadly invader, it was her time to go, and she died at the young age of forty-four in February of 1997. She held her spirits and hopes high until the very last day. I was blessed to have her by my side at a time when I really felt alone. She was a pillar of strength when I most needed it. Her guiding and helping hand were vital in regaining my spirits and hope. I was equally blessed to be able to be with her almost all the time during her illness, giving her my support and strength to fight and beat her sickness. But it was not to be. As I said, no one cheats death.

There are so many lessons learned, and I'm not the person who I used to be before November 15, 1994. In a way, that person died during that month, and a new me was reborn on Christmas Eve of that year.

I do not judge, for I believe that no one should do so. But I watch and analyze how people go about their daily lives. Unhappy and discontented with their lives, they fail to realize that the power to change lies within all of us. We measure our lives by what we accomplish and in the process are too busy to appreciate and be thankful for all the beautiful gifts life has given us. We aspire to accumulate material wealth and do not enrich our inner selves and accumulate those riches that no one can take away from us: inner peace, happiness, and love for others and ourselves.

We strive to educate ourselves about history, math, and other worldly matters, but we hardly take the time to learn about ourselves. We need to understand whom we truly are and the gifts each one of us has been blessed with that cannot be taken away. We feel inadequate because others can do things that we cannot, never realizing that each one has a special gift. We strive to fit into a model or image that is prefabricated for us by others instead of letting our real individual selves shine through. We are sold too many false ideas and idols, and, in our insecurity, we grab them, hoping that they fit. But they will not, because it is not who we are, and ultimately this will lead only to unhappiness and despair. The only true way to happiness and feeling fulfilled and content is through the exploration of who we are and through accepting ourselves as we are, with all our virtues and weaknesses. Once we let go of these false images and are who we are, we will finally find inner peace and the joy we all deserve.

I don't think about that episode in my life anymore. I have let it go and left behind the bitter memories. I decided I needed to move on, and dwelling on the past, which I cannot change, would not afford me any benefit. In fact, I felt it would be a roadblock to whichever road I chose. My memories can only imprison me in a world that no longer exists. I want to be free to savor my present, which is my gift. It's like trying to drive a car forward by looking in your rear-view mirror. It can't be done. I choose to drive looking forward and appreciating all the beauty life has to offer.

Many find it strange that I have forgiven my kidnappers and ask God to bless them and forgive them. I needed closure, and this was the final piece that was missing. I believe that those who inflicted harm on me live in their torment and desperation from which they have no escape. That is truly their punishment, and that can never be changed. They must confront what they have done, and the ghost of the past haunts them every waking day. There are no exits from this mental prison and no way to vanquish these demons and ghosts.

Many wonder how, after such an experience, I am able to function normally in society. The physical scars heal to a certain extent, but they contend that the mental scars do not. Others believe that time heals all wounds and we are able to gather the pieces of our broken lives and continue on. For me, the physical scars remain as a reminder of what I had to endure. Although they have faded somewhat, they are clearly visible as a reminder of human cruelty. It is a badge I wear that reminds me that I must always fight on and never look back. For me, it was a turning point in my life. I could choose to either wallow in self-pity or seek the pity of others. Or I could choose to use it as a springboard to make me a better human being and learn from the experience, no matter how harsh or bitter those experiences were. I chose the latter.

And so, those loose pages do not sit in that corner anymore, neither collecting dust nor yellowing. My story has now been told, and with the telling comes closure to that chapter of my life. I now turn the page. The ghost and demons that haunted me are now vanquished. My sincere desire is that by telling my story, I will give someone the courage and fortitude to face their own ghost and demons and vanquish them. If I have accomplished this, for just one fellow human being, then my reason and goals for writing this book have been fulfilled, and it has been a worthwhile endeavor.

Peace, Love, and Light Surround You Always,
And May Your Spirit Soar.

Marc Schiller

ABOUT THE AUTHOR

Marc Schiller was born in Buenos Aires, Argentina, and immigrated to Brooklyn, NY, with his parents when he was seven years old. An early entrepreneur, he started several small businesses by the age of nine. He attended high school in Brooklyn, participating in sports and as a member of the school's track team.

Marc received a bachelor's degree in accounting from the University of Wisconsin-Milwaukee and an MBA from Benedictine University. Marc has had a long and diversified career as both a professional and an entrepreneur. His professional career has spanned the US and the world. On an entrepreneurial level, Marc Schiller has launched several successful businesses, including two accounting practices both in Miami and Houston, a delicatessen in Miami, and an options and stock trading company.

Marc Schiller currently works as an accounting and tax resolution specialist for a national tax resolution company. He has two grown children. His son graduated from the University of Colorado-Boulder with a degree in economics, and his daughter currently attends Loyola Marymount University in California.

Pain and Gain — The Untold True Story is Marc Schiller's first literary publication.